"Her talent is evident." —*Bon Appétit*

"Simple, healthful, flavorful fare." —*Cooking Light*

"Gutsy, fresh, and flavorful [food]." —*New York Times*

"Kathleen has a gift for finding and delivering pure, bright flavor in healthy food everyone can enjoy."
—**Judi Rogers, author of**
The Zuni Café Cookbook

"Featuring Technicolor ingredients and beautiful presentation, her food fools the palate."
—*Los Angeles Times*

"An explosion of pure flavors and pleasing textures." —*Esquire*

"[Kathleen is] one of the top 2 percent of those in the know." —*Prevention*

Houghton Mifflin Company
Boston New York

200

Easy

Recipes

for

Healthy

Weight

Loss

Cooking Thin WITH Chef Kathleen

Kathleen
Daelemans

This book is not intended to replace medical advice or be a substitute for medical or other professional assistance. If you are sick or suspect you are sick, you should see a physician. If you are taking a prescription medication, you should consult your physician before making changes in your diet.

The author and publisher expressly disclaim responsibility for any adverse effects arising directly or indirectly from information contained in this book.

For information about permission to reproduce selections from this book, write to Permissions, Houghton Mifflin Company, 215 Park Avenue South, New York, New York 10003.

Visit our Web site: www.houghtonmifflinbooks.com

Library of Congress Cataloging-in-Publication Data is available.
ISBN-13: 978-0-618-62429-4 (pbk.)   ISBN-10: 0-618-62429-5 (pbk.)
ISBN-13: 978-0-618-22632-0   ISBN-10: 0-618-22632-X

Designed by Richard Oriolo

Printed in the United States of America

RRD 10 9 8 7 6 5 4 3 2 1

Mom and Dad,
there's not enough room in my heart
for the love and gratitude I feel for you both.
Without your love, support, and
tolerance for chicken pan supper six nights in a row,
this book never would have been possible.
You are my greatest heroes, my very best friends,
and the reason I'll never again live at the beach.
I will honor your kindness by passing it along.
What do you mean, "Start with my siblings"?

Contents

Acknowledgments

I'M NOT SURE HOW MUCH room they're going to give

me for this part but I know it can't be enough to properly thank everyone

who's helped me get to this point in my career.

To Judy Rodgers, for taking a chance on an aspiring chef who showed up

for the interview with two different colored shoes (I was trying to decide and

left the house before I did—talk about *embarrassing*). Thank you for tolerating me in the beginning, for believing in me along the way, and for never giving up even when I'd managed to back up the kitchen, *again*. Thank you for your love of pure authentic food, for your tireless devotion to your staff, and for providing us with the most important teaching environment a young cook could ever hope to work in. Thank you to my other Zuni mentors and friends who took the time to hold my hand and teach me, too: Ross Browne, John Clark, Robert Herarra, Gayle Pirie, Kelsie Kerr, Quang Nguyen, and David and Marsha McBride.

To Robbie Friedlander, owner and proprietor of Robbie's Tropical Farms, Maui, thank you for taking a gigantic leap of faith with me, for working tirelessly and developing organically grown specialty produce for the restaurant. And thanks for rushing down the volcano to our seaside café with handpicked, rain-or-shine harvests of the world's most tenderly grown, luscious produce.

Thank you to all the chefs and kitchen talent I've had the privilege to cook with and learn from along the way. I'm thankful for all you taught me: Meishan Anderson, Paula Benitez, Patrick Dunn and Joseph, Cindy and Gail, Irma Gonzales and Sandra, Tim Meyer, Alfonso Morin, Katarina Tualemoso, and Roberto Arguetta, one of the most skilled and talented chefs I've cooked with.

Thank you, Michael Perlman, for never giving up on me. Knowing you believed in me no matter what cockamamie idea I presented to you was enough to keep me moving forward on days the phone wasn't ringing. Thank you for always taking my calls, preventing falls, guiding the way, and for tolerating my payment schedule. Speaking of late payments, thank you, Ron Kawahara, for never turning me in to the late-payment police either. Thank you to my dear friend, David Kurzman, for the pocketful of lessons and all the great laughs.

Thank you, Grandpa Neil, for spoiling me rotten and for being the biggest kid of all of us. Thank you, Grandma Genevieve, for all the years of encouragement, for teaching me how not to be a quitter, and for sharing your hilarious sense of humor and sunny point of view. Thank you both for giving me my mom.

Thank you, Grandpa George, for pushing me to work harder and for saying to me very early on two things that shaped my life forever: "Kate, you eat too damn much," and "Kate, don't waste your life working at a job you hate." To my Grandma Helen, thank you for all the years of love and support and thank you for giving me my dad.

Thank you, Sharon, for being a great leader, a great teacher, a kind soul, and a generous spirit. Thank you for showing women that we *can*, all on our own. Thank you, Rainy Farrell and Jennifer Oberstein, for finding me that day and thank you for all your kind support every day since then.

Thank you to my family: Paul, for all your neat ideas, the special pet names, and all the Sundays with Emily. Carol, for your invaluable help and critical input no matter how crabby I got, and Talitha, for tasting and critiquing all the recipes honestly, especially when you knew I'd yell if you didn't "love" them. Thank you, Renie, for your quiet support; Marc, for keeping my computer purring; and especially Erin and Emily, for licking the bowls and spoons clean. Thank you, Uncle Albert and Aunt Carol, for your kind support. You're not still mad that my waiter spilled salmon down your back, are you?

Thank you to my dear friends, Jack Feliciano and Patrick Silviera, for supporting me every step of the way since the day we met, for teaching me that I could when I thought I couldn't, and for never giving up on what you knew was achievable.

Thank you, Doe Coover, for believing in the unbelievable and for taking this project on. Thank you for the encouragement along the way and for your kind and thoughtful guidance throughout. I can't thank you enough.

At Houghton Mifflin, thank you, Rux Martin. I'm a huge fan of your work! Your books are some of the most dog-eared in my collection. They are exceptional teaching tools; I am a better cook because of them. Thank you for nourishing, finessing, and refining my work. Thank you for making it a better book. Lori Galvin-Frost, thank you so much for all your contributions to this book, for your keen eye and your kind patience. Michaela Sullivan, thank you so much for all your beautiful design work on the cover.

Thank you, Gayle Pirie and Cleo Papanikolas, for styling the shoot, for waltzing in with your renaissance spirit and arms full of sweet, tender harvests from your Berkeley gardens. Thank you, Debbie Harder, for your generosity and wardrobe styling. Thank you, Terry McCarthy, for your ingenuity, creativity, and hard work.

I'm blessed to be a student of role models, mentors, extraordinary teachers, and friends. Thank you for your generosity: Mark Andrew, "Grandma" Bess and "Papa" Doc, Michael Bass, Dean Cobb, Carole Jacobs, Julie Camell, Carolyn Clifford, Roger Dikon, Angela Ebron, the Felicianos, Kim Gerbasi, Mariela Gomez, the Goodmans, Shep Gordon, Monica Gullon, DeAnne Hamilton, Barbara Harris, Florence Henderson, Peggy Katalinich, Michael Knight, Todd LaCoursier, Penelope Williams-Lent, Kim Marshall, Andrzej Milosz, Pam Peeke, Dede Perlman, Tajinder Reyatt, Richard Sax, Sue Perry, the Simons, Daphna Shalev, Nancy Smith, Joanne Sutro, Susan Ungaro, Elaine Willis, Deb Winson, and Terry at Powerhouse Gym in West Bloomfield.

At the Food Network, my sincere thank-you to Judy Gerard, who saw something in me no one else did. Thank you, Eileen Opatut, for believing in my work enough to allow me the opportunity to teach in the television format and, more important, to learn how to become a better teacher by allowing me the opportunity to learn from your best. Thank you, Jeanne Shanahan, for taking the project on and for nurturing it every step of the way. Your precision focus and expertise allowed the show to become what you knew it could be. Thank you, Sharon Bowers, Liza Hughes, Jill Novat, Kate Rados, Adam Rockmore, Susan Stockton, Amy Voll, and Carrie Welch.

Thank you, Alton Brown, for bringing the show *Cooking Thin* to life. Thank you, Marion Laney, for your vision and creativity. Thank you, Dana Popoff, for your dedication to the project, for your leadership and Herculean efforts. Thank you, Amanda Kibler, for your gracious, kind, and gentle ways, for your expertise, and for teaching me how to be a better person. Thank you, Maureen Petrosky, for all your great work and culinary contributions. Thank you, DeAnna Brown, Patrick Belden, Ginger Cassell, Lester Dragstedt, Stephanie Hammond, Sarah Mays, Jenny Maxwell, Jim McKinney, Paul Merchant, Whit Norris, Sarah Murphy, Denny Mooradian, Dede O'Reilly, David Traylor, Vanessa Parker, Drew Ponder, Derek Robertson, Cathy Rouse, Debra Rush, Vera Smith, Courtney Watkins, and Athalie White.

From the bottom of my heart, thank you to those who've taken the time to write to me because you teach me how to be a better teacher. Let's face it, I'm in this for us all, and if we're not learning or having any fun, *what's the point?*

Finally, I'd like to thank everyone who ever fired me. I learned a lot and am better and stronger for all the tough times. Had you not shown me the door, I never would have moved on and grown, so thanks for the kick in the pants.

Introduction

BEING HIRED STRAIGHT OUT OF Judy Rodgers's Zuni

Café kitchen to launch a seaside Italian bistro in a $790 million tropical para-

dise hotel in Hawaii, touted as "the world's most luxurious," didn't *seem* like a

bad career move. Turns out, trading swank San Francisco life for island living

nearly cost me my livelihood. Finding upon my arrival that I'd been replaced

by a chef flown in from Italy definitely wasn't the aloha greeting I'd been fantasizing. Tropical dreams were dashed by a tsunami-sized uncertainty.

Before I could phone Judy and plead for my job back, the resort owners whisked me off to a meeting and announced my new culinary appointment. "You will be the spa cuisine chef" is all I heard before I nearly lost consciousness. I spat the words right back, "Spa cuisine chef?"

"What *is* spa food and who eats it anyway?" I demanded. "Do I *look* like I eat low-fat foods?"

Did I mention I was 205 pounds and a size 22 at the time? A fat chef behind the stove of the resort's premier spa restaurant wasn't good for the overall image of the place. Not only did I have to invent a menu, I had to cook and *look* the part. No more food fests . . . no more late-night refrigerator raids . . . no more ice cream? Returning to the city-by-the-bay so soon was *not* an option. My mother didn't raise a quitter, or so she had pummeled into my psyche. Conceiving a future of fat-free foods had me trembling for Twinkies.

I couldn't imagine an entire restaurant dedicated to a cuisine that didn't exist. My best research efforts unearthed only three books on the subject, all out of print. No wonder, since they were filled with photographs of pea shoots and carrot sticks three ways. You know, the kind of pictures that leave you salivating *for something else*. Fearing my career path had crumbled for good, I rang up Judy.

She told me, "Look on it as a challenge and rely on basics. Grill and broil food, write your menus around vegetables, fruits, grains, and legumes. Choose leaner cuts of red meat, chicken, and fish. Get in your car and forage for island farmers. Use the freshest produce you can get your hands on and the food will speak for itself. Get advice from a doctor or nutritionist."

I knew she was right, but how much weight could spa guests lose in a week? And who goes on a vacation to lose weight? Most people planning island getaways start dieting so that they can fit into their "resort wear" the minute the travel itinerary is set. The trek back to pre-seat-assignment size begins when the stewardess sets that little bag of honey-roasted nuts before you. Your seven-day license to eat freely reigns supreme and doesn't expire until the plane touches down back in your hometown, right? We're *supposed* to come home fat from holidays, aren't we?

Spa-goers came to the resort to be pampered, rubbed, wrapped, and healed. Clientele forking out $450 a night certainly weren't used to hearing the word *no*—as in no Dom Perignon, no filet mignon, no lobster thermidor, and no crème brûlée. I had to find a way to send these people home happier, *not* heavier. And *I* had to slim down fast. Controlling my cravings, tempering my taste buds, and losing weight were simply a matter of preserving my paycheck.

I set out to create a cuisine I could be proud of and that guests could embrace. Having yo-yo dieted myself to distraction, I was determined to send guests back to the mainland with realistic tools to help them succeed at a life of healthy living. I found a nutritionist willing to help: Dr. Elaine Willis. I begged the good doctor to reinvent conventional wisdom by never mentioning the "d" word to our guests. Forward-thinking Dr. Willis indulged my instincts and deleted "dieting" from the official spa itinerary. I persisted in my pursuit to keep things simple by insisting that no one be required to weigh and measure their food or read a single book on health and nutrition.

Dr. Willis and I worked together until we came up with a formula that yielded outrageously delicious, nutritionally sound cuisine. The restaurant was an instant hit. Word of the sumptuous cuisine spread quickly. Spa guests, movie stars, recording artists, sports superstars, and supermodels flocked to the café's tables. The restaurant received dozens of culinary kudos and accolades from some of the nation's most respected food critics. A little culinary trickery and a lot of innovation proved once and for all that food with less fat and no unnecessary calories can please even the most discriminating palates.

If you're thinking that a spa vacation at a multimillion-dollar resort is the only way you can lose weight, think again, because the only thing you're likely to lose is a few grand. You *can* take advantage of all the secrets and amenities guests took home because everything you need to know is in this book. It's fair to say that this is one "vacation" that really can last a lifetime, and since your journey doesn't begin with a plane ride, you won't need your Visa or American Express card.

Okay, so there is no lei greeting, no limo driver, and no private butler in sight. Powerful personal trainers and private chefs catering to your every culinary whim are not part of the package. Room service, maid service, and in-room massage don't come with this book either. There's no one to draw your bath at night, and turndown service is definitely do-it-yourself.

The good news? Your journey to vitality doesn't involve debt, starvation, or exercise boot camp. It will, however, result in long-term success. Guilt be gone! Losing weight and getting fit are within everyone's reach. The program originally designed for the rich and famous has been simplified and refined for the very distinguished rest of us.

Because I'm the girl who had to be tutored in the principal's office in order to receive a just-above-failing grade to pass high school algebra so I could graduate with my peers, I haven't included cumbersome calorie counts or complicated nutritional breakdowns after the recipes. I'm deathly allergic to anything even remotely related to math, a genetic condition I inherited from my grandmother, as evidenced by the fact that *she* never opened a single bank statement or balanced *her* checkbook either.

The get-health-minded can be divided into two categories: those capable of understanding the stock quotes as they trail across the bottom of the TV set and those who cannot. Since I cannot, and because calculating every single morsel of food I ate was an insurmountable task and the very reason I had to enter Ben & Jerry's rehab in the first place, the only numbers you'll see here are page numbers.

Most of the recipes in this book are built around naturally healthful ingredients and are "clean." They do not contain any calories that don't bring anything to the party in terms of flavor. A few of the "comfort foods" come with warnings on them: these are intended to be once-in-a-while meals. Make room for the calories by making smart choices the rest of the week and adding a few minutes to your workout.

I can't stick to hard-core programs based on numbers. I've been able to enjoy the foods I love and achieve good health by making rules and setting rewards. I focus on balancing my calories, practicing moderation, and exercising regularly. Dr. Pamela Peeke, assistant clinical professor of medicine at the University of Maryland School of Medicine, gives this approach two thumbs up.

I'm living proof that modest lifestyle changes can result in weight loss, a greater fitness level, and a little freedom from stress. Don't get me wrong: you won't wake up looking like a Hollywood movie star on day two, but you *will* achieve results. In my wildest dreams, I never imagined *I'd* become a spa cuisine chef, let alone a weight-loss success story, 75 pounds and counting. If I can do this, you can too!

Kathleen's 1-2-3
Guide to the
Finish Line

YOU'VE GOT TO COOK THIN to win, but that's not all.

I flunked math, but I can count to three and so can you. Hold up three fingers.

To lose weight and get fit you've got to do three things. Your mother has been

over this with you, but let's review: eat right, exercise, and make up your

mind to do it. If you're wondering why "make up your mind to do it" isn't

first on the list, it's because it's never worked before.

Starting with your very next meal or snack, cut back a little on your portion sizes, drink gobs more water, and take a few brisk walks. In the precise moment that you're experiencing Stallone-style delusions of grandeur—you know, when you feel like Rocky running amok all over that city—take a front-row seat in your own (legitimate) glory, buckle up, and make up your mind to go all the way once and for all. Follow my guide to the finish line, cook thin, and you'll win your war on weight issues. And it'll stick this time. Trust me. It's snap-your-fingers, 1-2-3 easy.

Part One: Eat Right

COOK THIN, EAT THIN, START NOW (YOU HEARD ME)

Potato chips haven't made it to the moon. If you don't fuel your body with the right stuff, how do you expect to get anywhere? Lose the shame for good. Three by-dinnertime defining moments guaranteed to get you going.

The cabbage soup *diet wasn't good for my soul*

1. • **Eat right because there is no other way.** Fad diets work (for a nanosecond). I should know. I tried every one of them. I lost tons of weight. And sadly, it all came back, and then some. My maiden voyage was the total brownie diet at age thirteen. I was born with fat cheeks and spent the next thirty years growing into them. I realized I was different by age twelve, when everyone knew me as the Goodyear Blimp (thanks to my brother, Paul). I knew it wasn't "good" different because I never felt good about myself.

I was well aware of the differences between the size-2 cheerleaders and me. I was a double XL into Twinkies and Ho-Hos, and they were into boys and dating. They went to parties and proms. I baby-sat. Mostly so I wouldn't be home with my parents on the weekends in *case* the boy who sat next to me in algebra decided to date the fattest girl in the class and called. Mainly, I baby-sat as an excuse to eat myself back together again. Of course it never worked, and I only managed to eat the neighbors out of house and home. I chose my "jobs" by who maintained the best junk-food spread. No chips, no dip, no sodas? No sitter.

Needless to say, I kept growing. So I embarked upon my dieting years. The total brownie diet sounded like a sensible place to start. What could be wrong with twenty-six brownies a day? I lost a lot of weight. But as soon as I got sick of brownies, I went back to my old habits. Eating sprees. And the weight came back.

Once a year or so I'd get disgusted with my weight and go on another diet. There was the cabbage-soup diet, the steak diet, the pineapple diet, the seven-day diet, the shake diet, and the diet-pill diet. I tried them all, plus every fad diet the movie stars were touting and all the ones I saw on TV. I was either a size 18 or a size 14, until I crept up to a size 22. I stopped caring after that. I decided to accept my fate. I ate to celebrate. The "party eating" continued straight through to my twenties and didn't stop until destiny called in the form of my friend Jack, who'd come to visit me in San Francisco from his home in Hawaii.

Jack knew I was considering a chef's position in Maui and traveled across briny blue waters to assess my situation firsthand. A week after he returned home, I got a card from Jack with a one-way ticket to Maui and a note. "What are the chances of needing a change and getting a great job offer on the same tropical island that your best friend calls home?" So off I went. I had him, and you have me. It doesn't matter how you get started. It just matters that you do. Stay with me. You can do this.

Do you feel the way Willy Wonka's *Violet Beauregarde looked after she ate the fateful gumball?*

2. **Eat right to feel better about yourself.** Remember *Charlie and the Chocolate Factory*? Willy Wonka warned Violet Beauregarde *not* to eat the unperfected magical, complete-dinner-in-a-gumball, but she greedily swiped one anyway. She experienced a succulent dinner all right, but as she ferociously chomped her way through the dessert of blueberry pie, she expanded until she became a gigantic Macy's Thanksgiving Day Parade blueberry girl balloon. Guess whose brother used to call her Violet for the first sixteen years of her life? Where would we *be* without "support" from our families and friends?

I'm sure that I would never have gotten this far without the extraordinary help and guidance of my *much* younger and *more* beautiful sister, Carol, either. If not for

SUBJECT: I'M DESPERATE TO LOSE 80 POUNDS

SENDER: Monica

TO: email@chefkathleen.com

Dear Kathleen,

I just got pictures back from a family wedding, and I'm devastated at how much weight I've gained over the years. I guess I've been in denial about how bad things have gotten. My eating is out of control. I'm so upset. I'm beside myself about this. I am desperate to lose weight fast.

Monica

REPLY: TURN REACTION INTO ACTION

Dear Monica,

Asking for help is an important first step. Measure success not by pounds lost but by the number of healthful behavioral changes you make. Aim for new habits that you can live with for the rest of your life. Weight loss will be a wonderful bonus for work well done.

If you thought you'd have to wake up and run the Boston Marathon tomorrow, you'd never get out of bed. Most of us set our goals so high we can never reach them. Don't think about the numbers so much. Focus on how many things you can do right today.

Do three healthy things today. For example, drink eight glasses of water, go for a ten-minute walk, don't clean your plate at dinner (leave a truffle-size bite behind). Reward yourself handsomely for these small but hugely significant behavioral changes and challenge yourself to repeat them tomorrow.

Most important, love yourself today. Don't postpone the life of happiness you deserve today until you reach a certain dress size. Today you are the very same special person you will be when you achieve your goals. You'll be a little older and a little wiser, that's all. Please let me know how you're doing, Monica, and congratulations on a great start.

Kathleen

her, I would be eating out of Dumpsters behind low-class restaurants on the Vegas strip. In fact, just the other day she inspired me as I was folding laundry. She looked at all my jeans on the clothesline and queried in a feline tone, "Gaining weight again, Kathleen?"

"I most certainly am not! The dryer is running extra hot. It's shrinking everything I own," I practically shouted.

"Any of these jeans *new*, Kathleen?" she purred.

"No," I sullenly admitted.

"Preshrunk is preshrunk, Kathleen."

Six-month-old jeans don't suddenly start to diminish in size. Give up the late-night snacks. I bet your dryer will simultaneously start to "work" again.

The candid (usually unsolicited) "love" and "encouragement" I receive from each of my siblings has helped to keep me well grounded and offered new perspectives for my work, not to mention continued inspiration to pass up the third Krispy Kreme. Besides, food hangovers can be debilitating: headaches, bellyaches, dehydration, extreme fatigue, and bad breath. It's really a horrible thing to do to your body.

You don't need to see Violet in the mirror or wake up depressed because you don't like the way your body feels or the way your clothes don't fit. Even though you feel sick, you can't really "call in fat." Decide to be the master of your health and you will.

Do you really want to keep eating until you have to be **hoisted** *from your bed by a* **piano crane** *on live TV and shipped to the nearest hospital?*

3. **Eat right to get healthy.** I'm a cook. Mine is just to cook and fry, mine is not to reason why. I'm not a doctor, so I can't go on with any real authority about how eating right can lower your risk of heart disease and stroke, reduce your risk of developing type-2 diabetes, osteoarthritis, and gallbladder disease, or lower your risk of some cancers—uterine, cervix, colon, rectal, prostate, and breast cancer. According to the National Institutes of Health, "If you are overweight, losing as little as 5 to 10 percent of your body weight may improve many of the problems linked to being overweight."

Why trudge along in the slow lane when you can hop on the fast track? Change your shape for good. Three easy eating habits you can start today.

I.C.U. or I can do—the choice is yours

1. **Leave a snack-size bite behind.** I've found the only way to tackle a project I must complete but have absolutely no interest in is to break it down into manageable tasks. Start small. Reduce the portion size of each and everything you eat today. I didn't say eat according to National Institutes of Health guidelines for your age, weight, and height. And I didn't say *don't* eat the hot tamales. I simply said cut back a little. The calorie savings really add up.

   You can deal with one less bite, can't you? Attach an imaginary calorie count to each bite you don't eat. Do the math. Think of it this way: If you don't put it in your mouth now, you won't have to figure out how to fit it into your jeans later.

Boxed chocolates *keep better in your underwear drawer*

2. **Dump anything from your diet you're not passionate about.** Naturally there'll never be a really good reason to purge your underwear drawer of heavenly boxed chocolates, but there are plenty of things you can dump from your diet that you're *not* as passionate about.

   To guide me in my decisions to dump or not dump a particular food item from my diet, I developed a Ouija-inspired three-question quiz. For the sake of this exercise, let's put salt-and-vinegar chips on the block. Would I be tempted to maim a dining companion for eating even one chip more than her fair share of said chips even if she were my own mother? Would I behave like a three-year-old in a checkout line if I were denied access to said chips? If I were standing at the checkout and suddenly discovered I was penniless, would I be tempted to pilfer them anyway? If I answer yes even once, clearly it's a food I must love—an item I'm willing to "work" into my eating plan. Pity we can't have everything, but we *can* have some things.

What does it say about us that we can spell-check Doritos?

For me, salt-and-vinegar chips were in but something else had to go, so I dumped all other land mines in a bag. Out went the Doritos, Fritos, and Cheetos. Because I tend to lean toward the single-bag-must-be-a-single-portion mentality, I limit my portion sizes, too. If I eat one chip beyond the manufacturer's recommended serving size, I slap myself with a no-chips-on-next-week's-shopping-list citation. Stick to the rules and you'll get to your health goals.

Anyway, what's the point of eating if you don't taste and enjoy it? Make it a hard-and-fast rule to eat with all five senses. If it's chocolate soufflé, then savor it from the earliest whiff of dark-roasted cocoa, to the very first clink of your fork against the hot-from-the-oven chocolate-filled crock, to the last luxurious morsel. Pay attention. Drunkenly slither into the eating experience as if you were sliding into an oversize milk bath. Massage primal satisfaction from each and every creamy rich, decadent mouthful and bask in the afterglow.

Rather than give up on my favorite life-sustaining foods, I learned to cut back on meaningless (to me) calories. You can too. Start today.

Katie, bar the door!

3. **Start subbing good, better, and best choices for junk calories.** Everything's a trade-off. I was never addicted to soda but take my coffee from me and you'd better run for cover. Because I was a heavy-cream-in-my-coffee kind of girl, it was boo-hoo, no daily brew, or give up cow-luscious full-fat cream for good.

Truthfully, I used to reach for the heavy cream without thinking about it. I worked in a restaurant. It never occurred to me to walk three steps to the waiter's side station and grab much-lower-calorie milk to mix with my coffee. I never

SUBJECT: I'M DROWNING IN A SEA OF FAT

SENDER: Louisa

TO: email@chefkathleen.com

Dear Kathleen,

I've tried every diet I ever read about. I can usually make it one week. And then I quit and give up. Until I saw you on TV, I was convinced it was impossible for me to get healthy. Can you give me some advice to get started? Thanks.

Louisa

REPLY: FASTEN YOUR LIFE JACKET

Dear Louisa,

Establish goals that are realistic, moderate, and attainable. Having a clear vision of where you can realistically go will help you get there. Visions of size-2 ball gowns can make you feel like quitting. Focus on changing one habit at a time. Try walking for five minutes and push it up each day at your own pace until you're exercising thirty to forty-five minutes a day. You don't have to complete all your exercise in one session. Ten-minute sessions are just as good for you. Surely you can squeeze in ten minutes every now and then.

Adopt the can-do will-do mind-set. Forget about dieting altogether. Erase from your mind all the dieting "rules" you've learned—especially the ones that make you feel guilty, deprived, anxious, or like a cheater. Focus instead on making the best choices you can each day, choices that will lead you to your ultimate health and fitness goals.

Increase your consumption of healthful calories and slowly decrease the not-so-good-for-you stuff. Fill up on good food first; you'll have less room for foods you shouldn't eat too much of. Increase your daily intake of fruits and vegetables. Try this for starters and let me know how you're doing.

Kathleen

thought about calories—as was evidenced by the fact that I thought nothing of washing down a slice or two of leftover *gâteau victoir* (flourless chocolate cake) with my coffee. I never thought about calories, until the chub-grub spirit guides gave me an ultimatum: ice cream or coffee cream. I caught on real quick. To this day I'm a nonfat-milk-and-coffee girl, happy with calories to spare.

Building on my newfound calorie consciousness, I looked on food swapping as a way to legally cheat. Making room for my favorite foods was deemed fair and square by the nutrition police and the law is still on the books. It's like cleaning your closets. Ditch your college clothes for newer, better-quality duds. Why waste calories on oyster crackers when you might be in the mood for fries later? Why supersize the fries when you'd probably be satisfied with kid size? Skip the fries altogether and spend the calories on dessert or save them for later. If you're not quite ready to swap, mix and match. Try increasing the amount of good calories you eat before consuming wickedly delicious treats. You'll have less room if you follow the rule "good before evil."

Stay in your own lane and keep your eye on the finish line. Three no-fail ways to improve your overall performance by bedtime.

"Kate, you eat too *damn much"*

1. **Start reading labels with an eye toward nutritional content, calorie counts, and recommended portion sizes.** If there is such a thing as reincarnation, I was a fat, happy cow in my past life because I love to graze. I'll always eat to nourish my soul and will celebrate daily the sublime pleasure of consumption. I'm a food lover and see no reason why I can't have my cake and be fit, too. I'll never be a size 4 because of this deep-rooted desire to dine. The point is I've learned to accept the things I'm unwilling to change and have adopted strategies to live by. One is my calorie bank account, which exists solely in my head but couldn't be more real. I'm constantly running the numbers and checking the bottom line. I can tell you at any point in the day roughly what calorie range I'm in and how many I have left to spend.

Portion control isn't instinctive—it must be learned. I did it by reading labels and portioning out the serving sizes listed on packages. I didn't do it all at once, and I only do it now when I'm introducing a new food item to my repertoire. I hate constraints of any kind, so after I've done my homework and educated myself on how many grams of this or that "evil" thing the food has in it, I don't give it any more thought.

Educating yourself on portion sizes can be downright depressing, because chances are you eat too much. My grandpa used to say to me at breakfast every day, "Kate, you eat too damn much." I never understood what he meant until I measured a 1-ounce portion of cereal. This turned out to be the amount that fell to the floor as I dug my spoon deep into a gloriously overfilled, oversize breakfast bowl—the very same bowl I'd eat my ice cream out of every night—precisely the reason I was a size 22. I just didn't know any better or *want* to.

Label-awareness orientation is boot camp for people who, like me, were free-range foragers in past lives. Recommended serving sizes can't *possibly* sustain human life. Pea-size-portion shock eventually wears off. Nobody has actually *died* following the guidelines set forth by the nutrition police. Thankfully, there are ways around the establishment.

Pay to play *you must*

Each day, you wake up and *need* to consume *x* number of calories based on height, weight, and physical activity. The goal is to balance the calories over each day and each week—calories in versus calories out. I've found there's always room to play, which means you can never really blow it. This is a good thing since most of us will take any opportunity to beat ourselves up for eating even a spoonful of Ben & Jerry's. The only way to heal these self-inflicted wounds is to finish off the pint, right? And then there's no point in continuing on this "healthy path," so it's back to supersizing.

Wrong. Save up your calories for too-important-to-ignore food cravings.

Delectable nibbly bits at the occasional cocktail party, movie night, or Halloween are perfectly good excuses to indulge. But pay to play you must. Learn to scrape and save up calories for these glorious food occasions, limit portion sizes, and add a few minutes to your workout the days before and after.

You might be feeling overwhelmed by all this right now, but trust me, it's not nearly as hard as some of those crazy *diets* that you're expected to stay on until the end of time. Hardest of all is living life as an overweight person, which takes more courage, strength, and reserve than eating right and getting fit ever will. Apply those survival instincts to this expedition and you'll be living well and feeling great in no time. Don't forget, I'm a die-hard sugar junkie and couch potato at heart and I lost the weight and have kept it off. You can too.

Cupcake pajamas aren't a license to eat in bed

2. **Ditch mindless eating.** I got cupcake pajamas for Christmas. They have cream-filled Ding-Dongs, mile-high slices of chocolate cake, glazed doughnuts, princess pink coconut-covered Sno-Balls, and cartons of milk all over them. They're wintry delicious, 100-percent cotton, puppy-fur soft flannel. I just love them.

Naturally I like snacking in bed better than eating anyplace else on earth, too. In fact, I think restaurants should greet you at the door, hand you a pair of cashmere pajamas, show you to your bed, tuck you in, and take your order.

It was with great sadness that I gave up eating in bed, but I had abused the privilege. You see, I wouldn't stop at tea and cookies. I had to have the turndown truffle, which turned into the turndown petite box of chocolates. That wasn't enough, either. I loved pajama-dining so much I decided I should have dinner in bed, too. I started planning seasonal, eat-in-bed menus. Supping in bed was so glorious that it wasn't long before I didn't want to get out of bed in the morning. After all, breakfast in bed was socially acceptable, and lunch in bed is okay when you're sick, so why not all the time, I reasoned. With that decided, I nested on.

I already had a bedside phone. Laptops are portable, so there was no *real* need to walk clear across the house to my home office. And why wear street clothes during the day? Nothing in my wardrobe matched my sheets anyway. Besides, nonelastic waistbands are *so* confining. Sitting in too-tight pants forced my belly to roll up and over my pant waist. Wearing daytime pajamas became my saving grace.

Filling out my double-XL PJ's to maximum capacity was heavenly-hash fun, though I never realized elastic had such a fierce snapping point—just the wake-up call I obviously needed to cold-turkey myself out of that bad habit. Now the only things I eat in bed are all-fruit Popsicles (15 teensy calories each). Everything else is off-limits. You know what? Eating Popsicles in bed is fun, too.

Figure out what you're eating that you do not really taste. Don't eat it and you won't miss it. Oh, just pretend. You've set reality-based health goals and you're going to reach them. In order to do so, you've got to make mindless eating a non-negotiable. Plan for withdrawals and you'll make it.

Smokers trying to kick the habit need something to do with their hands, and withdrawing grazers need something to do with their jaws. Chew gum, yell at the TV, have a mint. Brush your teeth. Food doesn't pair well with Colgate.

Trains, planes, *and automobiles*

3. Eat to fuel your body and eat for fun, but follow the road rules. I can connect the dots on my steady weight gain through the years and across the country by marking Waffle House exits on a map. It was clearly God's intention to reward hungry road travelers or he never would have given his land over to Bill Knapp's and Howard Johnson's. Paper-lined plastic-basket cuisine, free birthday cakes, fried clams, and old-fashioned ice cream sundaes would never have been invented if we weren't meant to have them.

The very instant I knew I'd be traveling by air, I'd start craving honey-roasted peanuts and devising ways to get the stewardess to give me four packs instead of one. I'd start fantasizing about airport food even before I'd bought my ticket. If God didn't want me to have fourteen king-size candy bars before "now boarding" started to flash on the overhead monitors, he wouldn't have let them build concession stands every fifteen feet. No way would he have allowed Cinnabon factories, Ben & Jerry carts, or Wolfgang Puck cafés to set up shop between my seat assignment and me.

Any excuse to ditch my daily eating and exercise routines was an excuse to act like a kid on Christmas. My sentences started with "I'll start again on Monday," "I'm taking a break after the New Year," and "I deserve this." Well, guess who that backfired on? Miss Can't-Fit-into-Her-Pants, moi.

Swimming out to the buoys is one thing; navigating beyond takes strategy and strength. You're capable of both. It's critically important to plan ahead. Travel, fatigue, traffic jams, lack of enthusiasm, dinner dates, and dentist appointments are not excuses to stray.

Treat your health and eating goals as you would anything else on your calendar. Plan ahead. And plan to deal with the days that you have no plan. This is not only doable; it must become a nonnegotiable part of day-to-day life. If you can remember to pick up the kids, you can keep up with your healthy intentions, too.

Now, when I know I'll be too busy or unable to locate good food fast enough to feed the beast (my stomach), I pack healthful snacks to last throughout the trip. My granola goes where I go. I pack my own airline food, too. I keep peanuts in my purse and trail mix in the glove box. I opt for grilled chicken or fish, healthful salads, and appetizers when dining out. And I keep the freezer stocked full of homemade TV dinners. I'm not trying to be Martha you-know-who and I'm not as obsessed as I sound. I didn't get into these habits overnight, but the more I planned ahead, the less I fell off the wagon. Starting over got old for me.

Lie down and cry after the first lap and you'll never get to hear the national anthem. Three no-more-tears tricks for getting out of your own way.

Mind over Mallomars

1. Lead yourself not into temptation. You fell off the wagon? Boo-hoo. That's over, now get back up! Stop making excuses for why it's okay to eat too much of the wrong foods. A box of Thin Mints is not a charitable donation. No matter how cute she is or whose daughter she is, just because the Girl Scout is at the door doesn't mean you have to order an entire case of cookies. A box or two maybe, but only if you can control yourself in the presence of frozen Thin Mints. I cannot. I rely on friends to order them and then I invite myself over when they arrive.

This probably started because the principal let your child's school become a clearinghouse for PTA junk-food drives. Does getting fat on poor-quality junk food make for better parents? Who are we helping? It's with the best intentions that parents order a dozen wouldn't-even-eat-'em-on-my-death-bed chocolate bars, six rainbow-sprinkle-even-the-squirrels-won't-eat-'em cookie dough balls, and sixty-two kids-won't-touch-'em pizza kits.

SUBJECT: WHAT IS THE FOOD PYRAMID ALL ABOUT?

SENDER: Melinda

TO: email@chefkathleen.com

Dear Kathleen,

I am really upset. My doctor told me to follow the food pyramid. I was too embarrassed to ask him what it was but I know it's a diet because he said I have to lose 40 to 50 pounds. When I was in school we ate from the four food groups, but now there's a pyramid. Have you heard of it? Where can I find out about it? Once I make heads or tails of it how do I make myself stick to this? Do you eat from this?

   Melinda

REPLY: YOUR GOOD HEALTH

Dear Melinda,

The Food Pyramid Guide shows you the kinds and amounts of food that you need each day. Log on to www.nih.gov, click on Weight Loss and Obesity and then Weight Loss for Life. You can find a complete overview of the food pyramid and a breakdown of proper portions. If you don't have access to the Internet, your local library help desk can access the information for you. Or you can write to Weight-Control Information Network, 1 WIN Way, Bethesda, MD 20892-3665; or call toll-free: (877) 946-4627.

   Once you get all the information, don't panic. You're not going to starve. I was sure I was when I began learning proper portion sizes but I'm still here. Try to fill up on good calories first, cut back your portions a little at a time, and don't try to change everything overnight. Moderate, don't eliminate. Hang in there and read on.

   Kathleen

In this day and age who can afford to throw away food? So there we sit, packing away imitation Krackle bars, counterfeit caramel-filled Cadbury's, and bogus peanut butter cups. The price of all this junk in your house will cost a lot more than three dollars a bar. Write a check to the school instead.

   Sometimes it seems like we're living with the Keebler elves. To this day I can barely control myself in Target. They put all the new junk foods at the end of the aisles. I'm on a first-name basis with every brand. It's all I can do to put blinders and earplugs on and beeline toward my intended purchase. When those crinkly-wrapped foods do get the best of me, I limit the portions or give the rest away because I know that if I violate portion-control policies, there will be no treat next time.

If I could **wait** twenty minutes, I wouldn't have **gotten fat** in the first place

Restraint is something I really have to work at. To keep from stuffing my face with anything my hands can reach, I follow the twenty-minute rule, which I modified because practicing patience is another thing I'm working on. The twenty-minute rule says if you see it and want to eat it, wait twenty minutes and then eat it if you really have to have it. Twenty minutes is too long for me. I wait ten and have a glass of water. At the stroke of 10:01, I eat. I listen to my body and then restrict myself to the smallest quantity of whatever it is that I think will satisfy me. If I listened to my inner food demons (fueled not by nutritional needs but emotional wants) I'd never get ahead.

For the most part, I've made peace with the demons of junk food. Each morning I walk through my day mentally. If there are any cracks in my good-food foundation, I apply industrial-strength adhesive in the form of packed snacks and strategies for dining out. Let the chef know that you will flat-line right there in booth 47 if even one molecule of fat touches your food. But whatever you do, don't be rude when informing the waiter of your "life-threatening allergies." If you order like the world's fussiest diner or complicate things too much, the line cooks will rebel by deep-frying everything on your plate before they pan-fry it and then send it out. A more results-oriented approach is to look the waiter in the eye politely and explain that your mother died from ingesting a quarter teaspoon of the very same item you're asking to be left off your plate. And if he or she does get it right, tip handsomely. It's worth knowing you can come back and get it again. Be happy that you can have some of the junk, some of the time.

The little engine that could, *did*

2. **Get over it.** "Pity-party Polly, your fifteen-minute window to weep has been scheduled for 8:00 P.M." My mother used to say that no matter what we were depressed or mad about, we could whine and carry on for only fifteen minutes each day: "Whatever you're bellyaching about isn't worth more than fifteen minutes. Besides, your problems are still going to be there when you're done."

If pity parties aren't your thing, but quitting is, get over that, too. You're not helpless. You've done bigger and more important things in your life, especially if you have children or have cared for a sick loved one. You've demonstrated discipline, follow-through, strength, and resolve in tougher situations before and you can do it again. Besides, we're talking life *with* chocolate here.

So you binged. Turn off the tears and mute all negative internal dialogue. What set you off in the first place? Don't obsess yourself back to the cookie jar but think about it a little. Name three things you can do to avoid the M&Ms anesthesia next time. If you're unraveling at the same time each day, can you schedule a walk? A call with a supportive friend? Have water and healthful snacks nearby.

Pretend a friend had the exact same health fallout you did. What advice would you give him to get back on track? What's good for the goose is good for you. So heal yourself healthy. You can do this. Fifteen minutes every twenty-four hours is all you get, and that *includes* time crying in the shower. Be strong.

Bite off more than you can chew *and you'll choke*

3. **Reevaluate your motivations for getting started in the first place.** Wonder Woman is a fictional character, so stop trying to fit into her star-studded red, white, and blue bustier. Did you set impossible-to-achieve goals for yourself? What if someone you loved told you she wanted to fit into an itsy-bitsy teeny-weeny yellow polka-dot bikini by summer and she was going to cut out all sweets, chips, and alcohol, work out five days a week, take up yoga and twice-weekly weight-training sessions, and cook every meal from scratch in addition to her full-time family life and part-time career? Would you check her for signs of a high fever or what?

Make medical reasons for wanting to achieve good health your driving force. Losing weight and feeling better will be a natural by-product of healthy habits repeated over time. "Diabetes runs in my family, I want to lose weight to live

---

SUBJECT: I'M BACK ON TRACK, HOW CAN I STAY HERE?

SENDER: Mimi

TO: email@chefkathleen.com

Dear Chef Kathleen,
I saw you on a TV show recently and was so impressed with your approach to weight loss that I decided right then and there I could master good eating and exercise again. I've put off getting started for three whole years and now there's even more to lose.
Thank you,
  Mimi in Miami

REPLY: IDENTIFY YOUR TRUE MOTIVATION FOR COMMITTING TO GET FIT

Dear Mimi,
I'm so glad the show inspired you to get started. As you know, that's really the hardest part. The rest is easy. For your efforts to stick this time, identify the real reasons you want to lose weight.

For instance, in my case, I did it for my health. There's diabetes, heart disease, high blood pressure, and obesity in my family. A mostly healthy body is a miracle and a wonderful gift, and I was wasting mine.

Some people are inspired to start because the greatest gift they can give themselves, their children, and their spouse is good health. Getting started because you've got a family wedding and a burgundy bridesmaid dress to fit into is okay, too, but to make it stick, it's important that you're in touch with your true motivations. Flimsy motivations are easy to cast aside.

It's hard to make yourself and your personal good health a priority, but you can do it. Rely on friends and family for support when you need it. Congratulations!
  Kathleen

longer, I want to dance at my child's wedding, I want to enjoy retirement with my spouse."

Wrong: Visions of swimwear
dance in your head

A strategically softened pint of your favorite flavor ice cream sits on the counter. You scoop away. The fanatic spirit guide of vanity and pompousness screams into your ear, "What are you doing, you big cow? Bathing-suit season is just around the corner!" You freeze midscoop. The spirit of self-sabotage screams back, "I'll never look good in a bathing suit anyway, so what's the point?" You continue scooping. Soon you're in an ice-cream-induced stupor. The first few bites are out-of-this-world delicious, but as soon as you see the first strip of the bottom of the bowl, the spirit of self-sabotage flies into a rage: "You pig, you blew it! What were you thinking? You're worthless, you lack self-control, you're a pathetic sloth!" Naturally, your inner enabler tries to patch you up: "It's okay, you can start again tomorrow. No one saw you eat the ice cream, calories eaten alone don't count— besides, you didn't eat the whole pint but you really should finish it, you'll feel much better. Tomorrow's another day." You can guess who shows up again, the spirit of self-sabotage. Round and round they go. It's their idea of fun.

Right: Health *reasons are*
your driving force

Instead, imagine scooping away at that same pint of softened ice cream with the spirit of reason whispering in your ear, "Watch your portion size. You're doing great with your goals. You had a pretty good day today. A little bit is deeply satisfying. Everything is okay in moderation, and if you want to keep treats on the menu, you've got to mind the rules. Besides, you're setting an example for the kids; your husband had a mild stroke, and you're prone to diabetes. You don't really want to pedal this off at the gym later, do you? Eat slowly, taste, and enjoy every delicious bite." The spirits of self-sabotage and enabling have the night off. Challenge yourself to send them on a permanent vacation.

> **Is your fear of cooking making you fat? Take no action, see no results. Eat for good health and you'll outlast the Energizer Bunny. Three essential cook-thin mind-set strategies you already know.**

If you can scramble *eggs you can cook a goose*

1. **Have the confidence to cook.** Everyone's got someone in her life who's skinnier, prettier, and can whip up a ten-course meal faster than you can warm a TV dinner or make a decent piece of toast. If you've got a whopping case of culinary jitters, don't start with a dinner party. Start with something for your cat or cook Fido's dinner. He could probably use a little dog-chow deviation.

The truth is anyone can learn to cook thin (quick, tasty, and healthy meals). It's better for you in the long run if you can spark some kind of lasting love affair with your stove, but it's possible to get by with just a crush.

Don't start out cooking for critics and don't cook their recipes. That includes those from your mother and your mother-in-law. Wolfgang Puck couldn't get *their* recipes right. I've been cooking professionally for twenty years, but "that's not right, Kathleen" is the most-used phrase when I'm cooking alongside my mom. "Why are you doing it *that* way?" comes up a lot, too. Sure, moms do *everything* better and their way is the *right* way, but you need to eat, too.

Culinary disasters *make great mulch (or duck food)*

One day my dad went out and bought every book ever written on bread baking. To this day we don't know why. Unlike *my* usual approach—see one recipe, cook one recipe (read the book some other day)—my father's approach was to actually *read* the books start to finish. Thus we embarked on our "Please, Mom, can't we just have Wonder Bread?" years.

We lived in Florida, so my father blamed the first six months of failures on the humidity. Luckily we lived on a canal and had ducks. But they, too, tired of his bread. Bad bread, weeds, and seeds at every meal didn't seem tasty to my brother and me, so we thought the ducks might enjoy Dad's bread with peanut butter. It didn't take long for my mom to catch on, though. She looked out the window one day and saw the ducks gyrating in an effort to get their bills apart and demanded to know what we'd done. Needless to say, the ducks never got to try grape jelly.

The moral of the story is all my dad's culinary failures didn't destroy his career as a rocket scientist. So don't let a few kitchen failures hold you back.

Practice makes *perfect*

Learning to cook is just like learning to drive a stick shift. Kind of jerky in the beginning but mostly whiplash free after the first month. Except in my case. I wrecked my first and only five-speed car. Just when I thought I'd mastered shifting gears on the freeway it crapped out in the middle of an icy five-lane overpass. My little red Pinto spun like an airborne top until it jammed into a side rail. No one was hurt, but the car was a goner. Anyway, I can roast a good chicken, whip up a quick frittata, and bake a mean slab of salmon. With a little practice, so can you. Remember, Julia Child dropped a chicken on live TV and look at her now.

You get an A just for showing *up*

2. **Don't complicate matters.** Find a recipe with just a few ingredients, all of which you recognize and maybe even like. Imagine yourself making it, but if the first image that comes to mind is you swatting your fire alarm off the ceiling because there's a pot full of flames on the stove, it might be too complex.

While cruising through your cookbooks in search of your maiden voyage, look for a recipe you may have made before, something you've eaten before, a recipe with few ingredients and short instructions. Even if it's orange Jell-O. It's a great way to build your confidence. And then make it on a night when no one's home. Or make it on your day off. There will be another meal in less than eight hours. And there's always Cheerios if you really blow it.

Fly by the seat *of your frying pan*

3. **Listen to your instincts.** Every time I go to people's homes to teach them how to cook, they know the answers to their culinary questions before they finish asking me. Learn to listen to the voice inside your head. It's probably your mother's anyway, and when was she ever wrong?

Take your cues from the culinary pros. They almost never follow recipes as they're written—except when it comes to baking, which is science based. They're always improvising, swapping ingredients, and altering the outcome in one way or another.

The truth of the matter is many recipes aren't 100 percent dependable. Some work and some don't. Some are great, a few should be tossed, and others could use a little improvement.

A cookbook is really just a cross between a survival guide and a really good travel book. Use it as such. Decide where you want to go (pick the chapter you're interested in), check out the sights (settle on a recipe), and follow the instructions. Once you're on your way, you might want to take a side trip (deviate from the recipe) or skip the intended destination altogether (the dish looked good halfway through so you skipped the fancy garnishes or you used salmon instead of sea bass). Let your gut be your guide.

When a title catches your attention, read the little story at the top because there are usually a few good tips woven in. Then read through the ingredients list. If it sounds like it has too much or not enough garlic, it probably does. Write your comments and preferences down directly on the recipe.

Next, read through the instructions. As you read through each step, imagine yourself going through the moves, grabbing for the ingredients, and assembling the tools. Make notes of anything you don't have on hand. If on this dry run something doesn't sound quite right, it's worth a second read through. If it still doesn't make any sense, figure out what will and proceed *your* way. You're probably right.

Now cook already. Make notes as you go or after you've eaten what you've prepared. All my cookbooks are marked, highlighted, tabbed, and full of food. It's the only way I can remember things. I could live without the coffee-stained pages, though.

Part Two: Exercise

On your mark! Get in touch with your inner athlete (I had to make mine from scratch). Three get-off-the-couch-now tips guaranteed to get you to your healthiest self.

Lose a little, gain a whole lot

1. **Find your inner exercise voice.** I'm still looking for mine and had to move on without it. I hate exercise so much I skipped gym class twenty-three times in one semester of high school, almost flunking out because of it. It seems this particular malady is genetic *and* highly contagious. My mom hates exercise even more than I do. She makes it a policy not to sweat. My siblings don't exercise, either. My father purchased a pair of gym shoes back in '71 for five dollars and has "never had an occasion to wear them." I don't know anyone who *likes* to exercise, which proves the communicable theory. Or says too much about the company I keep.

My exercise epiphany came in the form of my friend Jack. My first week in Maui, he hoodwinked me into my first "walk" in six years by telling me we were going to see waterfalls.

Having lived in Yosemite National Park during a culinary apprenticeship at the Ahwahnee Hotel, I loved waterfalls and assumed they all had concession stands leading from the parking lot straight up to the base of their cascades, as in the case of Yosemite Falls.

I should have realized something was up when Patrick (an outdoorsy type whose very presence should have aroused my suspicion) made me trade flip-flops for gym shoes before we left the house. Clue number two was the absence of any sign of a waterfall or even mist when Jack stopped the car and called out, "We're here."

Skeptical, yet ever naive, I followed them. "It's just over here," Jack yelled as we headed down a pebbly path leading into lush green foliage, which I have to admit was intoxicatingly beautiful—part of their carefully plotted ruse, contrived "in my best interest."

Two hours and fifty-two blisters later, nary a waterfall in view, I was hot, starving, and mad. Out of my mind and out of breath, I was at the *bottom* of a deep ravine somewhere in the West Maui Mountains, tricked by my so-called friends

---

SUBJECT: NO TIME TO EXERCISE

SENDER: Missy

TO: email@chefkathleen.com

Dear Kathleen,

I'm a single mom working full-time with two teenagers and an aging ill parent living with me. I can't exercise and really need to just keep my sanity. The gym is too far away and too expensive for my budget. I'm going nuts. Please help.

Missy

REPLY: DELEGATE THE LAUNDRY BUT DON'T GIVE UP ON EXERCISE

Dear Missy,

You're swamped and maxed out but you probably know that. Take a deep breath. It's critically important that you eat well and get your exercise, especially during really hectic times. Exercise relieves stress, increases your energy, improves sleep quality, and it's time alone just for you.

Make exercise nonnegotiable so it never crosses your mind to cut it out. Exercise before work or during your lunch break if possible. Consider power walks around the neighborhood, a nearby park, or up and down the office stairwell if that's the best you can do. It works and it counts. What about an eight-minute workout tape before work, a ten-minute walk at lunch, and an eight-minute workout tape after work?

Consider saving up for an exercise bike or an in-home cardio machine. Sometimes a quick garage sale can yield enough extra cash. Your needs are just as important as everyone else's—don't give up on yourself. Anything is better than nothing but I'm betting you can work this out.

Kathleen

turned chain-gang guards, who doled out only enough food scraps and water to sustain life. One of the jailers barked, "Those wishing to sup on something other than wild berries and rainwater had best keep moving."

I hated them with all my might and begged the Hawaiian god of centipedes to dispatch swarms of the venomous creatures to their beds that night.

As the sun was setting over Haleakala, a sight I was sure I'd never see again, we made it to the car. I made it to my bed and fell asleep in my stinking clothes—*without* dinner. I woke up filthy, starving, and so sore I could barely make it to the table.

Gazing across green ocean waters to Molokai at breakfast that morning, feasting on Maui papayas and just-picked pineapples, I began to accept the things I desperately didn't want to change about myself but knew I had to.

There's just no excuse for being that out of shape, especially when all your parts are in working order. Life is a gift, and a body in generally good health is a miracle to be cherished, nurtured, and taken care of, by each of us.

Dragging your heels for the last time

2. **Get a second opinion.** Your inner voice voted for exercise a long time ago. And now that you've let thoughts of exercise into your head, you can justifiably stall your first workout another week or so by scheduling a visit to your doctor to get the official all clear. I have to say this because it's a good idea. Prepare yourself for this tête-à-tête because, unless you've been faithfully frequenting cardio blast class and eating perfectly balanced meals, chances are you're going to be given the inescapable "prescription" to sever all your favorite foods from your diet. But before you even get a chance to digest that bit of peachy news, you're going to get the rest of the remedy—exercise five times a week, thirty minutes a day, until Willard Scott is wishing you a happy hundredth: this, if you're lucky.

Keep in mind, as you fight the urge to head straight to McDonald's, somebody's always got it worse than you. Start realistically visualizing yourself more healthy and fit. Notice I didn't say Ken-and-Barbie buff. Setting unrealistic goals before you begin is self-defeating and serves no purpose.

Besides, you knew this was coming. Look at it this way—the more you move, the more you can eat. I exercise *to* eat, within reason of course. I eat for a living, and I'm not willing to pass up desserts, so I make up for it on the old exercise bike.

Most of those little aches and pains will magically disappear over time. You won't get tired climbing up the stairs as quickly as before. And picking up all those little toys won't be quite as hard. Of course, in the beginning you might be a bit too tired to cook but that goes away after the first day. Okay, I'm lying, which is precisely why you'll have to plan ahead a little. Stock a few dozen homemade TV dinners in the freezer to get you through the first few weeks of boot camp. Kidding! Exercise is not punishment; it's a privilege.

Mommy, I'm bored

3. There are some really good mental door prizes for working out. You know how at the end of the day if you hear anyone call your name even one more time you think you might not live to see morning? And let's not get into the plots you come up with to deal with impolite drivers, check-out clerks (just the ones from Mars), and phone solicitors. I've found working out to be a very good tonic for just such thoughts—which is a good thing because shrinks cost a lot, especially five times a week for thirty-minute sessions.

Think of workout time as "me time." I know it can be a stretch for some of you, and it was for me in the beginning, too. But it's true. No one yanks on your pant leg in the gym. The phone is never for you. The lady on the next treadmill over never asks for "just a moment of your time," no one asks you where her car keys are, no one accuses you of packing a yucky lunch, and no one asks for help with his homework. If you're lucky, no one will talk to you at all.

You're doing something really good for yourself and you get to check it off your list. Sure, you might be tired and you might be sweaty, but it's a selfish, all-about-you hour. Okay, so it's not the beauty salon, it's not a spa, it's not the movies, and it's not even a good sale rack at Nordstrom's. But you can never get in trouble for overspending at the gym.

Get set (setbacks out of your system). Three all-new-you exercise essentials you won't run away from.

The agony of **defeat.** *The thrill of shivering on a pool deck in a* **one-piece** *better suited for a sea lion.*

1. Invent a realistic exercise program. I used to put together overly ambitious exercise programs for myself. There was the time I wanted to be an Olympic cyclist. Lord only knows why I came up with that. Had I *ridden* a bike in ten years? Could my hubba-hubba hiney *fit* on one of those teensy seats? I went out and bought all the gear, stopping just short of a $1,000 racing bike. I opted for a $350 mountain bike with a real Mickey Mouse bell instead. Seemed more sporty and I couldn't resist that bell. *Ring-ring. Ring-ring.* I wanted the handlebar basket with fake plastic daisies but thought better of it—it detracted from the sporty look I was going for. Of course I didn't ride my new bike past the second day of ownership. I kept it in my bedroom because it looked cool. Made me *feel* more athletic. The thought of dragging it up and down the stairs every day took the wind right out of my sails. It made a much better towel rack anyway.

Flipping through *Vogue* one night inspired a craving for a much-needed Big Apple shopping excursion, so I set my sights on the New York City marathon. Thus, my Jackie Joyner-Kersee phase. It lasted as long as dinner and a show. Well, technically it lasted the length of time it took me to gear up, adjust my headphones, run down the block, and collapse in a hyperventilating heap on my neighbor's lawn.

One-dollar mermaid, me

Mark Spitz had just won seven gold medals, and the thought of a refreshing dip in a pool seemed appealing, so I embarked on my Esther Williams day. It was a quickie. When I looked in the mirror at the reflection of me in a swimsuit, one of the tutu-clad hippopotamuses from *Fantasia* waved back. Just when I thought I'd surely die of shame and humiliation, my mother stepped in. "Kathleen, do you *like* to swim?"

"Yeah, Mom."

"So swim."

She was right. I love to swim. There was a pool nearby, I could easily get in a swim before or after work, and it only cost a dollar. I really had no excuse except that I was embarrassed about the way I looked. Reason and the sound of my mother's voice took over my brain. "Kathleen, you can sit in your room and cry about it, or you can give it your best try. What's it gonna be? Those people aren't swimsuit competition judges enjoying a day off. Truth is, no one cares what you look like but you. And if you don't like how you feel, then do something about it. You're not helpless. You'll get through this. Be thankful that you can."

It worked for Forrest, Forrest Gump

2. **Set small goals.** I wanted to be able to run after my fleeing one-year-old niece and catch her *before* she got to the end of the driveway *without* feeling like a walrus chasing its prey. I thought it'd be nice to walk up a flight of stairs without feeling like I'd *earned* a nap. I wanted to walk around the block without calculating how long it would take paramedics to arrive in *case* I needed CPR.

So I went to the pool. Nary a Victoria's Secret model in sight. Except for the initial splash, no one even noticed me. No one rolled on the floor laughing at the sight of me in a bathing cap (which did nothing for my already chubby cheeks). They didn't give me my own lane, and they didn't offer to hoist me out of the pool with a crane.

It was pretty uneventful. I swam and got out of the pool. I even made it through the humiliating strip off your suit and get into your street clothes locker room scene. I went home and the world kept spinning on its axis.

Think of your exercise program as a giant heart-shaped box of chocolates (naturally the world's *best*-quality chocolates). Each chocolate represents a higher-for-you level of exercise. *Already* your appetite is gone? A cherry-filled chocolate (always hated those) means five extra minutes of cardio, dark chocolate coconut squares represent the introduction of weight training. Pecan clusters signal inter-

---

SUBJECT: MY HUSBAND EATS ALL THE FOOD I SHOULDN'T

SENDER: Trina

TO: email@chefkathleen.com

Dear Kathleen,
My husband buys junk food snacks and leaves them all over the house. I can't stay out of them. There are healthy snacks in the house but I'd rather eat the junk. Our freezer is jammed full of ice cream. Please help.
Trina

REPLY: IF GOOD SNACKS ARE IN YOUR SIGHT LINE, YOU'LL GRAB THEM FIRST

Dear Trina,

Who is doing the grocery shopping? If it's him, you're a little stuck, but if it's you, buy less or none at all. Ask him to pick up his own snacks on his way home. He'll probably bring less into the house or none if he's like my dad and too lazy to go to the store or just not interested enough.

Try to snack on good stuff before you go for less nutritious foods. You'll have less room. Surround yourself with good snacks you'll enjoy. Place bowls of trimmed fruit cut into bite-size chunks and veggies in easy-to-get-at locations, not molding in the bottom of the crisper drawer.

Buy snacks in smaller quantities, a pint of the best-quality ice cream at a time. If you've got three half-gallons, it's easy to graze from carton to carton without really knowing how much you've consumed. Take things a day at a time, reward yourself for all the good things you do, and don't place too many restrictions on yourself at one time.

Kathleen

val training, mocha creams indicate a total abdominal workout, rum nougats say triceps-biceps day, raisin clusters scream stretch and tone, raspberry creams declare race-walk day, milk peanuts equal push-ups, and dark chocolate truffles say sign up for a class.

Gorge through half the box of chocolates on the first day and your workout routine will be harder than the *Flashdance* girl's. So take it easy. A chocolate every few days or so. Instead of setting impossible exercise goals, set your sights a little closer to home. Do what you can handle, but you're going to have to push yourself a little to see and feel results. You didn't think you could do this from the couch, did you? Resist the urge to head for chocolate right now. I know you want some. Make a cup of hot tea or grab a huge glass of ice water with lemon and read on. No, it's not the same thing, but you bought this book because you're ready to change. So change. You can do it.

The dog ate your homework? Write on the blackboard one hundred times: I will think of a more believable excuse next time.

3. **Start today.** Today is the tomorrow you worried about yesterday. Too tired you say? Hmm. When haven't you been too tired? If we had to wait until we felt refreshed, relaxed, full of energy, vim, and vigor, we'd all be walking around in our pajamas. Too tired is a flimsy excuse and you know it.

No *time*? You can't find twenty minutes? That's the length of time you spend on hold with the DMV or staring out the window wishing for Madonna's yoga body or dreaming of full-time domestic help. Twenty minutes is the amount of time it takes to pick up the very same pile of plastic toys and puzzle pieces that are going to be right back on the floor an hour from now. And it doesn't matter how you do your time. Two tens equal twenty. Grab the mail and keep going. A brisk ten-minute walk after breakfast and ten minutes of marching in place during the evening news add up day after day.

Don't have the right equipment? Ran out of shoes again? Walking requires feet and the right mind-set. I find it hard to believe you're reading this barefoot. Put on the most comfortable shoes you have and get going. You're not going to walk that far today. Stilettos would be fine. If you really need new walking shoes, go get 'em tomorrow. The blisters will inspire you. The point is to move and to prove to yourself that you *can* get going. Because you really do have it in you.

Go already! Three reach-your-goal workout solutions.

Rita's great adventure
(Rita's my mom)

1. **Figure out what kind of exercise you can stomach.** I'll never forget the day I wanted to take my mom to Exercise Warehouse. I couldn't get her in the car. So I started negotiating with her. "Mom, you don't have to sign up for the gym if you pick out something to use at home."

"Kathleen, my life was just fine when you were in California."

"Mom, your doctor said you have osteoporosis and you need to move. Do you want to work out at home or at the Power House gym? Since you flunked swimming, I'm guessing the pool is out."

"Your father is the one who really needs to work out. He wants an exercise bike with a big seat."

"Mom, he's a cheapskate. He hasn't been shopping since the fifties. You can't *buy* anything at Exercise Warehouse for fifty dollars."

"Then find out how much it costs and I'll buy it for his birthday. He'll hate it but we'll put a big bow on it. He loves bells and whistles. You can talk him into getting one if it's got a lot of gadgets and you don't let him see the price."

"All right, fine, Mom. Like I *need* this kind of father-daughter outing. I'm doing this for you and believe me, it's going to hurt." So off we went on Rita's great adventure while she stayed home.

My mom figured out what would work for her and my dad and paid out enough cash to keep from using the bike as a towel rack. "With that kind of money I could have done something fun, Kathleen." Letting perfectly good money go to waste is worse to her than riding the bike. So she rides it every day and Dad does too.

SUBJECT: I NEED TO LOSE WEIGHT BUT I DON'T KNOW HOW TO START

SENDER: Laura

TO: email@chefkathleen.com

Dear Kathleen,

My doctor told me I need to lose 75 pounds. I'm totally overwhelmed and scared to get started. I don't know where to begin or what to do first. I live alone and have time to cook, but I've never been very good at it. Can you help?

REPLY: TRIM EXCESS CALORIES AND FAT ANYWHERE YOU CAN

Dear Laura,

Asking for help was the first step. Congratulations, you don't have to worry about where to begin because you're on your way now. Start by cutting out any excess calories and fat you won't mind giving up. For instance, would one slice of cheese on your sandwich satisfy you? Would you really notice 2 teaspoons less of mayonnaise? How about cutting your salad dressing back by a tablespoon? Every spoonful helps. A tablespoon of olive oil has 14 grams of fat and 130 calories—that's a big savings. Can you switch from whole milk to 2 percent?

Cut your portion sizes back a little bit at a time, too, but start slowly. Inch your way toward recommended serving sizes. Increase healthful calories wherever you can. Up your daily fruit and veggie intake. Cut back on meat meals if you eat too many. Up fish and chicken meals and try an all-veggie night.

When you're cooking, keep in mind that recipes often call for way more fat than is necessary. Listen to your instincts when you're trying to determine if the recipe could work with less fat. If a recipe calls for ½ cup oil, try using ⅓ cup this time and ¼ cup next time. Make notes directly on the pages to keep track. (This won't work with baking, though.)

Start watching cooking shows, reading culinary magazines, and logging on to food web sites. You'll find a lot of great ideas and information.

Kathleen

Sometimes she calls me up and says, "Kathleen, this is your mother. Thanks to you, I'm riding my new refrigerator."

Knowing that my mom gets on her stationary bike five days a week and rides for twenty minutes, no matter what, means that if she can do it, I'd *better* do it. Besides, if I skipped a workout, she'd sense it and there'd be a message on my machine: "Kathy, this is your mom. I know you're there, and I know you skipped the gym. If this is how you're going to make a living, you're going to have to set a better example for people. And you really should give up coffee."

Figure out if working out alone, with a partner, or by conjuring up the voice of your mother (my mom's never rests) is best for you. And stick with it. Joining a gym is not for everyone and really isn't for me, either. I hate it. But I'm into my tenth year of this and have as hectic a schedule as anyone. Knowing that I can get to the gym in three minutes, work out for an hour, and be done for the day was my driving motivation to face my Ken and Barbie phobias and sweat indoors.

Mirror mirror *on the wall, who's the* frumpiest *of us all?*

2. **Brave the jungle gym.** One should not be made to feel like "Sarah plain and fat" walking into a beauty pageant when entering a gym. There's something so intimidating about women wearing two-toned lipstick, teardrop diamond earrings, and clothes that can't possibly absorb sweat to work out in.

The reality is that they aren't there to scare us. They've got their own agendas and are busy living their lives the way they see fit. *I* was the one who had to get over it. My armor became *my* workout gear. Someone had to level the playing field and since I couldn't afford Saks Fifth Avenue workout sets with matching T's and diamonds, I thought it might as well be me.

I dress to kill. Can I help it if my "paint the house" spandex doubles as workout wear? Wearing beat-up baseball caps, "Trix Are for Kids" T-shirts, and real athletic shoes sends the message to my brain that it's time to work. We can't all be dressed to the nines.

Joining a gym is not for everyone, though, and I can still hardly believe I go every week. Don't talk to me about gym bliss and exercise highs. How anyone can get "addicted to working out" is beyond me. I go because I have to go. I go to achieve my best health. I go because I don't want to deal with brittle bones and Lord knows what else later on. I go because I'm way too tired to worry about work or complain about some idiotic project when I'm exhausted from exercise.

At least you've never been **called** a "big chewy **rump**" by a pierced punk rocker sporting a rainbow Mohawk

3. **Come up with an exercise plan.** For heaven's sake, you're not house hunting. You're not choosing the baby's name. And you're not sifting through job offers. Walk or don't walk. Work out indoors or outdoors. Swim, hike, cycle, tae kwon do, or do si do, just *do* something. You'll *feel* better. You're never going to ditch your sluggardly ways unless you make a move. Besides, you can change your exercise plan any time you want.

Listen, I feel your pain. I know how hard this is but I know, too, that you can do it. You don't need to feel like crap about it any longer. And I know you do. Because I did too. And I do every time I get lazy and skip the gym.

When I was going to college in California, I used to zip around town on a moped. Stopped at a red light one day, I heard a bunch of hooting and hollering as a car full of college boys pulled up alongside me. Naturally I turned to check out the ruckus (and to see if any of them were cute) just in time for one of them to look me dead in the eyes and call out to the others, "Fat chick on a moped." If *that* didn't send me straight to Mee Heng Low's for moo goo gai pan and fortune cookies.

You can turn off negative internal dialogue faster than you can mute the commercials. It's important not to use the hurt you feel as an excuse to give up, because you just end up feeling guilty. Next thing you know, in waltzes your spirit guide of self-sabotage. It's not the best idea to beat yourself up for *anything*, let alone skipping your exercises. Guilt and shame magically blossom into self-confidence after the first five minutes of any form of self-care, especially exercise. And that's what you need to cling to: feeling great about yourself.

> **Medals are great but these rewards are even better. Three confidence-boosting, prizewinning benefits guaranteed to send your self-esteem soaring.**

Buy me some peanuts *and Cracker Jack. At least there was a* prize *in every box.*

1. **Attitude adjustment.** When my spinning teacher told me I "really ought to buy a heart-rate monitor" he might as well have told me to feed a fifty-dollar bill to the cat. I can't say I love spending perfectly good money on shoes and exercise gear I otherwise wouldn't be caught dead in. I can't say my favorite part of getting in shape is getting out of bed at the crack of dawn to go work out, especially when it's 14 degrees with a wind chill factor of 40 below zero. I don't like the feel of sweaty clothes on my skin and despise the fact that Lester the drowned rat shows up in the gym mirror instead of me. I hate the way my hair gets wet and forms to my scalp like papier-mâché to a balloon. Naturally my baseball cap usually falls off at the exact same moment Mr. Tall and Perfect walks by. I pretend the reason he doesn't ask for my number is *not* because he's writhing in horror at the sight of my hair but because he can't find a pencil.

What I *do* like about exercising are the many benefits. The intangibles. If you can just make it past week one, horrible hunger pangs, pass-out-tired feelings of fatigue, and minor cash setbacks, everything gets markedly easier. Energy levels soar. If you *wanted* to put forth more effort at the office, you could. You won't fall asleep before the kids do anymore. You might actually be able to count to ten before you explode and kill someone in the family. I'm not saying you'll prance through life, but you'll count the hours until bedtime on fewer days. The excess energy is yours to spend as you please.

SUBJECT: LOW THYROID

SENDER: Sue

TO: email@chefkathleen.com

Dear Kathleen,

I have a lot of weight to lose. I recently found out that my thyroid level is low and that I have too much calcium in my blood. Any suggestions?

REPLY: WORK WITH YOUR DOCTOR

Dear Sue,

I'm not qualified to address your thyroid and calcium conditions, but I strongly urge you to learn as much about your diagnosis as possible. Call your doctor's office and ask if they can recommend any particular books and sources of support. The Internet is a great resource, too. Log on to the National Institutes of Health web site, nih.gov, and see what you can find. Formulate a list of questions. Make an appointment to discuss them with your doctor and all the different treatment options and solutions.

Once you've been given the medical all-clear to keep losing weight safely, reevaluate the calories you're consuming versus the calories you're burning. You've got to burn off more than you consume to achieve weight loss. Challenge yourself to make the numbers work. Good luck.

Kathleen

Mall stamina

I prefer to take my Energizer Bunny stamina to the mall with my sisters. We can cover a lot of ground together. In the old days we used to get so tired we'd have no choice but to meet at the Häagen-Dazs bench. We refueled with Swiss chocolate almond cones or in my case an Oreo blizzard. I pretended it was a "healthier" choice. The fact that the volume of a blizzard was three times that of a single scoop never seemed to bother me. Never mind that it had three times the calories as well. It was made from nonfat yogurt—*had* to be healthy. Not!

The best part about taking control of your health is that you don't feel bad about yourself anymore. You're finally doing what you should have been doing all along. And did it take more than two seconds for the guilt to go away? The turnaround is instant. I started feeling better as I was lacing my gym shoes for the very first time because I knew I was on my way. I finally got up enough courage to get up and go. And I built on that teensy spark of confidence. I liked the way it felt and wanted more of it. When I'm totally down in the dumps and discouraged, I think back to those shoelaces, and it usually gets me going again. It's very important to acknowledge every single thing you do right. We certainly don't hesitate to beat the tar out of ourselves for the teeniest mistake. Use that same skill to uncover all the good stuff you do.

Being healthier and having more rest and energy give you the patience to deal with life's daily blessings. If you have more confidence in your physical appearance, you have more confidence in how you are, period. It pours over into every area of your life. When you feel good about yourself, who you are, and where you're at in life, you're there, which is why it's important *not* to compare yourself to others. Compare your improved body to your old body. Listen to your body getting stronger. Hear the greatness from within. And appreciate it for the miracle that it is.

No more weigh *station for you*

2. **The light years.** You see it coming up on your calendar. Instead of the annual preexam tremors and anxiety, you feel pretty good about things. When Nurse Ratched calls your name, you'll be able to waltz up to the notoriously inaccurate scale that suddenly has become fine-tuned for your annual weigh-in. Naturally she automatically whips the weights to the 300-pound mark from your last visit but much to her chagrin finds that she has to move them back down. Feeling smitten with yourself, you start humming. It takes all your self-control not to launch into nah-nah-nah-nah-nah-nah!

Next, she takes your blood pressure and says in a patronizing singsong voice, "It's down a little bit from last time. Have you been exercising?" Just as you're about to launch into a victory speech she stabs you with a needle to draw blood for your cholesterol check.

In walks Dr. Feel-Good. In his too-little, too-late voice he says, "I see you've dropped some weight. That's good. Keep it up. Only 100 more pounds to go." Of course you're feeling like someone let the air out of your tires until you notice that his lab coat can't close over his belly. You consider lecturing him on his diet and suggesting a good exercise program but think better of it, because he really does have your best interests at heart, even if he could use a bedside-manner refresher course.

The fact is you're making progress and that's all that counts. You're moving forward. You didn't get here in a day; it's going to take time to get back to reality. Slow and steady wins the race, unless you're competing with Marion Jones, and what are the chances of that?

You look mah-ve-lous!

3. The little things. You'll be able to wear your wedding ring again, your socks won't make marks around your ankles, you'll be able to trade the expansion band on your wristwatch for something more fashionable, and you won't look like you're storing acorns for winter in your cheeks. Never again will anyone look to your closet for shirts big enough to shelter the Boy Scouts overnight in bad weather.

Even before better-fitting jeans you'll notice your underwear fits right again. Six o'clock will come and go without your fearing death by underwear strangulation. The expiration time on your bra will be longer, too. You'll be able to spend more waking hours in your brassiere without feeling the need to tear it off your body and fling it out the car window at the first private moment.

Looking good in your skinny jeans is just a bonus. There's going to come a day when you're not going to look good in your jeans, no matter what you do. How many centenarians have contracts with Guess? This is all about good health. *Feeling* good in your jeans is much more important.

Mr. Ed's bride **doesn't**
live here

You'll look your best when you *feel* your best. When you feel your best, you'll stop obsessing over how you look because you won't care anymore. Not the kind of I don't care, what's the point, I'm the real Mrs. Ed, so why brush, floss, drag a comb through my hair, or get out of my pajamas, for that matter. It's a carefree I-don't-care. You *know* you look good.

Part Three: Make Up Your Mind to Do It

BECAUSE WHO WANTS LIFE

WITHOUT BOSTON CREAM PIE?

You can't get to the finish line if you don't take the first step. If you want change, make change. Three get-up-and-go-today

Find or fake the right **mind-set** *to get started*

1. **Ready, set, go!** People who live on the other side, where the grass is greener, wake up the first day of their journey toward better health and fitness by saying, "Today I'm going to throw out all junk food, hire a personal trainer, and get thin in six weeks." And they do. Yippee for them. I can't relate to that and have proven beyond a reasonable doubt that I could never be that disciplined. So I've come up with a way around that unrealizable level of perfection that's worked for me and can work for you, too.

Not only do you *have* to do this for yourself but you eventually have to *want* to do this for yourself, two very different mind-sets. Self-imposed scare tactics, a family reunion or swimsuit season, are an okay way to get started. But do yourself a favor now that you've made the commitment to eat better, cook thin, and get fit. Before you get started, shelve your baggage. Just for a little while anyway.

Skinny people think overweight people eat too much because we're dragging around too much emotional baggage. While this may be true, everyone knows food tastes better when there's a heartfelt reason to eat. I, like most everyone else on the planet, am an emotional eater. If I chucked my luggage, I'd be in danger of death by starvation or, at the very least, severe malnutrition.

I had to teach myself to separate weight loss and health goals from emotional issues. It really is the key to lifelong success, but I'm telling you now, it's not easy. It's achievable, but for me, it's a constant struggle. I have to steadfastly remind myself not to feed my emotions or use them as an excuse to quit. It's very easy to let stress block the only way out of town. Don't let it. Once you've made some progress in the physical health department, you'll feel better equipped to deal with emotional issues, but one thing at a time.

If your little red wagon is full *of dirt, plant tulips*

2. **Let go of excuses or work around them for now.** Everyone's got a figurative little red wagon. They're given to us around the time we take our first steps. Somewhere in the instruction book of life, *I* thought it said to fill them up with childhood hurts, teenage guilt, and adult woes. I didn't actually *read* there was a prize for the wagon with the highest pile of pain, but I tried to win anyway. The more-is-better mind-set proved once again that it isn't always. I've still got the wagon but I try to keep it empty.

No one can do this for you. If you need to hit rock bottom to get started, lower your standards. How long do you want to let this go on? Do you want to dance at your kid's wedding or what? Do you want to spend your retirement money on trips, cars, and cruises or on upper GI tests? Do you want to become one with your pharmacist or your travel agent? Don't make me call your mother!

Yankee Doodle handy

There are calorie crooks around every corner and fat grams waiting in the shadows. We had to call in the government to sort it all out with tougher labeling laws and to spell out dietary guidelines and fitness recommendations. The information and resources are all there, backed up by science and medicine. We now have

email@chefkathleen.com

SUBJECT: I CAN'T SEEM TO LOSE ANY MORE WEIGHT

SENDER: Bea

TO: email@chefkathleen.com

Dear Kathleen,

I need to lose at least 100 pounds and I've only lost 51. I've been walking on the treadmill and dieting, but I can't seem to lose any more. I've been stuck at the same weight for one month, and I'm getting discouraged. What should I do?

REPLY: INCH YOURSELF TO THE NEXT LEVEL

Dear Bea,

Losing 51 pounds is a phenomenal achievement, so you should be very proud.

Small changes can make a big difference. Burn 250 calories in physical activity and trim 250 calories a day from your diet, and you can lose about a pound a week. Trimming 250 calories isn't as hard as you think and can be as simple as cutting out coffee break calories. Not the coffee but those darned Krispy Kremes. Skip the fries at lunch, cut out the regular soda, or just say no to dessert. At each meal, try leaving behind 1 tablespoon of everything you consume. Do you really think you'll notice 1 tablespoon less of mashed potatoes?

How often do you work out, for how long? Aim for thirty to forty-five minutes a day five times per week. Can you inch up your workouts by five minutes a session? Add an extra day to your regime, get in a weekend walk? Can you increase the pace or intensity? How about a little cross-training? Can you walk a set of stairs at lunch? Sign up for a once a week class?

Keep up the great work, Bea. Keep challenging yourself to go to the next level.

Kathleen

access to exactly what's in foods, how much of what we should be eating, and how long we need to keep our heart rates up each day. You've heard everything your doctor has to say on the subject, so it's time to make up your mind to do it. The time for excuses has expired.

Be the Phoenix rising out of the ashes of your bad habits. Get motivated, make your culinary game plan. Start with foods you like, and weave in things you know you should be eating. It's not as simple as bacon, eggs, and cheese for breakfast anymore. These recipes are going to make your life a lot easier. Rely on them. I did the thinking and testing for you.

If you don't want to do this for you, it's just not going to work. You have to find the motivation within yourself. Of course you have the option of slamming the book shut right now and using it as a doorstop, but aren't there enough of those in the house already? You've got some motivation because you're reading this. Keep up that momentum. See where else you can find reasons to keep moving forward.

I got a D– in algebra, **flunked** *cheerleading tryouts, and* **never** *got asked to the prom*

3. **Keep at it.** Everyone graduates, eventually. It takes four years, all of your parents' patience, and sixty-four tubes of zit cream to graduate from high school. Consider yourself back in school. That's the journey. Don't put more expectations on yourself now than you had back then. We all had different study habits, but everybody made it out alive. Whatever you do, don't set yourself up to fail by taking on more than you can handle.

Focus on small behavioral changes, tiny little things you can do each day that over time will produce tremendous results. Trust me, if you do the work, you'll get healthier. It's not going to happen overnight, but you're in control of your ride. Take on as much or as little as you want to.

For instance, your exercise routine has to fit into your day or it will be too easy to talk yourself out of doing it. It's got to become a nonnegotiable. So while you're thinking about what and how you want to work out five times a week, thirty minutes a day (the more I say it, the sooner you'll believe me), go for a walk.

Start small. A walk to the mailbox is too small but a walk around the block is a great start. Bottom line, it's got to fit into your day and meet your health criteria, too. You might as well deal with this now, or you're just going to have to come back to it later. You can do this. Focus on health reasons.

The weatherman can't always promise sun. Three all-weather tough-it-out coping strategies guaranteed to keep the spring in your step.

Do you **make** your own nail polish?

1. **Access medical information.** Do you make your own shoes? Did you paint your car? Do you make duct tape from scratch? Hello. Rely on the pros, access information they've collected, and utilize all the great tools out there. Take charge. Determine your destiny. You're not on a mystery tour. Health professionals are at

---

SUBJECT: I'M ADDICTED TO SNACK CAKES

SENDER: Sharon

TO: email@chefkathleen.com

Dear Kathleen,

I'm embarrassed to admit it, but I'm addicted to any kind of snack cake. I love those Little Debbies, Hostess Cupcakes, Twinkies, Sno-Balls, and anything soft and creamy. I feel very bad that I eat them, and know I shouldn't. I buy them for my kids' lunches, and I guess they remind me of my childhood or something.

Sharon

REPLY: TWINKIE DETOX COULD BE IN ORDER

Dear Sharon,

I can totally relate. I love a good Ding Dong, too. I've found the only way to kick those kinds of habits is to purge my cupboards of foods I can't control myself around. It's a little drastic, but I know my limits. Do it for you and do it for your kids. You mentioned that the cakes remind you of your childhood, which indicates to me that your mom packed them for you. Your kids could end up with the same kind of problem you're having, so try to set a good example for them. Stop with the cakes already.

If cold turkey is too hard to come to grips with, whip up Karen's Angel Food Cake (page 351). It's an easy, satisfying alternative.

Kathleen

---

your fingertips twenty-four hours a day. All you have to do is call on them. And lots of times you don't even have to leave the house. Everything starts and ends with your personal physician. That said, there are plenty of other ways for you to access the latest health news.

Start with the National Institutes of Health. Log on to www.nih.gov. "Begun as a one-room Laboratory of Hygiene in 1887, the National Institutes of Health today is one of the world's foremost medical research centers, and the Federal focal point for medical research in the U.S. . . . From a total of about $300 in 1887, the NIH budget has grown to more than $17.8 billion in 2000." So they're spending lots of money to figure things out for us.

When you get to their site, click on Health Information. Next, click on NIH Health Information Index 2001 health topics A–Z and the Institutes that research them. Follow the instructions for the information you seek. You'll find a comprehensive page of health information related to the condition you're researching, including health-education programs, special reports, news of the latest information, clinical trials, in-depth topics, and additional resources. And it's all free.

For instance, under "obesity," you can access articles on weight loss and control, binge-eating disorders, safe and successful weight-loss programs, dieting and gallstones, the health risks of being overweight, programs for overweight children, dietary guidelines for Americans, physical activity, weight control, and much, much more. It's a fantastic resource. If you don't have access to the Internet from your home, it's worth making a trip to your local library.

Playing Easy-Bake Oven **alone** *is fun but then* **you** *gotta do all the dishes yourself*

2. **Have friends or at least a good crowd to run with.** When I was seven, my mom put me out with the empty milk bottles one morning and told me to go make friends. The neighborhood was swarming with children of the same age who went to the same school and who lived within spitball target range of my front door, but we'd just moved into the neighborhood, and my Susie Homemaker kitchen wasn't even unpacked yet. Nobody wants to play with a kid with no toys. On top of the tyke strikes against me, I was terribly shy and certain I'd never meet anyone like my best friend Charlotte, who was probably my "best" friend because she let me boss her around.

The milkman came and went. I couldn't make myself leave the front stoop, so I was forced to eat lunch outside. My mom opened the door just wide enough to hand me a PB&J on white and a glass of milk. Her summer plans didn't include a whining child hollering, "There's nothing to *doooo*, Mommy," when there was something out there I *could* be doing. She wasn't budging on this. I could come back in when I made a friend, period. After drinking all that milk I couldn't "hold" it anymore. So I went next door and knocked. A little girl my age answered. "Can I use your bathroom?" I asked. "Sure," she said. "What's your name?" "Chatty Kathy," I answered. And the rest is history.

Too bad our moms aren't always around to make sure we go out and do the things we already know are best for us. The point is, you can do this on your own and you really need to learn how to rely on yourself, but it's also important to seek out supportive friends and to get the good advice of friendly acquaintances.

Health-conscious party of one, your table is ready

3. **Don't be afraid to dine alone.** Don't be surprised when the people you live with don't jump up and down for joy about your newfound commitment to health and wellness. I don't think you'll come home from a hectic day to a three-course healthy dinner prepared by an enthusiastic spouse on day two, but it *could* happen. The kids aren't going to break out in, "Kumbaya, Mom, we love this spinach. Kumbaya, Mom, we love this kale. Kumbaya, Mom, can we have more broccoli? Oh Lord, we love these peas."

You're going to have to win their support. But don't count on getting it. And don't let the absence of it sabotage the goals you set for yourself. Ann Landers says if your spouse won't go to counseling with you, go yourself. If your spouse won't commit to get fit with you, get fit yourself. Expect it to be hard to deal with others' lack of enthusiasm and support because it will be, but you can survive it. Family opposition is not a reason to give up. See your goals, see yourself working toward your goals, say your goals out loud, and see yourself crossing the finish line.

Lead by example. Don't get too pontifical or you'll lose them. You're not a short-order cook. If the troops don't like what you fix, let them fend for themselves. Don't buy separate groceries for everyone. If something's too tempting for you to have around, don't have it around. The kids don't *need* the latest lunchroom fad foods. Let them buy lunch at school with their allowance.

If your spouse could use a little dietary discipline and a bit of exercise, too, but will have none of it despite your progress, there could be a little turbulence. He could be feeling bad about his own health and resentful. "Things were just fine around here until you got on this health kick," he might be thinking. Remember that just because you made a decision to change doesn't mean everyone has to change with you or that they want to hear about what you're doing, what you're eating, or how much weight you've lost. Respect boundaries. Love your family like you've always loved them. We don't all move at the same pace. This is a very personal path.

This old house wasn't rebuilt *in a day*

You'll feel and probably start to act differently. You might start doing things you haven't done in years. Perhaps you'll feel like catching a movie midweek or you'll take a trip to a museum that you've never visited. Naturally your family will look at you in a funny way. Your appearance will change, too. You may decide to color your hair, paint your fingernails, or buy new clothes. Maybe you'll suddenly buy plaid pants, red sneakers, and bedazzled tiny tops. Of course your family will suspect mental illness.

This is the mixed-blessing-in-disguise part of getting healthier. Your spouse will be married to someone new. Change disrupts everything and can be very hard on a family. The comfort zones are blown apart, schedules are ruined, and the food's different. You're not going to be the most popular person on the block. They won't know how to act around you. They may "have liked you better the old way." Some families deal with this better than others. It will take time for everyone, including you, to adjust.

> No one said you had to work without a coach. Boost your self-esteem by lunchtime. Three instant sources of support you can access now.

And the Oscar for Best Supporting Actor goes to . . .

1. **Turn to friends.** It's a one-man show without a cast. Day-to-day mini-exchanges are essential for good health survival. When I exercise with my sister, Carol, our treadmill workout flies by. When I run in Central Park with Jack, we're finished before I'm through babbling on about whatever he wasn't paying attention to in the first place. When I'm exercising to really good music on my CD player, my workout is over before I get to my favorite song. When I know I can look like the lady next to me if I just work a little harder, it inspires me to push myself to the next level.

Sometimes I chat with a few of the ladies after exercise class. We trade survival tips and encourage each other. The give-and-take exchanges are motivating and inspiring. When I was working my way toward an awful knee injury, one of the members told me about some shoes that might provide better leg support. Someone else gave me the name of a good doctor.

My butcher knows I'm always trying to eat healthfully, so every time I walk in, he's got another tip to "keep it lean" that he's overheard from another customer. My sister-in-law and I trade health and fitness magazines back and forth, and my mom and I are forever trading delicious recipes with each other (of *course* they're healthy).

I don't think I would have been able to stay on track all these years without this kind of a support system. I'm related to some of my sources, friends with others, and don't necessarily know the names of many, but they're all very important.

SUBJECT: MOM OF FOUR HOME-SCHOOLED KIDS,
NO TIME TO COOK

SENDER: Tammy

TO: email@chefkathleen.com

Dear Chef,

I would love to see more suggestions on how to provide healthful meals for a very busy family. We are a family of six with all four of our children into sports, so it's always hectic. I work part-time from home and also home-school all four of our children. God bless you for helping us.

Tammy

REPLY: BUILD COOKING INTO THE LESSON PLAN

Dear Tammy,

Life certainly sounds busy at your house, but it seems you may have a very unique opportunity to build family meal planning and preparation into the children's daily curriculum. In planning and preparing meals children can learn hand-eye coordination, how to read and follow instructions, chronological order, math (adding, subtracting, and fractions), budgeting money, weights and measurements, and a little science, too (baking powder, baking soda).

Health activities could include: understanding the food pyramid, learning proper nutrition, searching for simple recipes, making a shopping list based on the ingredients called for, planning food purchases, shopping, organizing the kitchen, properly handling and storing food, preparing food, freezing meals for later, balancing flavors with salt and seasonings, and more.

Perhaps you could develop an overall monthly plan of the family's weekly meals. The children could each work on different parts of the project according to age and maturity, with everyone ultimately working toward the same goal—quick and tasty, seasonal, healthful meals.

Good luck!

Kathleen

The church lady

2. **Open your eyes.** I get support from unlikely sources. Some people have changed my life forever and they don't even know it. Sometimes they don't even know my name, nor I theirs. The lady at church with the severely handicapped teenage son is a constant source of strength for me. She is one of the most dignified women

I've ever admired from afar. Though it's easy to see how some people might choose to institutionalize such a child, she is driven to provide her son with the best life she can, at home. I've seen noble courage, fierce determination, deep love, and a few tears in her eyes over the years, but I've never seen the face of a quitter.

If she can devote her life to that child and if she can get up every day and face what she does, I have no excuse for fleeing my responsibilities and commitments to good health.

Fortune 500 man

3. **Open your ears.** My spinning teacher is va-va-va-voom, hunka hunka of burning calories, fierce. We heard he was coming to our gym weeks before he started teaching. His no-excuse-is-acceptable-in-my-class approach to getting fit *will travel*. And for me it does. When I got kicked out for not showing up with a heart-rate monitor for the sixth class in a row, things began to sink in.

"If you don't know how much or how little your heart's working, Kathleen, are you going to put forth more or less effort? Do you want to work out strategically and achieve maximum results or are you looking for an excuse to give up? Do you want to be in control or out of control?"

I've never spent more than five minutes talking to him before or after class but I've gotten way more than my money's worth from his teaching. I do know that he's lost a considerable amount of weight because he told us once. He chooses to spend some of his spare time teaching others. It's obvious he doesn't do it for the cash. He seems to have made a commitment somewhere along the line to help others.

Sit up and pay attention and you can use his insights for the rest of your life: "You see those people talking on their cell phones on the treadmill? What kind of results do you think they're seeing?" "You made the effort to come to class, so give it everything you've got and if you're not willing to, you might as well go home and watch TV." "If you want to see change, you've got to earn change." "It's mind over body, people. You can talk yourself into this or you can talk yourself out of it." "Focus on the finish line. If you don't see it, you're going to get lost."

"Believe you can and you will." "Give it 50 percent and you'll get 50 percent back."
"You're 100 percent in control of your ride. Where do you want to go?"

Michael Jordan worked with a team of experts and he didn't
wear bedroom slippers on the basketball court. Three won't-
bust-your-budget benefits that gym bucks buy.

Honey, did you notice the scale *is broken again?*

1. **Invest wisely.** I decided to join a gym after two years of exercising on my own, one minute after discovering that my bathroom scale suddenly began reporting "false" readings again. I'd reached yet another plateau. Plateau in my case is synonymous with halfhearted workouts and subconscious cheating—entirely different from blatant cheating. I can recognize blatant cheating—like those times when I've made too many trips to the buffet too many days in a row, *again.*

Subconscious cheating for me is usually brought on by some unforeseen disaster—too many long hours at work, not enough sleep, my favorite show's being preempted for a lousy football game, whatever. It doesn't take much to get me going. Quicker than a tornado forms in the flat plains, the spirit of self-sabotage takes over my ability to eat for the right reasons.

I start incrementally increasing my serving size of, well, just about everything. I splash a little more milk in my coffee and add another cup of cereal to the bowl just for good measure. When lunch rolls around, I help myself to a few extra slices of meat, which naturally leads to another slice of thick-cut cheese and a fistful of chips (which cannot be washed down with plain old water, so I grab a soda). Instead of an apple as an afternoon pick-me-up I settle on peanuts, which wouldn't necessarily be bad, but I go for four servings. I start having second helpings at dinner and dessert six nights a week.

I'm 100 percent unaware of my behavior on a conscious level until denial screeches to a halt at the exact same moment the dryer begins to shrink my clothes again. But by then I'm in deep trouble. My pants are too tight and my

SUBJECT: I HAVEN'T EXERCISED IN TWENTY-FIVE YEARS

SENDER: Grace

TO: email@chefkathleen.com

Dear Kathleen,

I never exercise. I'm a "woman of a certain age," if you know what I mean, and I don't want to exercise. I know I should but I can't think of how.

Sincerely,

   Grace

REPLY: IT'S NEVER TOO LATE TO START

Dear Grace,

Take a walk. Go get the mail and keep going. Start with five minutes. Go ten minutes the next time. Challenge yourself to work your way up to thirty minutes. Or consider exercise videos. A friend recently lost 20 pounds exercising in her living room. There are videos geared toward every age and fitness level. Rent a few exercise tapes from your local video store so you can get a feel for the type of tape that appeals to you.

My mom, who is also "of a certain age," hates exercise but has made it a nonnegotiable. Gyms are not her thing and classes aren't, either. She walks outside in the warm weather and rides a stationary bike in front of the television on rainy days and throughout the winter. She hops on the bike during the last half hour of *Today* and knows that as soon as the show is over she's done for the day. She's lost 40 pounds since she started riding.

You might consider setting up a mini home gym—nothing fancy, just a few free weights and a bench. Hire a trainer for a session or two to help design a program for you and to show you how to safely perform each exercise. You could combine walks outside with weights indoors to achieve a well-rounded fitness program. To find a trainer, call a local gym and ask for a reference.

   Kathleen

shirts are way too small. I feel like Godzilla trying to fit into Barbie's clothes. I don't know about you, but when my waistband pierces my belly and cuts off my air supply, I get mean on top of being stressed out. Ill-tempered on my way to chubby is just not comfortable.

I'm not saying you should go out and spend a thousand dollars on a membership you won't use or classes you won't attend, but investigate your options and consider the possible returns on your investment.

A bucket of hot **buttered** *popcorn, an XL Coke, and a good movie, or an hour with a* **physical** *terrorist?*

2. **Throw good money after bad habits.** Facing life without movie candy was more than I could bear, so I decided to weigh my options. My friends Jack and Pat have been into weight lifting for years. They suggested I consider working with a personal trainer—a very hard concept for me to come to terms with. The thought of paying a trainer for something "I could do perfectly fine on my own" didn't sit well. I was totally intimidated by the money factor, I was very fearful of making a complete fool of myself, and frankly, I was a bit skeptical. But my pants were too tight. It was time to go to the next level of self-care.

Jack and Pat told me not to pick the trainer with the biggest muscles. "Not someone with no body fat and scary veins sticking out all over the place, just someone who looks to be in very good shape. He or she will have a complete understanding of the different muscle groups, results-oriented methods of training, and probably some nutrition basics. Make sure the trainer is certified, too." And not the Cracker Jack kind of certified.

There were trainers at the gym who fit the description, and they were all certified because my gym insists on it. I found that out by asking at the desk, always a good place to inquire about such things. They directed me to the wall of "worship," as the trainers (no egos there) like to refer to the space where their individual photos, list of credentials, and contact information are posted.

I'd learned by observation that all personal trainers are not created equal. As in all professions, some are good, some are great, and some are downright scary. If the gym member cried out in pain or grimaced too many times in a five-minute period, that trainer was eliminated as a possible candidate—why anyone would pay good money to be tortured is beyond me. I crossed out the trainer I overheard telling a client, "All I eat is tuna fish and egg whites." I also had to pass on the trainer whose only client quadrupled in size—although in-depth engaging conversations in the midst of fitness equipment seemed like a fun way to get in shape, it was obviously ineffective. I settled on Todd because I'd heard other members say nice things about him, and none of his clients ever left the gym in an ambulance.

Miss Know-It-All,
didn't

3. Learn new tricks. I never expected to really learn anything from a trainer because I never believe "health fads." Besides, I'd been working out for two years. I "knew" how to get in shape. My skepticism quickly faded and has disappeared. Sessions with a trainer taught me a huge range of new exercises, how to safely use gym equipment, how to achieve and maintain proper form, and how to execute each exercise for maximum results. I learned how many reps of what I needed and how often I needed to do them to achieve my goals safely.

I also learned how to visualize, concentrate, and focus on fitness goals. Lifting weights requires discipline, which I can always use a good dose of, and has given me a greater sense of self-confidence. I'm definitely a lot stronger.

Sisterly *love*

My sister, Miss No-Way-Would-I-Ever-Use-a-Trainer, works out with Todd now, too. She'll be the first to tell you that her idea of fun most definitely *isn't* a day at the gym. She's the super-busy mom of a super-active five-year-old, so time was always her "reason" for skipping the gym. But she's always been a schedule keeper. She can remember, keep, and show up on time to an appointment made a year ago.

After my first session with Todd, I realized keeping an appointment with a trainer was no different than keeping a doctor's appointment, a great solution for my super-organized, scheduled-to-the-max sister. I told her she ought to consider making appointments to work out. "Are you out of your empty head, Kathleen? I'd rather spend money at the dentist!" So I made an appointment *for* her. I stole one of her checks, wrote it out to Todd, made sure he cashed it, and then told her when he'd be expecting her. I felt I had no other choice, being the big sister and all.

She's too cheap to throw money away, so she went. I guess it wasn't awful because she's still going. And now her husband, Mr. Dot-Com-Work-Out-of-My-Home-Office-All-Day, does too. As far as I can tell, it's the only time he sees daylight.

Sisterly advice

Knowing how extremely busy my sister's life is and how she'd prefer to clean the ductwork in her house than exercise, I asked her how she's been able to keep her commitment to continue going to the gym. "Well, I have to say that sitting around looking for excuses is *much* easier and more fun than actually going there. But it takes about the same amount of time and isn't *quite* as fulfilling, since it doesn't help me hit my health mark for the week. I do have a family to think of."

We all have our own set of reasons for not being able to make it to the gym, and all of them are valid. It really is just a matter of budgeting your time. Weave your workout right into your schedule, and make it take the place of something else, preferably something you don't like or something you can do at the same time. Is *Wall Street Week* or *Martha Stewart Living* your favorite can't-miss show? Then watch it at the gym from the treadmill. You still get to see your shows, and your workout will go by without your even noticing.

It might be a good idea for you to schedule one workout at a time if every Tuesday at 4:00 P.M. is too much. This way you can build yourself up. Continue the walks around the block and use the gym for more serious stuff—weight training and classes. Carol's reason for getting a personal trainer was twofold: "I didn't know the first thing about using all of those torture-chamber-looking machines and it's one more person I'll have to tell that I'm *not* working out today."

Making your local gym and/or a favorite park a regular part of your fitness regime is a good idea because you see the same people all the time and they see you. You can draw inspiration from them because you see that they are coming every week and you know that they will notice if you don't show up for a month.

Sisterly retaliation

One more tip from Carol: "Another way to schedule your gym hour is to fit it in just before something good. Plan a trip to some place *more* fun than the gym on your way home, which leaves the possibilities *wide* open. I know Kathleen uses this method. She'll stop at Starbucks on her way home for a nonfat, no-flavor-ain't-no-fun-without-the-mocha-whip latte. Don't tell Todd or Kathleen, but I think my reward should be a little better. There is a really nice gourmet grocer on my way home. I like to stop in and pick up something extra special there. Maybe just some imported low-fat (I'm *sure*) cookies, which I'll have only one of (yeah, right). My all-time favorite is to pick up a quick solution for dinner. I try to cook without my stove as much as possible. I was lying about the cookies, but not about deserving something better."

Photo finishes count. Three navigate-the-terrain tactics to ensure your seat at the awards banquet.

Raggedy Ann **wasn't** *much fun to play with when her* **stuffing** *fell out*

1. Strip away the final layer of excuses. The only thing hard about taking charge of your health is listening to that lunatic taking up space in your brain. Give her a three-day notice to quit. Say your bye-byes and move on.

When the doctor tells the mother of a boy with a broken leg, "It's going to take eight weeks to heal and then several more months of physical therapy," the mother doesn't start bargaining: "Listen, Doc, two weeks is all I can devote to this. I just don't have the time, the will, or the discipline. Frankly the whole thing bores me just thinking about it. If permanent damage is the outcome, so be it. I'm busy." Without question she takes on the task. She's 100 percent committed to the child and his care.

Why would it ever be okay to give up on yourself? Why is our commitment to our own good health the first to go? This isn't cancer. It just isn't anywhere near as hard as the real tough stuff in life. You don't stop bathing when your husband loses his job or someone you love is diagnosed with a terminal illness. No stress, no matter how intense, is a reason to abandon your health. You need your body to work *for* you, not against you.

No one is taking anything away from you. No one is telling you you can't enjoy all the same foods you've always enjoyed. You still get to enjoy every holiday, every family picnic, date nights, and all the same food and social occasions you always have. Moderate, don't eliminate.

Sure, you have to exercise. It's up to you to put on your creative thinking cap and make it fun. You might want to consider boot camp as an option, but it's not mandatory. A sunny fall day spent crunching through leaves on a wooded path in a nearby forest or park is exercise. A lazy day of canoeing down a river brimming with wild birds and exotic plant life is exercise. Mall walking, window-shopping, and zoo excursions count, too.

Danger, Will Robinson! Vending *machines ahead.*

2. **Anticipate land mines.** Personally, I think vending machine calories shouldn't count. The very reason you're eating out of a vending machine in the first place is usually not a happy one. Most likely, you can't break away from your office, you're in between classes, or you're on the go and just can't get to food that makes sense. Admittedly stressful and albeit unpleasant, these are not gold pass occasions to eat—they're not even silver pass occasions. You get no pass to overindulge when you've had plenty of time to plan ahead.

Is your career making *you fat?*

Are church meetings plumping you up? Do you leave PTA gatherings three pounds heavier? It's so unfair. Do we *look* like Hansel and Gretel in need of fatten-

SUBJECT: I'M SO SICK OF HEALTHY STUFF I WANT TO QUIT

SENDER: Darlene

TO: email@chefkathleen.com

Dear Kathleen,

I'm so tired of worrying about what to eat, when to eat, how much to eat, and I'm burned out on exercise. I have so much weight to lose and have tried everything. It's just so hard. I feel defeated all the time. I know I shouldn't give up again, and that's why I'm writing. I'm desperate for help. Do you have any suggestions? Thank you.

Darlene

REPLY: TAKE A BREAK

Dear Darlene,

It's very important to take time off physically and mentally, so take a day off every now and then from your normal routines. Try to maintain what you've accomplished when you're "off." Don't use a day off as an excuse to binge.

When I'm really in a funk, I focus on something else for a while. I've made a deal with myself. If I absolutely want to take time off in one area of healthy living, I devote that time to something else. When I've had it up to my eyeballs with exercise, I take the day off but spend gym time researching new recipes, reading through a new cookbook, or checking out the latest health articles or web sites. I might log on to a healthy chat room to see how other people cope with burnout.

Try to determine exactly what it is that's driving you to feel like quitting. Are you exercising too much? Are you giving your body enough time to recover between workouts? Are you getting enough rest? Have you been doing the same exact exercise routine every time you work out?

Have you placed too many dietary restrictions on yourself? Are your overall goals too ambitious or unrealistic? Keep your focus on the small picture when you feel overwhelmed. I'm going to eat healthy all day. I'm going to work out four times this week. I'm going to get all my servings of vegetables in today. I'm going to drink eight glasses of water every day this week. I'm going to lose 5 pounds in five weeks.

When was the last time you rewarded yourself for doing the right thing? All movement in the right direction is positive change that deserves recognition. Be patient. You didn't gain the weight overnight. You don't want immediate weight loss: it won't last, and it's not the main goal anyway. Weight loss is a side effect of good healthful habits. Move forward every day, but take it slow.

Kathleen

ing up? Learning to tame that spirit of impulse eating in work and social settings is a drag. It's bad enough we have to face so many awkward gatherings surrounded by people we wouldn't necessarily choose to spend time with in the first place. Food was my only vice. Technically, there have been other ways of coping all along, but none of them tasted good dipped in blue cheese.

I'm not saying it's easy to walk into the break room and pass up fresh dough-nuts. Believe me, I know how hard it is to dash past a Dolly Dumplings giant jar of foil-wrapped chocolate kisses without grabbing a handful. I'm still practicing.

It was either spend spare calories on food I truly love or start purchasing my clothes at Omar the tent maker's shop. I learned to cut way back on the water cooler calories pretty quickly. Let's face it, nobody brings his or her best stuff to share anyway. Besides, Betty's birthday cake is nowhere near as satisfying as the German chocolate cake my sister makes me every year for *my* birthday. Now that's good cake.

If Mama ain't happy, ain't nobody happy

3. **If you don't make good health your number-one priority, you won't have it.** Society isn't coming to your funeral. Naysayers, Judy Judgmentals, and the finger-pointer sisters won't be there, either. Toss out the instructions that came with your first baby doll and pram; they're obsolete. It's not a mom's duty to take care of her family's needs before her own. It is not selfish to nourish *your* body first so that you have the energy and peace of mind to nourish your family, too. Remember the part about faking the right mind-set until you can find it? This is the part where you focus on finding it. Because, if you don't visualize it, you won't find it and eventually everything *will* fall apart.

Repeat after me: you deserve all the love you give freely and then some. I can't hear you! You deserve all the same love you give freely and then some. Now say it this way: *I* deserve all the same love I give freely and then some. It's up to *me* to give it to *me*. I have to accept responsibility for taking care of myself first. If I don't take care of my own needs first, I will not be able to take care of my family in the way that they should be taken care of. If I don't take care of my own needs first, I will not be setting a good example for my family, they will never learn to take care of themselves properly, and then they'll never leave home.

Your good health and fitness are your family's good health and fitness, too. You will have a higher level of self-confidence; you will feel stronger mentally and physically. You will laugh and giggle more. Look at it this way: when the teacher's in a good mood, class goes by faster, and the kids are more receptive to learning. You have more patience for "Mommy, Mommy, Mommy" when you're happy. When Mom's in a good mood at dinner, the conversation is light and lively and just plain fun. You and your spouse will "date" more when you're happy. Everything is better when your frown is upside down.

This feels totally unnatural and goes against every episode of *Leave It to Beaver*, but it's time to get with the program, and you know it deep down. Better the laundry should be a little wrinkled than you should collapse in a heap. Believe it in your head first, and your heart will follow. Make it happen, allow it to happen, don't feel guilty for putting yourself first. It will become second nature after a while. It just has to. If you program yourself to make *your* good health your number-one priority and if you believe you can achieve it, you will.

Keep the YO-YOS *in the toybox*

After ten years of this, I'm in the groove most of the time. Sure, I yo-yo, but it's 5 to 7 pounds, not 50 to 60. When you find yourself pedaling backward, focus on maintaining what you've learned until you're able to turn maintaining back into progress. When I get off course, I go right back to the basics and grab on for dear life. I don't always start at square one, either. I normally get a little lost when life is throwing me a curveball, so I latch on to whatever part of the program I can deal with at the moment.

It doesn't matter how you find your way back to the path; it just matters that you try. If you try, you will succeed. Once you get started, the payoff is instantaneous. Your confidence builds back quickly. The first step in the right direction naturally leads to the second, and before you know it, you're back in the groove.

Anyway, it's a lot easier and safer to work your way back through these good behavior basics than to launch another ultrarestrictive fad diet that just can't work. Make up your mind to do this and you will.

Please pass the tofu

I'm kidding. None of the recipes in this book contain tofu, although I really do like it, especially fresh from the tofu factory in Wailuku, Hawaii, where I used to live. A little slivered scallion, a little soy sauce, mmm. Maybe in book two. I didn't want to scare you off with wacky recipes and oddball ingredients your kids would sooner clean their rooms than try.

SUBJECT: WHAT DO YOU THINK OF LIQUID DIETS?
SENDER: Jane
TO: email@chefkathleen.com

Dear Kathleen,
What do you think about the different liquid diets? I need to lose a lot of weight and was thinking of getting a headstart. I am considering one of the diet-shake plans. You eat one full meal a day plus two chocolate shakes. I want to see pounds drop quickly. What is your opinion of these diets? How did you do it?

REPLY: DON'T GO THERE

Dear Jane,
Remember Aesop's fable "The Tortoise and the Hare"? The biggest braggart in the forest lost to the determined turtle. I lost the weight pound by pound. It took a while but I've had great success.

To maintain good health for the rest of your life, you need to modify your behavior until you achieve good eating and exercise habits. Essentially you're retraining your palate and your body to expect, crave, anticipate, and enjoy the right foods. Do it gradually by making small methodical modifications to your diet while incrementally increasing physical activity at the same time, and the changes won't be so drastic you can't live with them.

Wouldn't you rather eat delicious foods than drink a shake? Who wants to give up meals you're "allowed" to have?
Kathleen

Round Up the Tin Pan Bangers, the Spoon Lickers, the Chocolate Chins, and the Dirty Bibs, It's Time to Cook Thin!

Special orders **don't** *upset us because we ignore them*

restaurant meals can be

worked into your weekly eating plan, but if you want to lose weight and stay healthy *you've* got to cook thin. With a little advance planning and organization you won't have to stand at the foot of the stove for hours to enjoy home-cooked meals most nights. To keep motivated and on the fast track to good health, make eating meals out a reward for cooking in.

Beg for no butter, cry life-threatening allergies, and plead your case 'til the cows come home, but keep in mind that restaurant employees aren't really concerned with your health and dietary restrictions. No fat, no oil, no way. Most restaurants don't use nonstick pans. The coating wears off much too fast because of rough wear and tear, so metal pans are usually the norm. Some sort of fat must be used to keep food from sticking to the metal.

Chocolate soufflé or fryer grease—where do you want to spend fat calories?

Seared, broiled, roasted, or grilled food bound for your waistline *is* cooked with at least one splash of liquid fat, probably a ladle's worth. If you're lucky, the fat they're using is good-quality olive oil or drawn butter. Most often, though, it's the cheapest oil owners can get their hands on. Although technically it's USDA approved and digestible by humans, it's fat you don't need but will consume *and* have to work off later.

The most common small-size ladle in the restaurant kitchen is a 2-ounce ladle. Do you really think super-busy line cooks pushing out hundreds of plates per meal have the ability to take the time to use anything less than the easiest amount to scoop, you guessed it, the full 2 ounces? That's roughly 500 calories and 60 grams of fat. Even if they use the rarely stocked ½-ounce ladle, that's still 125 calories and 15 grams of fat before the first ingredient hits the pan.

It takes a very high culinary skill level to achieve eye-appealing proper doneness with little fat. Most kitchens aren't staffed with three-star chefs. When the kitchen is backed up, line cooks can be working half a dozen sauté pans, the grill, and the ovens all at once. To keep food from burning and to buy them a little time until they can flip your "chicken, no oil," "fish, very dry," or "vegetables, no butter," they have no choice but to add another ladle of fat. Sure, a lot of kitchens are responsible and will try to accommodate your requests, but the only way to truly control your calorie intake is to prepare most of your own meals.

Don't let this be you

Clipping, snipping, and bleaching away at my do one day, my hairdresser, who's forever remodeling his home, said in all seriousness, "I was thinking of taking out my stove and putting stools there instead." He's the married father of twin boys. "My wife hates to cook and I don't know how, so what's the point? I think we could get by with a little griddle or something, don't you?" He was dead serious.

Kitchen? *I know we have one. I think it's where we keep the mail.*

If the most important item in your kitchen is the phone book, your favorite kitchen tool is a fork, and your waistline is wandering in the wrong direction, you might hold on to your skinny clothes by giving your kitchen a low-cost, do-it-yourself, total makeover.

Situate yourself where you can eye your kitchen from every angle, and open all the drawers and cupboards. Now *stand* back. Do you see organized cabinets, shelves, and sideboards with easy-to-get-at appliances utilized regularly? Are countertops strewn with last week's mail, car keys, and a cell phone? True, every home *needs* a "mission control" drop-off location, but the kitchen isn't it.

Nifty new gadgets and countertop appliances could be just what you need to whisk your way toward good health. Before purchasing the latest kitchenware wonders, consider your actual needs based on available space, foods you love, and daily time allotted for cooking. Think of counter, cupboard, and drawer space as oceanfront real estate.

That said, counters and surfaces really should be declared debris-free zones. Never-used espresso machines, dusty decorative bottles, newspaper stacks, school

Round Up the Tin Pan Bangers

homework, and cookie jars (talk about needless temptation)—all have a place they can call home *outside* the kitchen. Chuck the vase of dead flowers and pitch the rotten apples in the requisite fruit bowl while you're at it. You'll be more inspired to cook in a clean kitchen you can freely move around.

Kitchen yoga

If you have to perform Cirque du Soleil moves to get to your skillets, then it's time for a ten-minute tidy. Organize pots, pans, and lids together. Get rid of unopened wedding gifts or breadmakers you've never used. Dishes, plates, and bowls are best stocked near the dishwasher. Take a tip from restaurant pros: create your own cooking stations. Systematically reorganize for speed and ease. Store all the gear you'll need to sauté, pan sear, braise, boil, or fry in one place. Spoons and forks, tongs, whisks, spatulas, and meat thermometers should be neatly stored nearest the stove. Create a mini pastry kitchen within your kitchen by stocking baking supplies (ingredients and tools) together, too.

Not tonight, dear, I have a headache

No one wants to cook in a filthy, dingy, depressing environment. Create a space you want to be in, a space that draws you in and just feels great. Cooking is fun, creative, and relaxing. And, if you don't think so, pretend you do. It's in your best interest to embrace it. Bring in a small TV, a CD player, a portable phone, a vase of fresh flowers, luxurious tea towels, a candle or two. If the phone drives you nuts, make it a phone-free zone. Designating it a kid-and-spouse-free zone during prep time might not be all bad either. Don't attempt to cook in the dark. Open shades and shutters; remove window dressings altogether if it will bring in significantly more light and you can get away with it. Use higher-watt bulbs or halogen lights, the best you can afford.

Install inexpensive under-the-cabinet lighting, spots, or lamps where you need them. Just because the house came with the chandelier hung smack dab in the middle of the room doesn't mean you have to leave it there. Consider installing a skylight or enlarging the windows when the budget permits.

Honor thy icebox

Eliminate refrigerator chaos and curb the urge to graze on the wrong things by deep-cleaning and reorganizing your fridge. Store foods you'll forage to find, no matter where they're crammed, in harder-to-reach locations like the vegetable drawers and the back shelves. Buy smaller quantities of "necessary" high-calorie items and keep them out of sight.

Merchandising *matters*

Make like a grocer—market items to hungry grazers by making everything appear mouthwatering. Fruits and veggies front and center at eye level, washed and pop-in-your-mouth ready, set in small decorative bowls or bundled in easy-to-grab packages. Keep lots of healthy snack items reachable and in plain sight. Consider individual yogurts, cottage cheese, turkey slices, hard-boiled eggs, healthy leftovers, carrot Jell-O, and Chocolate Pudding (page 386).

Arctic disclosures

If the gigantic ice mass in your freezer *isn't* preserving another woolly mammoth, then it's time to defrost, explore, and excavate. Purge unidentifiable foil-wrapped freezer bombs from your life. A healthy freezer is full of individually wrapped chicken breasts, chicken or turkey burgers, hamburgers, a few lean steaks, pre-portioned pounded pork tenderloin, and meatballs. Dinner-size portions of chicken broth, tomato sauce, pizza sauce, pizza dough, and tart dough have their rightful place, too. Homemade bread crumbs, grated mozzarella cheese, crisp topping for fruit (page 382), nuts of all kinds, and TV dinners you made yourself should take up the rest of the space. Naturally you'll have a pint (keyword: *pint*) of your favorite ice cream tucked in there somewhere. And maybe some frozen cookie dough; better you should slice off and cook single portions than eat all the raw dough or the entire baked batch.

Garana-meals

Remember Garanimal clothes, the mix-and-match tops and pants for kids? You need "garana-meals," mix-and-match cupboard supplies you can use to whip up quick and tasty meals. How many of your kitchen shelves are devoted to junk food right now? Five, you say? Make it one or less if you're ready. Missed the weekly trip to the grocery store? Not a problem if you stock up on enough go-together ingredients that can morph into the evening meal *without* a last-minute mad dash to the market. Make it a priority to shop and cook from pantry supplies. Organize shelves and ingredients by meals you can get on the table fast. Pasta, canned tomatoes, capers, and olives to the left; tuna fish, white beans, and bread crumbs to the right.

On your mark, get set, *shop*

Now that you've cleaned up the joint, evaluate your cooking arsenal. If a piece of equipment isn't used, it's got to go. Do you own the best you can afford? Does the piece perform efficiently? Calling for carryout won't be so tempting if dinner doesn't take all night to make.

There's no secret formula for figuring out which hand tools and small appliances you need and which ones would be nice to have. Longing for the flavors of the great outdoors more often than you can muster the energy to master the barbecue? Consider an indoor grill. If rice is twice as nice to you, check out the latest rice cookers. If that task is a stovetop snap, your money might be better spent on a state-of-the-art mixer fitted with every imaginable attachment. Too many fancy parts you say? How about a juice extractor? Can't be bothered? Try a wok pan.

The very best kitchen tools to buy are ones you'll actually use. How much is too much to spend? How much would you pay for a few extra minutes of story time with your kids? Or increased leisure time? You may have to save up for the Mercedes of all food processors, but there are plenty of items under thirty dollars you shouldn't live a minute longer without.

As seen in Kathleen's kitchen

Knives. You don't have to own the ultimate knife set, and just for the record, I don't. A paring knife, a good serrated bread knife, and an 8- or 10-inch chef's knife are all you need to tackle just about any task. Choose the best knives you can afford. Go to a specialty kitchen store and grill the staff on the pros and cons of the knives they carry, then shop around for the best price and make your buy.

Pots and pans. A dream collection will eventually include 8-, 10-, and 12-inch nonstick sauté pans and a basic pot, with matching lids, sold just about everywhere. Sets usually include a little saucepan, a medium saucepan, a 3-quart pot, and a pasta pot, all fitted with lids. Pick up the best stainless steel pots and quality nonstick pans that you can afford. No matter what pie-in-the-sky promise those late-night infomercials make, nonstick *always* wears off and the entire pan will have to be replaced after a few years anyway, so don't spend your money on the "best" quality, high-priced sets.

Start off with cheap skillets and an inexpensive pot and lid kit. Figure out which size pots and pans you use most. You'll know which pots and pans to trade up and which ones to drop from your collection. A cast-iron pan or two and a stovetop griddle might be something to consider, too.

Pizza stone. This is not a must-have, but I wouldn't want to live without one. Buy one the size of your bottom rack. Keep it in the oven always. Food cooks faster on the hot stone. Onions caramelize, soufflés soar, casseroles brown and bubble. Note: If you can't find a square stone the size of your bottom rack, take your rack dimensions to a stoneyard and tell them what you're looking for. They'll sell you something that will work just fine. A single layer of unglazed tiles or fireplace bricks will work too.

Plastic mandoline. Slice, shred, and julienne yourself slim. Serve up quick-dish savory salads without a single leaf of lettuce. Try fennel, beets, carrots, celery root, and jicama. Craving salty baked potato chips? Waffle-cut your own.

Digital thermometer. When supper's a disappointment because it was left in the oven too long, late-night food forays are more likely. Digital thermometers are inexpensive and easy to use. Time-consuming sauces aren't necessary when you're serving perfectly roasted chicken, moist meat loaf, and fork-tender fish.

Mini chopper. Diced onions, minced garlic, and chopped parsley all in the same recipe? Cookies call for chopped chocolate and nuts? No prep cook on staff? No problem. Chop your workload in half with this kitchen wiz.

Salad spinner. Wet lettuces won't water down dressings once you give them a whirl. Spin beet greens, turnip greens, Swiss chard, and fresh herbs, too. Perk up salads, soups, and sauces in seconds with clean fresh herbs. You'll find it hard not to add them to everything in sight. Wilt clean greens right into your next pasta dish or sauté them in a little olive oil with slivered garlic, red pepper flakes, and a sprinkling of salt. Added bonus: clean, lush greens have a longer shelf life.

3-quart saucier with lid. I know we've talked about pots and pans already, but since this is my absolute (can't-function-without) favorite, it deserves a special mention. Good for just about every job, this pot has sloping sides and it's not too big or too small, making it perfect for sauces and just right for soup du jour, pasta, risotto, and chili.

Cutting board. Bigger *is* better. There's nothing worse than chopping on a board that's too small. A 14 × 20-inch board fits on most countertops. Note: Always keep a damp dishcloth underneath your cutting board during use to prevent slipping.

Kitchen scale. When in doubt, weigh it out. Two pounds of eggplant got you stumped? How many apples in a pound? What do 6 ounces of chocolate chips look like? Who knows? Suddenly all those recipes written in weights can be measured accurately. If a recipe calls for 1 pound of beef and 1 tablespoon of oil and you eyeball a pound and a half instead, you'll use more oil, and calories will be over the top.

Kitchen linens. The dish on kitchen laundry? Stock up. Minimize health risks by changing them daily. Good-quality tea towels, hot pads, and dishrags are essential. Absorbent, durable towels make kitchen cleanup a cinch. Thick, fireproof hot pads that fit over hands or oven mitts are fundamental to kitchen safety.

Refrigerator dishes and wraps. Do yourself a favor and buy clear, stackable, microwave-proof, freezer-proof, dishwasher-safe, food storage containers. If you've got a collection of mismatched, melted, scratched, stained containers missing half their lids, use them as drawer organizers but don't store food in them. It's not worth the hassle and who wants to guess what's inside? Keep on hand an assortment of parchment paper, wax paper, plastic wrap, sealable plastic bags in several sizes, and good-quality aluminum foil. You don't need the hassle of junky products. There are coupons for all this stuff.

Cookbooks. I have four thousand. A little over the top, I know, but books inspire, educate, and entertain. Choosing ones you can actually use is easy when you know how. If, on the first thumb-through, you don't find six recipes you like right off the bat, the book's probably not for you. Can't pronounce and/or get your hands on the ingredients? Don't buy it. Directions doable? Give your potential purchase a final once-over, and if you think you can have some fun getting a few new dishes on the table, add it to your cart.

Are we supposed to eat this?

Your family isn't going to jump for joy and beg for extra veggies at dinner just because you decide to cook thin. Casually announce your intentions, expect a revolution, but hold your ground. They won't notice half the changes. Gradually introduce the ones you know they will. This kind of transformation isn't easy and people get testy when you start messing with their food, so don't make them go cold turkey or you'll lose them early on. Focus on making incremental changes over time. Introduce a new veggie side dish on Monday, encourage everyone to take a walk around the block after dinner on Tuesday, serve a real dessert on Wednesday, and see if you can get away with serving a fruit dessert on Thursday. Try fish for dinner and a walk around the block on Friday. Reward everyone with a meal out on Saturday. Ask them to keep an open mind and to be patient. You, too. Rome wasn't built in a day. This lifestyle is about making good, better, and best choices each day and bettering those choices at a comfortable pace. Push yourself a little, too.

Round Up the Tin Pan Bangers

Kids, honey, how about if we all go to bed hungry tonight? I'm bushed.

Your favorite NFL team doesn't function without a game plan, and neither should you. Nothing will sabotage your good intentions quicker than a lack of focus. Don't make it easier not to cook. Four P.M. *isn't* the time of day to start thinking about cooking and shopping. The eventual goal is to plan meals a week in advance so you can formulate shopping lists from actual recipes, thereby custom-creating and automating your family's road map to good health.

I'm not saying you have to lay out every meal and side dish on Sundays when you'd rather be lounging, but planning ahead is critical. How do you start? Read the recipes and make your shopping list from what you'll actually be cooking. Keep the cookbook someplace you'll actually read it. I can think of worse bathroom reading material.

Don't get discouraged if you can't nail down a weekly menu just yet; make your list from recipes you think you might want to try. If everything's at your fingertips, it will be harder to talk yourself out of cooking.

There are no coupons for vegetables

Food costs good money and I don't know anyone who has enough to waste, so I'm not going to tell you to ditch the marshmallows, mac 'n' cheese packets, or the mayonnaise lining your cupboards. You'll have to make those decisions on your own.

Focus on buying more good-for-you foods that will help you lose. Expect your grocery dollar to be spent differently. You might just end up saving money. Seasonal fruits and vegetables are cheaper than Pop-tarts and gourmet chips. However, if you're new at this shopping-cooking game, then you might end up buying more healthful convenience foods, such as gourmet vinegars, good-quality olive oil, fresh spices, individual healthful snack-size products, and perhaps a frozen entrée or two. You might end up doling out a little extra cash, but how much is good health worth to you?

The mad market dash is chaos you just don't need in your life

Schedule time for shopping. This means driving time, shopping time, time for unloading groceries, and, if at all possible, time to clean the veggies *before* you stash them in the crisper. Every able body listed as a resident at your address should participate in these rituals. No one person should be stuck holding the bags.

My sister shops, and her husband and my five-year-old niece (she's *so* helpful) greet Mom in the driveway to unload the car, and they all clean the vegetables together. It's not as perfect as it sounds, but you get the idea. My brother, his wife, Renie, and my six-year-old niece, Emily, shop together on weekends. They have a ball. After Emily puts enough "healthy stuff" in the basket, she gets to choose one treat (or ten, if Mom isn't paying attention). My parents wrangle and shop their way through the markets on Saturdays. I say wrangle because my dad *is* the guy on that antacid commercial popping all the spicy samples in his mouth when my mom's not looking. Figure out how to make shopping a weekly ritual, an appointment you don't break, and line up the troops to do their fair share, too.

Pretend you're shopping at Fauchon (a Paris supermarket for millionaires)

When you finally get to the market, stroll through the aisles with the same sense of adventure and curiosity you have when you're shopping someplace new. Wander down aisles you normally skip; peruse shelves you'd otherwise pass by.

Every time you shop, pick up something new. You don't have to spend a fortune. A budget of two, three, or even five dollars extra each week will go a long way toward jazzing up comfort foods. Pick up a spice you've never tried, a new kind of vinegar, or a nutty oil. Buy one new fruit or veggie each week. Don't bring home more than you'll use and if you're too busy to cook, buy something new that doesn't require cooking. Plan your first meatless meal. Soften the experience with a real dessert, especially if it's your family's first all-vegetable feast. Select a new cut of meat or a different variety of fish each week. Choose an unusual shape of noodle or a new brand. Upgrade to pasta made in Italy when you've got some spare change. Note the difference. Change from instant rice to whole-grain rice or from white to brown rice. Grab a bag of lentils or beans you can cook from scratch. Add a new kitchen tool or foodie magazine to your cart for inspiration.

Reward yourself when you follow through on these mini assignments. It does take a little bit of effort, but you will increase your good calories. Keep yourself challenged and entertained. Relax, enjoy, and have fun.

Honey, what's this slimy stuff in the vegetable drawer?

Speaking of perishable produce, it's not impossible to buy seven days' worth of vegetables at a time. Buy a combination of delicate and long-lasting veggies: lettuces, corn on the cob, tomatoes, green beans, mushrooms, and sweet potatoes. Consume the most perishable veggies in the beginning of the week and save the heartier selections for the week's end. Or send your spouse to the market midweek. Easy, hold on. I know what you're thinking: my husband couldn't pick out a good green bean to save his life. Probably true, but he does know how to pick out the very best of what *he* likes. So when you're doing the weekly shopping, don't buy any of his favorites.

Pots and pans can't fly as far as I'd like to throw 'em sometimes

Just because the recipe title says soufflé doesn't mean that's what's going to come out of the oven. Of *course* it's not your fault. Cooking is no more or less hit-and-miss than eating out. It's cheaper to throw away a meal you've cooked than to chuck one you paid for at a restaurant; besides, it's healthier to eat at home, so just keep at it. For every dozen or so recipes you try, you're probably going to love only two. If you're lucky, a few will even end up on your "I'd make again" list. But chances are you'll hate some of what you try. It's not your fault and it's no excuse to quit. Sadly, there are lots of recipes in print that are just awful. Some were probably just lousy ideas in the first place and others might have been tested in an institutional setting, which just doesn't translate well for home cooks. Worse, some recipes are never tested at all.

Some kitchen failures turn out to be really great. The Simple Corn Cakes on page 285 were supposed to be fritters. The batter didn't turn out thick, and I didn't think adding glue could have helped, so I switched gears and developed corn cakes. They're really, really great. Don't expect perfection, whatever that is anyway. Keep an open mind. Know that recipes aren't perfect—they're really just a guide.

Culinary cheaters *prosper*

Listen to your inner culinary voice. Improvise, cheat, cut corners, or substitute ingredients anytime you think you can get away with it. Chances are you will. When you're reading through an ingredient list and you come across something you don't like, such as green peppers, don't use them. If two cloves of garlic sounds like too much, use one. If you love basil and ¼ cup doesn't sound like enough, use more.

Anytime a recipe calls for raw garlic or raw red bell peppers my mom and I always cook them. She despises the taste of raw garlic, and I hate it when people add red peppers to a recipe strictly for color; it's a waste of money and time. I despise the taste of raw red peppers, so if I think roasted, peeled red peppers will add a flavor element to a dish, I'll keep the peppers; otherwise, I delete them altogether. There's less room for experimentation in baking, though. As a rule, I don't mess around with those recipes too much.

To cut down on catastrophes, read recipes start to finish in advance. And do it the night before, if you can. Visualize yourself making the recipe, grabbing for the ingredients, and picking out your pots. This kind of advance planning eliminates what's-for-dinner-blues, which are usually followed by big-bad-binges.

After you make a recipe for the first time, make notes directly on the recipe. If you think it's worth making again, write that down. If you hated a particular element of the dish or it took longer to cook than the directions indicated, write that down, too. Perhaps a different herb or an added ingredient might make the recipe better—write it in. I've got lots of recipes with "yuck" noted on them, but way more with "great" written in the margin. When something doesn't quite work the way you wanted it to, either pretend it was great or think of all the bad restaurant meals you've paid for. You haven't stopped eating out, and you shouldn't give up on cooking.

Top ten cooking survival *tips*

1. **Lose the complicated entrée mind-set.** Keep dinner simple, especially if you're time starved. Quick oven-broiled fish with microwave veggies is dinner.

2. **Who's on the sauté station tonight?** Build your culinary team. Enlist help, divide up the chores, make lists, delegate tasks, and follow through. Every able body should participate regularly in some aspect of meal planning, shopping, cooking, or cleanup.

3. **Build menus around naturally healthful ingredients.** Three ounces of steak can be consumed in four bites and two minutes. A heaping bowl of Sesame Ginger Shrimp and Spicy Black Bean Salad will take many more bites than four and a lot longer, too. Don't underestimate the psychological and emotional reasons we eat. They're just as important as our nutritional needs.

4. **Cheat any way you can, but don't compromise your waistline.** Any shortcut you can pull off is worth it. If something from a can, bag, or box will mean the difference between your eating in or ordering out, by all means go for it. Read product labels carefully, though, and make the healthiest choices you can.

5. **Fill up on the good stuff.** Increase good calories wherever you can. Can you get an extra serving of veggies by tossing a handful of corn into the salad? How about peas and mushrooms in the mac 'n' cheese? Roast asparagus in the same pan with the potatoes, and you've got two veggie sides instead of one.

6. **Use of high-impact flavor ingredients is highly encouraged.** Resuscitate, invigorate, acidulate—use sea salt, kosher salt, ginger, citrus, vinegar, garlic, capers, anchovies, olives, fresh spices (no, they do not have the shelf life of books), and freshly cut herbs. Grow your own. They're pretty and cheery. If the plants die, remember seeds are cheap, and dirt is free.

7. **Pare down prep.** Ten minutes in the kitchen after dinner tonight is easier to pull off than ten minutes before dinner tomorrow when you're tired *and* starving. Peel the potatoes tonight. Cook the noodles. Whip up the dressing. Wash the veggies. Marinate the chicken. We're not talking the whole meal here. Just a task or two.

8. **Plan to morph meals.** Plan tomorrow's supper today by making a double batch. A salad can become an entrée if you add a piece of chicken or fish. Grill extra veggies tonight and top your pizza with them tomorrow. When you're cooking black beans from scratch, they can morph from soup to chili and from salad to salsa. Challenge yourself. See how many meals you can make from a single recipe.

9. **Supersize—make your own TV dinners.** Attack an overscheduled week head-on. On nights you're not so rushed, make a double batch of something you know freezes well. Store the second half in microwave-proof containers, clearly marked, with the full title of the dish and the date. A sumptuous title will inspire you to actually *take* the frozen dinner *out* of the freezer and eat it on one of those nights you're tempted to pick up the phone and call for the next-pants-size-up, er, carryout.

10. **Choose the right tools.** Use the right tool for the task and you'll slash culinary frustration. Dull knives, the wrong spoon, a melted spatula, a fork with a broken handle, or a pot that's too small creates kitchen stress. Who needs it? Keep your tools in good working condition and handy.

So cook already. Plan to cook and you will. Plan not to and you won't eat. Or worse, you'll eat poorly.

Breakfast

Wake up and smell the Krispy Kremes

YOU'VE HEARD ALL YOUR LIFE that breakfast is your

most important meal. Well, it is. If you're tired to death of cereal, here are

some options. But remember that cereal's a pretty good choice, too. And I'm

not referring to sugary kid cereals. If there's a prize inside the box or the

cereal is mixed with miniature rainbow-colored marshmallows, it's probably

not the healthiest choice. You don't need to start your day like that. Besides, a "single serving" isn't enough to sustain bird life, so you're just setting yourself up for a day of bad eating.

Don't skip breakfast—it's false economy. You can't "save" calories in the morning and "spend" them later. You'll rob your brain of fuel, and if you also haven't had enough sleep (who gets enough?), you'll find yourself too tired to cook. Calories deemed for breakfast expire after breakfast, so use them. You'll just end up ordering supersize burgers and fries because you skipped breakfast, and where's that going to get you?

Don't run around claiming you don't have time for breakfast. Carve 3 minutes off your shower, don't shave, and don't read the paper. Who sends kids off to school with empty stomachs? You've got time, too. No matter what you tell yourself, you're never left with no choice—only the worst choices. Doughnuts, oversize bagels, and Mc-fast fried breakfast sandwiches are cop-outs.

Make your own eat-on-the-fly breakfasts. Grab a banana; pack Crunchy Granola (page 81) or healthful cereals to go; make your own English muffin sandwich; make a Fresh Fruit Smoothie (page 92); buy regular-size bagels, toast them, and go. Eat-on-the-run breakfasts are fine.

For those of you who are tired of eating the same old thing every day, you have options. Change your mind-set or change your eating habits. Personally, I love eating the same thing every day: homemade granola with fruit and nonfat yogurt. I know exactly how many calories I'm consuming and I don't have to think about what to eat. It's brain food, I'm not hungry in an hour, and I've got enough fuel to keep me going until lunch. Besides, I've made a commitment to cook most of my other meals at home. I don't have time for a complicated gourmet breakfast du jour. But if you do, check out the recipes. And no, Cranberry Apple Pecan Loaf (page 86) isn't a balanced breakfast by itself. Use your head.

Crunchy Granola

I lost my first 30 pounds by snacking on this instead of bonbons, Ho-Hos, candy bars, and doughnuts. I keep individual portions of it with me at all times. It's not the only healthy snack I eat but it's one of my favorites. I never leave home without it, especially when I travel. ▪ If you're a seed person, skip the almonds and use pumpkin or sunflower seeds. Once the granola is cooked and cooled, I add my favorite combinations of dried fruits: raisins, dried cranberries, dried blueberries, chopped dried apricots or pears.

20 SERVINGS vg

1 cup firmly packed dark brown sugar

½ cup water

4 teaspoons pure vanilla extract

1 teaspoon salt

6 cups old-fashioned rolled oats

1 cups chopped pecans, walnuts, or slivered almonds

Dried fruit (optional)

PREHEAT oven to 275°F. Line two cookie sheets with parchment paper and set aside. Combine brown sugar and water in a 4-cup microwave-proof glass measuring cup or bowl. No smaller—it could boil over. Place in microwave on high for 5 minutes and cook until sugar is completely dissolved. Remove from microwave; add vanilla extract and salt. Stir to combine until salt dissolves. Place oats and nuts in a bowl and pour brown sugar syrup over them. Stir until thoroughly mixed. Spread mixture on cookie sheets and bake 45 to 60 minutes, or until golden and crunchy. When mixture comes out of oven it is still very pliable. You may choose to add dried fruit as a finishing touch at this time. When granola has cooled completely, store in an airtight container.

MORPH Sick of plain old granola? Mix in other healthful cereals you like. I cut my batch with Grape-Nuts and All-Bran. WARNING: Read the labels on the cereals you're considering—sugary cereals with marshmallows and peanut butter puffs might not be the best choices.

Here's the skinny on this recipe: you can make it with 1 cup brown sugar and it won't be as clumpy or you can make it with up to 1½ cups brown sugar and it will be clumpier. Manipulate the raw granola just before you put it in the oven by squeezing it together in your hands as you drop it onto the cookie sheets. The granola will clump together; however, once it is cooked, handle carefully or your delicious nuggets will turn to dust.

Muesli

This recipe is easy to customize. Try blueberries and blueberry yogurt or peaches and peach yogurt. Use your imagination. If you discover you're a muesli lover, keep at least a double batch in the refrigerator at all times. ■ There's no cooking involved but you do need to soak the oats overnight, which requires no more thinking than dumping milk over oats and stashing them, tightly covered, in the fridge. Surely you can handle that, no matter how tired you are.

1 SERVING

½ cup old-fashioned rolled oats

½ cup skim milk

Dash ground cinnamon

1 tablespoon raisins

½ apple, peeled, cored, and diced

1 tablespoon plain low-fat yogurt

PLACE oats, milk, cinnamon, and raisins in a bowl; stir to combine. Cover tightly with plastic wrap and refrigerate overnight. Just before serving, stir in apple and yogurt.

Lactose intolerant? Substitute ¼ cup apple juice and ¼ cup water for the skim milk.

Wild about bananas? Blend ½ ripe banana and ¼ teaspoon vanilla extract until smooth. Add to muesli in place of cinnamon, raisins, and apple. Or top muesli with any of your favorite fruits: peaches, plums, apricots, pears, or berries of any kind. Try different dried fruits, such as blueberries, cranberries, or currants. Toasted nuts are a great addition, too.

Cooking Thin with Chef Kathleen

Baked Eggs with Cooked Vegetables and Herbs

Unless you've got a ton of time on your hands, the only reason to make this recipe is because you want something delicious and just happen to have a bunch of leftover vegetables on hand. Or better, you're finally listening to my incessant shtick and you actually prepared extra veggies a few days ago just so you could morph them into this savory meal.

4 SERVINGS

Eight ¼-inch-thick slices zucchini, grilled

Eight ¼-inch-thick slices Japanese eggplant or 4 slices larger eggplant, grilled

1 red pepper, roasted, peeled, and seeded, cut into quarters

¼ cup loosely packed, roughly chopped fresh herbs (parsley, basil, oregano, or thyme or combination)

4 large eggs

½ cup tomato sauce

¼ cup freshly grated Parmesan cheese

Coarse-grained salt and cracked black pepper

PREHEAT oven to 350°F. Spray a 9 × 9-inch baking dish with non-stick cooking spray. Layer vegetables into pan, sprinkling each layer with fresh herbs. Using the back of a large spoon, press to make four indentations in layered vegetables for eggs so that they don't all run together. Crack eggs and put one in center of each indentation. Distribute tomato sauce evenly over eggs, being sure to cover each yolk with some sauce. Sprinkle with cheese and bake until eggs are just set, 7 to 10 minutes. Season with salt and pepper just before serving.

SHORTCUT CHEF

Cheat and use tomato sauce from a jar if you don't have your freezer stocked with the world's easiest Microwave Tomato Sauce (page 247) for just such occasions.

The recipe calls for grilled vegetables but they can be baked, broiled, or pan cooked. If you've got other vegetables you think could work in this dish, use them.

Talitha Anne's Microwave Applesauce

When my little sister was very young and not allowed to use the stove, she asked our dad to peel and cut up two apples, then added a little bit of cinnamon and a tiny bit of sugar and cooked it in the microwave on high until it was applesauce. Try different kinds of apples until you find a favorite. Good eating apples won't necessarily be good cooking apples. ■ This applesauce is absolutely outrageous stuffed into crepes or served over potato pancakes, Sunday morning flapjacks, French toast, or Belgian waffles, topped with a teensy spoonful of real vanilla ice cream.

6 TO 8 SERVINGS

2½ pounds apples

Dash cinnamon (or more to taste)

2 tablespoons sugar

Water or apple cider or apple juice if necessary

PEEL and core apples. Cut into quarters and place in the largest microwave-proof bowl you have that fits into your microwave. If you have only smaller bowls you may have to cook in two batches. Add cinnamon and sugar. Microwave on high for 15 minutes. Remove from oven and stir. If applesauce is soft and the consistency you like, you're done. If not, cook it longer. If it's too thick, add juice or water by the tablespoonful until it's right.

Great-Granny's Banana Nut Bread

A favorite of my mother's since she was a child. On special days, Great-Grandma sent Mom off to school with her favorite lunch box feast, banana nut bread and butter sandwiches. The very mention of this recipe in our house results in a batch made on the spot. (Don't I wish!)

ONE 9-INCH LOAF; 12 SERVINGS

2 cups flour

1 1/2 teaspoons baking powder

1/2 teaspoon baking soda

8 tablespoons (1 stick) butter, softened

1 cup sugar

3 large or 4 medium bananas

2 eggs

1 1/2 tablespoons yogurt or milk

1 teaspoon lemon juice

1/4 teaspoon salt

1 cup pecans (optional)

PREHEAT oven to 350°F. Grease and flour a 9 × 5-inch loaf pan. In a large mixing bowl, sift together flour, baking powder, and baking soda. Set aside. In a large nonreactive mixing bowl, cream butter, sugar, and bananas. Add eggs and mix until combined. Add yogurt or milk, lemon juice, salt, and pecans (if using). Mix thoroughly. Add dry ingredients to wet and mix until just combined. Pour into prepared pan. Bake for 1 hour 25 minutes, or until a toothpick inserted in center comes out clean. Start testing for doneness after 50 minutes.

SHORTCUT CHEF

Measure out the dry ingredients ahead of time and get all your ingredients and tools out. Even little steps will save lots of time.

To reduce the calories and sugar, use 1 egg plus 2 egg whites instead of 2 eggs. Use 1/4 cup butter and another 1/4 cup bananas instead of 1/2 cup butter. Use 3/4 cup sugar instead of 1 cup. But there's nothing like the real thing. So if you really don't have room for banana bread calories, don't make it today. Wait until you do.

Breakfast

Cranberry Apple Pecan Loaf

When my grandmother died, we found thirty bags of cranberries in her freezer. When she'd come to visit from Florida she used to make my mom buy them for her because she swore she couldn't get them at home. She carried them back on the plane because she was always afraid they'd lose her luggage. ▪ The only other person who loves cranberries as much as my grandma did is my dad. In fact, the only thing he cooks is cranberry relish and he won't give out his recipe. My mom says it's the one that's on the back of the cranberry bag. ▪ Cranberries aren't just for Thanksgiving dinner. They're a wonderful addition to pumpkin bread, bran muffins, lemon cake, hot fruit cobbler, and pancakes. Cranberry sauce is great on cereal and toast, and spread on chicken sandwiches instead of mayo.

ONE 9-INCH LOAF; 12 SERVINGS

Finely grated zest of 1 orange

⅓ cup fresh orange juice

⅔ cup buttermilk

3 tablespoons unsalted butter, melted

¼ cup unsweetened applesauce

1 large egg, slightly beaten

2 cups flour

½ cup sugar

1 teaspoon salt

1 teaspoon baking powder

¼ teaspoon baking soda

1½ cups coarsely chopped fresh cranberries

⅓ cup coarsely chopped pecans

PREHEAT oven to 375°F. Grease and flour a 9 × 5-inch loaf pan. In a small nonreactive bowl, stir together zest, orange juice, buttermilk, butter, applesauce, and egg. In a large nonreactive mixing bowl, sift together flour, sugar, salt, baking powder, and baking soda. Using a rubber spatula, stir wet ingredients into dry until just moist. Add cranberries and pecans and mix until just combined. Do not overmix. Pour mixture into prepared pan. Bake 20 minutes, then reduce heat to 350°F and continue to bake until golden brown and a toothpick inserted in center comes out clean, 35 to 45 minutes more. Cool in pan 10 minutes, then turn loaf out onto a wire rack and cool completely before serving.

Guyometer:
I love anything with
cranberries.
It's guy-tested. If a
real guy likes it, your
husband will, too.

SHORTCUT CHEF
Measure out the dry ingredients ahead of time. Lay out the rest of the ingredients and all your tools.

MORPH This wholesome bread is wonderful in the morning toasted or served as a light dessert à la mode with a teensy scoop of vanilla ice cream or lemon sherbet.

Sweet Potato Bread with Cranberries, Currants, and Pecans

Though we'd cook these loaves four at a time, we couldn't bake this bread fast enough at my Maui restaurant. Guests went crazy for it and started lining up even before the sun had a chance to come up. ▪ Yes, you can use fresh or canned pumpkin or even sweet varieties of squash. The recipe calls for dried cranberries and currants and, while delightful, they're sometimes hard to find or just too expensive. Use plump raisins instead if you want.

ONE 9-INCH LOAF; 12 SERVINGS

2 cups flour

1 ½ teaspoons baking powder

1 teaspoon baking soda

¼ teaspoon salt

1 large egg

2 large egg whites

1 cup firmly packed light brown sugar

1 ½ cups cooked and pureed sweet potatoes, pumpkin, or squash

¼ cup vegetable oil

1 ½ teaspoons pure vanilla extract

1 cup fresh cranberries

½ cup dried cranberries

½ cup dried currants or raisins

⅓ cup chopped pecans

PREHEAT oven to 350°F. Lightly grease and flour bottom and sides of a 9 × 5-inch loaf pan; set aside. In a large mixing bowl, sift together flour, baking powder, baking soda, and salt. Set aside. In a separate nonreactive bowl, whisk together egg, egg whites, brown sugar, sweet potatoes, vegetable oil, and vanilla extract. Add dry ingredients to sweet potato mixture. Stir about five strokes, then add fresh and dried cranberries, currants, and pecans. Mix until just combined. Do not overmix. Pour batter into pre-pared pan. Bake until a toothpick inserted in center comes out clean, 50 to 60 min-utes. Cool in pan 10 minutes, then turn loaf out onto a wire rack and cool completely before serving.

If the queen's coming for brunch: This delightful special-occasion breakfast bread is lovely on chilly afternoons with a cup of tea, if you've got a few calories saved up for just such a splurge.

SHORTCUT CHEF
Measure and sift the dry ingredients in advance. Lay out all other ingredients that don't require refrigera-tion and the necessary tools. You'll be amazed at how quickly the job gets done when you get around to it.

COOK ONCE, EAT TWICE Bake two loaves and freeze one. It won't take any extra effort.

When the oven is hot for something else, throw in a few sweet potatoes or squash halves, enough to make 1½ cups, for this recipe. Sweet potatoes don't seem to taste "warmed over" the next day, so they're another thing you can cook ahead.

Cinnamon Apple Streusel Muffins

Weakness #457: crumb cakes. You know the ones. Those little four-packs loaded with crumb topping. I used to love to go to the half-off bakeshop and load up on crumb cakes. It was one of my worst pre-weight-loss habits because I couldn't stop myself from eating way more than a portion, whatever that was. ▪ These muffins helped me kick my coffeecake addiction. I'm not suggesting for a minute that you replace a more nutritious breakfast with **Cinnamon Apple Streusel Muffins.** Not at all. These are special occasion calories you need to plan for.

12 SERVINGS

FOR THE TOPPING

⅓ cup firmly packed brown sugar

3 tablespoons flour

2 teaspoons ground cinnamon

2 tablespoons cold butter, cut into tiny cubes

FOR THE MUFFINS

1¾ cups flour

⅓ cup granulated sugar

2 teaspoons baking powder

¼ teaspoon salt

I large egg, beaten

¾ cup apple cider or apple juice

I apple, peeled, cored, and diced

I teaspoon pure vanilla extract

¼ cup vegetable oil

PREHEAT oven to 400°F. Line a 12-cup muffin tin with paper baking cups; set aside.

PREPARE THE TOPPING: In a small mixing bowl, stir together brown sugar, flour, and cinnamon; cut in butter with a fork. Set aside.

PREPARE THE MUFFINS: In a medium mixing bowl, mix together flour, granulated sugar, baking powder, and salt. In a small mixing bowl, combine egg, apple cider, diced apple, vanilla extract, and oil; add all at once to flour mixture. Stir until just moistened. (Batter should be lumpy.)

Spoon about 1 tablespoon batter into each prepared muffin cup; sprinkle with 1 teaspoon topping. Fill evenly with remaining batter. Sprinkle tops of muffins with remaining topping. Bake about 20 minutes, or until golden brown. Remove from pan; cool slightly on racks.

Guyometer:
Can I have a couple more?

SHORTCUT CHEF
Mix the dry ingredients together and gather all your tools. Muffins are pretty easy to whip up after dinner, plus it's always best to bake treats when you're not hungry.

If you can't be trusted not to eat the whole batch yourself, the minute they're completely cooled off, wrap them up individually and place them in the freezer. Don't leave anything to chance.

Fresh Fruit Smoothie

At the beginning of my weight-loss journey, I relied heavily on smoothies to keep me out of the cartons of ice cream in the freezer that shouldn't have been there in the first place. Today my ice cream rule is to keep no more than one pint of the very best quality in my freezer at a time. Ice cream is my absolute weakness. I have to limit myself to ¼-cup portions or I'll go bonkers. ▪ Boy, was it a sad day for me when the media exposed the real calorie, sugar, and fat contents of all the different commercial smoothies. I find it much safer to make my own.

1 SERVING

SHORTCUT CHEF
Keep frozen fruit on hand, especially bananas. Bananas and frozen fruit give homemade smoothies that desirable creamy texture often achieved with the use of frozen yogurt, sherbet, or ice cream by smoothie vendors. Papaya, mango, and kiwi also yield a creamier smoothie.

MORPH Use skim milk, ice, fruit, and a teensy bit of sugar and you've got more of a milkshake. Keep in mind when you're making smoothies that you're not competing with McDonald's here. You're going for a delicious, naturally healthful drink.

1 large ripe banana

3 to 5 ripe strawberries

½ cup crushed ice

2 tablespoons apple cider or juice

PLACE all ingredients in a blender. Blend until smooth.

Soups

SOUP FOR DINNER? IF YOU'RE thinking, "Where's the

entrée?" keep an open mind. Change your definition of dinner and change

your perception of soups. What could be more divine than a hearty bowl of

soup and a chunk of crusty bread? And I did say hearty, which doesn't mean

made with heavy cream or thickened with cheese and eggs. Think about how

you feel when you eat like that anyway. I'd rather get a food hangover from chocolate I can see and savor than from cream so lost in soup I can't properly enjoy it. But that's just me.

If soup is going to be the star attraction, it should be a feast for the eyes and for the belly. Contrary to popular belief, it's not hard to make, especially if you get into the habit of throwing chicken and veggie scraps in the freezer for making batches of soup stock later. If you haven't quite mastered quick homemade stocks (pages 95 to 97), there are plenty of good-quality stocks you can buy.

Either way, stocks on hand make soups a snap to prepare and you really don't even need to follow a recipe. A few hearty handfuls of fresh or frozen veggies, a cup of noodles or rice, and dinner is done. Check out Mom's Quick Chicken Soup on page 98—it doesn't get any easier than that. Soups morph. Make a double batch, freeze half, and add different ingredients when thawed. No one will ever know you're serving leftovers.

In our house, soup dinners mean divine desserts are sure to follow. A light and brothy soup is just right on a hot August night followed by a generous serving of Washington Street Inn's Peach Batter Cobbler (page 380) or my mom's favorite, Rhubarb Crisp (page 382). À la mode shouldn't be out of the question if you're sticking with the dessert rule of thumb—higher-calorie desserts on light meal nights only.

Two Recipes for Chicken Stock

"Mom, how do you make your chicken stock?" "Well I don't do it the way you do, that's for sure." "Mom, I throw a whole chicken (one with the head and feet attached if I can find it) in a pot and cover it with water and bring it to a boil. I skim off the foam, throw in a little salt, a peeled onion cut in half, a peeled carrot cut in half, a celery stalk or two, and a bay leaf. I bring it to a boil again, skim off any foam, and reduce it to a simmer. I cook it until it tastes good, about 2 hours. What's wrong with that?" ▪ "Kathleen, nobody can get chickens with the head and feet attached, and who'd want to anyway? That's just gross. And why should anyone want to waste a perfectly good chicken just to make broth? And what? Then we should throw it out? What a waste of money, Kathleen." ▪ "How do you make chicken stock, Mom?" "I empty the freezer. I use the bones from roasted chickens, backbones left over from split-roasted chicken, the wings and tips left over from chicken wings, and dark meat I didn't feel like eating. I throw all that in a pot with any leftover vegetable scraps I can fish out of the freezer without killing myself and cover it all with water. I try to remember to put a carrot and an onion in the pot and some salt and pepper. It's the same as my vegetable stock, only with chicken. I just hope that it comes out more chicken-y than vegetable-y. I strain it in a colander and then again through cheesecloth and let it cool in the refrigerator overnight. The next day I skim off the fat, divide the stock into dinner-size portions, and freeze it." ▪ "That's it?" "That's it, Kathleen. Cooking doesn't need to be fancy or complicated."

Vegetable Stock Rita's Way

This is hard to admit, especially since I'm a chef and I might have to apply for a cook's job again someday, but I hate my vegetable stocks. I've tried other chefs' recipes and I don't particularly love anything they've come up with, either. Besides, buying vegetables for the purpose of making vegetable stock is too luxurious for my pocketbook. I'd rather go to the movies. ▪ But my mom has vegetable stock down. She makes the best vegetable soups I've ever tasted in my entire life. There's just one teensy little problem. She doesn't use a recipe. ▪ "I do too have a method, Kathleen. Take all the vegetables out of the freezer, dump them into a pot, and cover them with water. Put some salt and pepper in there and cook until just before it smells bad. Strain it through a strainer and then through cheesecloth. Cool it, refrigerate it, and then divide it up and freeze it in dinner-size portions." ▪ "Mom, I can't write that." "Why not, it's the way I've always done it." "I need amounts, Mom, techniques, precise cook times." "No, you don't. If I can operate this way, so can anyone else. You don't always have to have a recipe for things, Kathleen." ▪ So I did what any roving reporter would do—I followed her while she made stock one day. I ended up with the same kind of notes a rookie reporter would wind up with after a day of sleuthing organized chaos. The ingredients list reads like her chatter. They're direct quotes. You can't make this stuff up.

Scraps of red peppers

First and last slices of onions

Any leftover dinner vegetables that didn't have sauce on them (steamed green
  beans, peas, carrots, etc.)

Tomatoes that had too many bad spots minus their bad spots, and first and last
  slices of other tomatoes

Stalky ends of fennel

Celery just before it gets bad; the tops and the bottom inch (leave out the dirt)

Outside leaves of cabbage—a few

No potatoes (too gooey), broccoli, cauliflower, or Brussels sprouts (too strongly flavored)

If I bought a rutabaga for something I put the leftovers in because Lord knows I can't get your father to eat the whole thing. Rutabagas only come in humongous, so there's always some left over.

The same goes for leftover turnips.

Beets are out unless you want bitter purple soup.

If you have any other stuff hanging around, throw it in. You'll know if it works.

Make sure you always have an onion and a carrot in there, and who cares about the rest of it?

FROM MOM'S LIPS TO YOUR EARS Part of the reason to make vegetable stock is to use up those vegetables you don't feel like eating. It's either the little bit left from dinner that your conscience won't let you throw away or the stuff you brought home and know you're just never going to fix for whatever reason or the carrots that are getting limp. So instead of throwing them out and feeling guilty, put them in little bags in the freezer. When you can't get into the freezer anymore, make stock.

Mom's Quick Chicken Soup

Mom and I are having dinner and she says, "How do you like the soup?" "It's great, Mom. I love it." "Really? It's from a box." "Huh? Mom, a box? What do you mean?" "The broth, I didn't make it." I couldn't believe it! "I was too tired to make the broth from scratch and I thought this was as good a time as any to see if it's possible to make good soup from store-bought broth." She definitely proved something I deemed impossible (but then what do daughters *really* know anyway?).

4 SERVINGS

1 tablespoon olive oil

1 cup diced onion

Coarse-grained salt and cracked black pepper

6 to 8 cups canned chicken broth (the best you can afford)

One 10-to-12-ounce boneless, skinless chicken breast

3 cups sliced carrots (about 4 medium)

1 cup orzo or any other small pasta or noodles

1 to 2 cups peas (frozen are fine)

1/2 cup loosely packed, roughly chopped flat-leaf parsley

IN a medium soup pot, heat olive oil over medium-high heat. Add onion to pot and stir until evenly coated with oil. Season with salt and pepper. Cover, reduce heat to medium-low, and cook, stirring occasionally, until translucent, about 15 minutes. Add a splash of chicken broth or a teaspoon of water to pot if onions are ever in jeopardy of burning.

WHEN onion has completely softened, add chicken broth, chicken breast (left whole), and carrots to pot. Cook uncovered for 10 minutes, or until chicken breast is cooked through. Remove chicken breast and shred when cool.

MEANWHILE, add orzo to soup and cook 10 minutes, until al dente, then add peas. Cook for another 5 minutes. Return chicken to pot, along with the parsley. Taste and correct seasonings. Cook 1 minute more. Serve immediately.

Guyometer:
I like the rice and peas combination.
Why bother explaining again that orzo is pasta, not rice?

If the queen's coming for dinner: She probably won't be happy with just chicken soup. Garnish this delish dish with a few lemon or lime wedges and generous sprigs of parsley or cilantro.

FROM MOM'S LIPS TO YOUR EARS

You're already using canned broth, so at least cut up the carrots and onions yourself. And don't skimp on the parsley. It's delicious in chicken soup.

Corn Soup with Zucchini, Tomato, and Basil

Sometimes a bowl of soup is dinner. Your family will probably roll over and faint the first time you serve them a bowl of soup and a salad for supper but it's very important to balance out heavy meals with lean meals. It's a price I gladly pay to enjoy luscious dinners like Split-Roasted Chicken and Potatoes (page 346) or a sensible portion of real dessert. ■ Balancing calories daily and weekly is key. Anyway, it's not like this soup is a light snack. It's quite substantial, very delicious, and satisfying.

4 TO 6 SERVINGS

*Guyometer:
More filling than I
thought.*

1 tablespoon olive oil

1 medium onion, finely diced

4 cups homemade Chicken Stock (page 95) or canned broth

1 pound zucchini (about 2 small or
  1 medium), cut into ¼-inch cubes

2 cups cored, peeled, seeded, and chopped tomatoes

2 cups fresh corn kernels (about 4 ears)

Coarse-grained salt and cracked black pepper

½ cup loosely packed basil leaves

SHORTCUT CHEF

If you don't want to fuss with fresh tomatoes or corn, or if they're out of season, use a 15-ounce can of chopped tomatoes with the juices or frozen corn.

MORPH Give yourself a night off next week or the week after. Make extra and freeze it. Add extra veggies, such as sliced mushrooms, peas, cubed carrots, or cut green beans, the second time around. Make it stew-like by adding shredded chicken, cubed cooked stew meat, small cooked pasta, or cooked rice.

PLACE oil and onion in a large pot over medium-high heat; stir onion to coat evenly with oil. Add 2 tablespoons of stock to pot, stir, and cover. Reduce heat to medium-low and simmer 15 minutes or so, until onion is soft and almost cooked through. Add zucchini and tomatoes, stir, and cook uncovered about 5 minutes, until zucchini begins to soften. Add corn and season with salt and pepper to taste. Add remaining stock to pot, increase heat to high, and bring to a boil. Boil soup for 1 minute and then turn off heat. Taste and adjust seasonings. Cut basil into small strips. Ladle soup into serving bowls and garnish with basil. Serve immediately.

Lentil Lemon Soup

Red lentils always want to become thick, mushy soup, whereas brown lentils keep their shape. Since I don't mind thick soups I use red lentils in the winter, when homey thick soups seem to comfort cold bones, and reserve the brown ones for warmer days. If you're lucky enough to stumble across petite French lentils, try them. They're positively delicious and worth the extra money. As with any recipe that calls for a stock, the better your stock, the better the end result. But if you're in a hurry or homemade stocks aren't part of your culinary repertoire yet, use the best purchased broth you can get.

4 SERVINGS

- 1 cup lentils, rinsed and cleaned of impurities
- 4 cups Vegetable Stock (page 96), Chicken Stock (page 95), or canned broth
- 2 dried chili pods or ¼ teaspoon crushed red pepper flakes (optional)
- Juice of 1 lemon (or lots more if you like it lemony)
- Coarse-grained salt and cracked black pepper

PLACE lentils, stock, and chili pods or red pepper flakes (if desired) in a pot. Bring to a boil and immediately reduce to a simmer. Simmer, stirring occasionally, until lentils are soft, about 30 minutes, or depending on how soft you want your lentils. The type of lentils will determine cooking time. Add more stock or water if soup is too thick. Add lemon juice just before serving. Taste and adjust seasonings with salt, pepper, and more lemon if you want. Serve immediately.

Guyometer:
I really like this one.

MORPH Stir in leaves of fresh spinach 5 minutes prior to serving. It's really quite good. Roughly chopped Swiss chard and beet greens are very good, too; add them about 10 minutes prior to serving because they're a little heartier than spinach.

Add chili spice or not. It's up to you. Add a little lemon or a lot—it's all a matter of taste. Cook to please yourself.

If you want to complicate matters, you can cook the lentils in water but add a peeled carrot cut in half, a celery stalk cut in half, half a peeled onion, and a bay leaf. Once the lentils are cooked, discard these additions and proceed as directed.

Green Bean, Potato, and Tomato Soup with Lots of Pasta

It's soup with enough pasta to call it a hearty main course. Serve it with a simple salad of garden lettuces and call it dinner.

4 SERVINGS

1 tablespoon plus 1 tablespoon olive oil

2 cloves garlic, minced

1 pound green beans, trimmed, cut into 1-inch pieces

3 medium potatoes, peeled, cut into ½-inch chunks

One 14-ounce can whole tomatoes with juice, crushed by hand

4 cups Chicken Stock (page 95) or canned

6 ounces uncooked spaghetti, broken into 2-inch pieces, or any small pasta

Coarse-grained salt and cracked black pepper

¼ cup loosely packed basil leaves, minced

2 ounces freshly grated Parmesan cheese

Guyometer: I'll eat it as long as we're having steak tomorrow. "Off the record, Kathleen?" "Sure, Dad." "Not as skimpy a meal as some of the things you and your mother come up with."

IN a large soup pot, heat 1 tablespoon of olive oil over medium heat, add garlic to pan, and cook but don't brown. If necessary, add 1 teaspoon of water to prevent it from browning. Add beans, potatoes, tomatoes, and chicken stock to pot all at once. Bring to a boil, reduce heat to a simmer, and cook 25 minutes. Add pasta to pot; season with salt and pepper to taste. Cook over low heat 30 minutes more, or until pasta and vegetables are tender. Stir frequently so pasta doesn't stick together and potatoes don't sink and stick to pot bottom. The soup is very thick. Just before serving, stir in basil and remaining 1 tablespoon olive oil. Stir in cheese now or grate it over each serving if you're feeding both cheese lovers and cheese haters.

If the queen's coming for dinner: No need to cook a crown roast—this is enough food to please Her Royal Highness, the king, and all his men. Garnish the soup with sprigs of fresh basil and curls of Parmesan cheese. Drag a metal carrot peeler over a block of Parmesan cheese to form showy curls.

The recipe calls for you to cook the beans and potatoes for the same length of time, which causes one to think that the beans will be way overcooked. By some chef's standards they may well be; however, it's a matter of taste and getting dinner on the table with the least amount of fuss possible. If you're into crunchy beans, add them to the soup when the potatoes are halfway cooked.

Open the can of tomatoes, then holding your hand over the top, drain the juices right into the soup pot (at the appropriate time). Crush the tomatoes by hand and drop them into the pot, too, or crush them with a spoon right in the pot if you were never fond of finger painting.

FROM MOM'S LIPS TO YOUR EARS

Soup should be overcooked. The pasta overcooks too. If you don't like things overcooked, make something else. Hey, she's raised four kids, she tells it like it is.

SHORTCUT CHEF
Prep all or some of the veggies the night before, and if
you get that far you might as
well cook the soup the night
before, too. Cooking all or
part of tomorrow's dinner
after the dinner dishes are
cleared is a great habit to get
into. You get the next day off.

MORPH Make a double
batch and freeze the leftovers. By now, if you've
been listening to me at all,
your freezer is probably
overflowing with healthful,
home-cooked, ready-to-
reheat-and-eat meals. Use
good-quality containers that
will protect the foods from
freezer burn and label them.

If you like potatoes that hold
their shape when cooked, use
Yukon Gold potatoes or waxy
potatoes. I love the texture of
cooked russets in this soup
because they break down and
thicken the soup, absorbing
all the wonderful flavors along
the way and making each bite
all the more grand.

You owe it to yourself to use
homemade chicken stock
whenever you can. Chicken
stock is a no-brainer (page
95). Freeze it in dinner-size
batches. It's great to have on
hand for soups and sauces.

Potato and Cabbage Soup

I could have called this cabbage and potato soup but I figured you'd turn the page quicker. At least this way you might humor me and look through the recipe. Listen, there's bacon in this soup, and it doesn't take a lot of time to prep. It's really quite easy, but it does require 2½ hours on the stove, so keep that in mind.

4 SERVINGS

2 strips bacon, cut crosswise into matchstick-size strips

1 large onion, finely diced

½ large head cabbage, cut into ¾-inch slices and then into
   ½-inch chunks

1½ pounds Idaho potatoes (3 to 4 medium), peeled and cut into
   ½-inch chunks

2 carrots, peeled and cut into ½-inch slices or chunks

⅓ cup apple cider vinegar

½ teaspoon coarse-grained salt

3 cups Chicken Stock (page 95) or canned broth

Cracked black pepper

IN a large soup pot, cook bacon and onion over medium heat, stirring often, until onion begins to soften. Add cabbage, pota- toes, carrots, vinegar, and salt, and stir until combined. Add chicken stock. Bring to a boil, immediately reduce to a simmer, cover, and cook 2½ hours, or until potatoes have broken down a little and cabbage is completely cooked. Taste and adjust season- ings with salt and pepper. Serve immediately.

Pumpkin and Cannellini Bean Soup

Make the soup. Don't look at the ingredients list and turn the page just because it says to peel and dice a pumpkin. If you can peel and dice an apple you can peel and dice a pumpkin. True, it's a little harder but it's worth the trouble. This soup is so good and good for you. The dried beans aren't a problem either because they take the same amount of time to cook as the squash.

4 SERVINGS

1 teaspoon extra-virgin olive oil

1 ounce pancetta or country bacon, diced

2 cloves garlic, slivered

4 sprigs fresh thyme

2/3 cup dried cannellini beans, soaked overnight and drained

1 1/4 pounds peeled, seeded, and finely diced pumpkin or butternut squash (about 1 small cooking pumpkin)

1/2 teaspoon crushed red pepper flakes

5 cups Chicken Stock (page 95) or canned broth

If the queen's coming for dinner or even if she's not: Serve this soup with toasted bread croutons or thin shavings of Parmesan cheese and freshly cracked black pepper.

IN a large soup pot, combine olive oil, pancetta, garlic, and fresh thyme. Turn heat to medium and cook, stirring often, until garlic is golden, about 5 minutes. Add beans, pumpkin, and red pepper flakes to pot and stir to coat evenly. Add chicken stock. Bring to a boil, then reduce heat to a strong simmer. Cook until pumpkin has disintegrated into broth and beans are cooked through and fork-tender, about 1 hour. Discard thyme sprigs. Serve immediately.

SHORTCUT CHEF Peel and dice the pumpkin ahead and the rest can be thrown together pretty painlessly.

MORPH Make extra and freeze it in dinner-size portions that you label. You'll be glad the day you remember you've got it somewhere in the bowels of your freezer. You may have to dig a little but you won't have to cook.

Butternut squash can be used in place of cooking pumpkin for this recipe. Other winter squash varieties will work too, but keep in mind they may be difficult to peel and dice.

If you forget to soak the beans a day ahead, place them in a pot, cover with water, and bring to a boil for 1 minute. Turn off the heat and let stand 1 hour. If you don't have time even to do that, rinse them and go for it. Cooking takes longer but you'll get the job done. You won't win any culinary awards for perfect, evenly cooked beans but so what? Or use a 15-ounce can and add them near the end of cooking.

Minestrone

I thought minestrone had to have noodles but my mom says I'm wrong. When your mom tells you you're wrong, you're wrong. "Minestrone is an Italian word meaning big soup, Kathleen. Big soup doesn't mean noodles. If you want noodles, add noodles. What do I care? Just don't skimp on the beans—they're better for you than noodles. If you're going to fill up on noodles you might as well throw a loaf of bread in there too. Eat your vegetables, Kathleen. Set an example for people. Live what you preach or I'll tell." "Yes, Mom."

4 TO 6 SERVINGS

1 tablespoon olive oil

1 medium sweet onion, chopped

2 stalks celery, chopped

2 small carrots, peeled and chopped or thinly sliced

2 cloves garlic, minced

1 tablespoon plus ¼ cup loosely packed, roughly chopped flat-leaf parsley

1 tablespoon plus ¼ cup loosely packed, roughly chopped basil leaves

One 28-ounce can plum tomatoes with juice, chopped

2 cups dried cranberry beans, soaked overnight and drained (page 107)

1 quart Chicken Stock (page 95), canned broth, or water

1 bay leaf

1 tablespoon sage leaves, chopped

2 cups peeled and diced potatoes (any kind)

2 cups roughly chopped cabbage

¼ pound prosciutto or ham, finely diced (optional)

Coarse-grained salt and cracked black pepper

SHORTCUT CHEF

This is not a soup you can come home from work and make in time for dinner unless you prep all the vegetables the night before. Otherwise, this is great to make on the weekend. Get-ahead prep jobs: peel and dice the carrots, celery, garlic, and cabbage the night before. Clean the parsley, soak the beans, and peel the potatoes (store them covered in water).

MORPH Make a double batch and freeze it in dinner-size portions. When you just can't face another night in front of the stove you won't have to.

HEAT olive oil in a large soup pot over medium heat; add onion, celery, and carrots, and cook 15 minutes. Add garlic, 1 tablespoon parsley, and 1 tablespoon basil. Cook 1 minute, stirring often. Add tomatoes with their juice, beans, stock or water, bay leaf, and sage. Bring to a boil, then reduce heat to a steady simmer and cook 30 minutes. If soup is too thick now or anytime during cooking, add another cup of broth or water. Add potatoes and cabbage and cook 40 minutes more, or until beans and potatoes are cooked through. Add remaining ¼ cup parsley, remaining ¼ cup basil, and prosciutto; taste and season with salt and pepper. Cook 5 minutes more to blend flavors. Discard bay leaf.

Guyometer:
My grandmother used to make this but hers had noodles. This is good, too.

Cranberry beans are hard to find sometimes. Use any kind of dried beans you like—pinto beans, white beans, navy beans, black beans, whatever. If you can't find fresh sage, skip it or find a substitute that pleases you, fresh oregano or marjoram perhaps.

If you don't feel like chopping the canned tomatoes, squeeze them between your fingers directly over the pot when you're supposed to add them.

FROM MOM'S LIPS TO YOUR EARS

If you can cook pasta, you can cook dried beans. Just remember to soak them the night before. And now that you didn't do that, place dried beans in a small pot, cover with water, bring to a boil for 1 minute, and let them sit for an hour off the heat. Or use canned.

Roasted Butternut Squash and Apple Soup

I look forward to fall's glorious harvest each year, just as mothers look forward to the first day of school. The flavors and textures of the different squashes are marvelous and the nutritious benefits are definitely a plus, but mostly squash is so darn simple to prepare. Roasted, steamed, baked, or pureed into soup, squash doesn't require much prep time and the results are really wonderful.

4 SERVINGS

2 pounds butternut squash (I medium)

2 Northern Spy, Rome Beauty, or other
   baking apples

I teaspoon olive oil

Coarse-grained salt and cracked
   black pepper

4 to 6 cloves garlic, peeled and cut in
   half lengthwise

2 sprigs thyme

4 cups Chicken Stock (page 95) or canned broth

*Guyometer:
What's for dinner
tomorrow?*

PREHEAT oven to 375°F. Cut squash in half lengthwise. Remove seeds. Peel, core, and cut apples into quarters. Brush cut surfaces of squash and apples with olive oil. Season with salt and pepper. Set apples aside. Place squash on a cookie sheet cut side down. Lift squash and tuck half of garlic and 1 sprig of thyme into cavity of each half. Bake 15 minutes. Place apples on cookie sheet with squash and continue baking until squash and apples are completely soft and tender, 15 to 20 minutes more.

WHEN squash is just cool enough to handle, scrape meat from skin and place in a medium pot along with apples and cooked garlic; discard thyme sprigs. Mash with a potato masher or, if a smoother texture is desired, pass through a ricer or food mill.

Add only enough chicken broth to achieve desired consistency. For a thinner soup, use more stock; for a thicker, heartier version, use less stock. Heat over medium-high heat, stirring constantly, until soup comes to a boil. Taste and adjust seasonings. Serve immediately.

If the queen's coming for dinner: Swirl a little sour cream or crème fraîche into each serving if you want a devilishly good bowl of soup that will impress your guests. The white swirl in the center of the soup is very pretty.

SHORTCUT CHEF
While someone else is cleaning up tonight's dinner dishes, cook the squash and make this tomorrow's dinner. If it's tonight's meal, cook the squash after breakfast. Ten minutes here, ten minutes there, and you're done before you know it. Lay out the rest of the ingredients and gather your tools.

MORPH Get ahead on tomorrow night's veggie side dishes; cook an extra squash and reheat it in the microwave or add it to mashed potatoes. Leftover squash puree is perfect for Sweet Potato Bread (page 88). (No one will know the difference.)

Tomato and Bread Soup

Now you can never say there's nothing in the house to eat. Who doesn't have stale bread and a can of tomatoes in the cupboard? My Neapolitan grandma told me, "Kate, we never used fancy breads to make this soup; nobody had that kind of money. We used biscotti. Not the sweet kind, the savory kind." Since I'm sure none of you are reading this from your Italian villa either, any stale bread will do.

4 SERVINGS

½ pound stale country bread, crusts removed, sliced or pulled into big chunks

3 cloves garlic, minced

1 tablespoon olive oil

Herb stems (parsley, basil, oregano, and thyme), minced (optional)

One 28-ounce can tomato chunks in puree

1 quart Chicken Stock (page 95) or canned broth

½ cup loosely packed, roughly chopped basil leaves

Coarse-grained salt and cracked black pepper

Guyometer: Pretty good. (You know guys hate to let on that anything that's not downright greasy is any good.)

SHORTCUT CHEF

Spread bread in a single layer directly on the oven rack or on a cookie sheet and let sit in the oven overnight with the light on or while you run errands. You're just trying to dry it out. Think Thanksgiving bread for stuffing.

Speaking of fresh herbs— while you're sautéing the garlic it would be lovely to add a few herb stems to the pot to flavor the sauce, but if you don't have them handy, skip it. And don't give it a second thought. Yes, they make a difference, but no, it's not worth the time and money if it's at all inconvenient. I'm sure you have a windowsill full of potted herbs to choose from. Ahem. They're cheap and cheery.

You can use canned whole tomatoes and their juice. You'll just have to squish or roughly chop them.

PREHEAT oven to 250°F. Place bread in a single layer on a cookie sheet and toast until it dries out but doesn't color, 20 to 25 minutes. If it does color, so what, the soup will still be great. Remove bread from oven and set aside.

IN a 3-quart pot, place garlic, olive oil, and herb stems (if using), turn heat to medium, and cook until garlic just begins to turn golden. Add tomatoes and bread and cook, stirring occasionally, until bread falls apart and combines with tomatoes, about 20 minutes. Add chicken stock, reduce heat to low, and cook, stirring every now and then, for 10 minutes. Add basil, taste, and adjust seasonings with salt and pepper as needed. Serve immediately.

Cooking Thin with Chef Kathleen

Vegetable Soup

I was going to call this summer vegetable soup but the truth of the matter is you can
make delicious vegetable soup year-round. You know I'm going to tell you to use the
best vegetables you can get your hands on. Always keep your eyes peeled while
you're marketing and take advantage of roadside stands, farmers' markets, and specialty produce stores. Richly satisfying, healthful meals will sway your palate away
from craving the wrong foods. Before you know it, you'll be consumed with veggie
hankerings day and night. Well, maybe not exactly.

4 TO 6 SERVINGS

8 cups Vegetable Stock (page 96), Chicken Stock (page 95), or canned broth

12 scant cups any vegetables OR:

> 3 to 4 small potatoes, peeled and diced (about 1 cup)
>
> 1 large carrot, peeled and sliced (about ¾ cup cut ¼ inch thick)
>
> 1 medium fennel bulb, cored and diced
>
> ⅓ pound green beans, trimmed and cut into
> 1-inch pieces (about 1¼ cups)
>
> 1 pound Roma tomatoes, chopped (about 3 cups)
>
> ½ pound zucchini, cut into 1-inch pieces
> (about 1½ cups)
>
> 1 ear corn kernels (about ½ cup)

Coarse-grained salt and cracked black pepper

¼ cup loosely packed, roughly chopped herbs

If the queen's coming for dinner: Garnish the soup with a teaspoon of pesto and sprigs of freshly picked herbs.

PLACE stock in a large pot and bring to a boil over high heat. Add
the 12 cups vegetables or the potatoes, carrot, and fennel;
reduce heat to a strong simmer. Cook 15 minutes. Add green
beans, tomatoes, zucchini, and corn. Cook until all vegetables
are tender, 5 to 7 minutes more. Season to taste with salt and
pepper. Add herbs and cook 1 minute more. Serve immediately.

Warm crusty bread and a
simple green salad round out
this meal beautifully. Not too
much bread, mind you, and
easy with the butter if you
use it at all. Dip the bread in
the soup.

**FROM MOM'S LIPS
TO YOUR EARS**
Eat your vegetables.

Roasted Vegetable Soup

Especially delicious in colder months when you're craving the kind of comfort foods you shouldn't overindulge in. This hearty soup is great the night you make it and even better the next day.

4 TO 6 SERVINGS

1 ½ pounds potatoes, washed and cut into 1-inch pieces

1 large sweet onion, cut into 1-inch pieces

½ pound carrots, peeled and cut into 1-inch pieces

½ pound parsnips, peeled and cut into 1-inch pieces

6 cloves garlic, unpeeled

1 tablespoon olive oil

Coarse-grained salt and cracked black pepper

6 cups Vegetable Stock (page 96), Chicken Stock (page 95), or canned broth

1 tablespoon balsamic vinegar

1 sprig rosemary or thyme

PREHEAT oven to 400°F. Throw all vegetables and garlic into a large plastic bag. (One of the bags you brought them home in. You may have to use two bags.) Pour 1 tablespoon oil into bag with veggies and shake until well coated. Spread vegetables on a rimmed baking sheet, season with salt and pepper, and roast, turning once or twice, until nicely browned, about 45 minutes.

SCRAPE vegetables but not garlic into a large soup pot. Peel garlic and place it back on baking sheet. Set baking sheet on largest burner you have over medium-high heat and pour ½ cup vegetable or chicken stock and the balsamic vinegar into pan. Deglaze by stirring and scraping bottom and sides of baking sheet. Magically, all the tasty nibbly bits will come loose and the garlic will disintegrate into the pan juices. Pour this viscous sauce directly into soup pot with vegetables.

ADD remaining 5½ cups stock to soup pot with rosemary or thyme. Bring to a simmer, taste, and adjust seasonings. Cover and cook slowly until flavors are blended, about 20 minutes. Add water as necessary to thin soup. Remove herb sprigs and serve immediately.

Guyometer:
Great soup.

SHORTCUT CHEF

Peel and chop vegetables the night before while you're watching TV or listening to the radio. Store them in a plastic bag with oil and pepper. Do not salt the vegetables or they will release their water and steam instead of roasting to golden brown. Salt the vegetables just before you put them in the oven.

The recipe says to cut all vegetables into 1-inch pieces. Unless you've studied culinary arts abroad, this is practically impossible. The point is to keep the vegetables uniform in size so they'll cook evenly.

Sandwiches, Pizzas, and Frittatas

BELIEVE IT OR NOT, HOMEMADE pizza is a really fast

meal. The dough keeps well, frozen in large sealable plastic bags, so on your

way out the door in the morning, throw a frozen dough ball on the counter.

When you come home all you have to do is roll it, pat it, and mark it with a P.

Put it in the oven for your family and wheeeeeee! You just made dinner in a

hurry.

We sometimes have pizza for dinner after an early movie. By using the oven timer to turn it on while we're out, we come home to a pizza stone that is hot, hot, hot, and we're eating within 30 minutes. You can't get pizza delivered faster than that, and you'll never want take-out pizza again once you've mastered homemade. You do have to plan ahead by keeping grated cheese and tomato sauce in the freezer, but you can handle that.

Too tired to lift your fork? If you can make scrambled eggs, you can make a frittata. Even teenagers can master these. Pick up a whisk, beat some eggs, throw in some frozen peas, a slice of bacon cut into tiny strips, and a few cooked potatoes, and call it a frittata. Leftovers make great frittata fillings, too.

Sandwiches are another can't-cope-with-dinner, quick-and-light meal solution. It doesn't matter how you get the job done; it just matters that you do. Pretty soon this will all become second nature and four o'clock "what's for dinner?" dilemmas will be a thing of the past.

Mozzarella-Tomato Sandwich

We almost didn't put this in the book because it's good only if you can get your hands on peak-of-season tomatoes; also, fresh mozzarella can be hard to find in some parts of the country. We decided to leave it in, though, because it's really, really delicious. If you can find these ingredients, great—if not, skip this recipe.

4 SERVINGS

1 large tomato, peeled (or not) and thinly sliced

½ pound fresh mozzarella, buffalo milk if you can get it, thinly sliced (about 2 balls)

Coarse-grained salt and cracked black pepper

4 Italian rolls, split, or 8 slices country bread

1 clove garlic, peeled and cut in half

4 teaspoons Pesto (page 250; optional)

1 ounce arugula (3 to 4 leaves per sandwich)

2 red bell peppers, roasted, peeled, cut in half, and seeded

PLACE tomato slices and cheese slices in a single layer on a plate. Season with salt and pepper to taste; let stand for at least 15 minutes. Toast rolls or bread. Rub toasted halves or slices lightly with garlic. Spread pesto, if using, on bottom half of rolls. Begin to build your sandwich by placing a few leaves of arugula on the bread, followed by roasted peppers. Lay slices of tomato and cheese over peppers and cover with top of roll.

Guyometer:
If we can have meat tomorrow, this is okay for "healthy."

MORPH Turn this into a hot sandwich by first placing cheese on bread and running it under the broiler until the cheese is melted. Remove from broiler and proceed as directed. Try drizzling a little balsamic or red wine vinegar over the tomatoes if it sounds good to you.

Since we made you go look for buffalo milk mozzarella, we didn't think you'd mind looking for arugula (a salad green sometimes sold near the herbs and sometimes called rocket or roquette). But if you can't find it, substitute any tender salad green or leaves of fresh basil.

The recipe calls for you to rub a raw clove of garlic over the bread. If you don't think you'll pick up much garlic flavor this way, think again. Practice on a slice of toast. Cut a garlic clove in half and press lightly on one side of the toast and harder on the other. Taste them. You will notice a huge difference.

Grilled Chicken Sandwich with Onion, Tomato, and Arugula

Esteemed cookbook author Richard Sax enjoyed this sandwich so much when he ate it in my Maui restaurant that he included the recipe in his book *Lighter, Quicker, Better*. His love for the sandwich was largely due to the exceptional quality of the locally grown ingredients nurtured and harvested by Robbie Friedlander of Robbie's Tropical Farm, located on the slopes of Maui's Haleakala volcano. I've been known to make this twice a week when tomatoes are in season and sweet onions and tender young greens are available.

4 SERVINGS

8 thin slices large ripe tomato

Coarse-grained salt and cracked black pepper

¼ cup loosely packed, chopped basil leaves

2 teaspoons olive oil

12 ounces boneless, skinless chicken breasts, pounded thin (¼- to ½-inch thick, or to size of bun)

4 thick slices sweet onion (Maui, Granex, Walla Walla, or Vidalia)

8 thick slices whole-grain or Italian bread or something equally good

1 clove garlic, peeled

2 cups lightly packed, trimmed arugula or baby lettuce leaves

4 teaspoons fresh lime juice

ARRANGE tomato slices on a platter. Season with salt and pepper to taste. Sprinkle with half of chopped basil; set aside. Let stand up to 1 hour but not much longer or tomatoes will become watery.

PREHEAT broiler. Season chicken generously with salt and pepper to taste. In a 10-inch nonstick skillet, heat oil over medium-high heat. When it is hot but not smoking, add chicken to pan and cook until golden brown, about 3 minutes per side. Remove and set aside. Add onions to pan and cook until golden and tender. When chicken has cooled, slice it thinly.

TOAST bread on a cookie sheet under broiler—this happens quickly, so watch the toast carefully. Rub one side of each toasted slice with garlic clove. Place one slice of bread on each plate and arrange a bed of arugula or lettuce on each slice.

DIVIDE sliced chicken into four servings and place on lettuce. Squeeze fresh lime over chicken. Top with tomatoes and onions, separating the onions into rings. Sprinkle with remaining basil. Top sandwiches with remaining bread slices. Serve immediately.

Guyometer:
Mmm. At least
there was some
meat to this
dinner. Sometimes
all she serves is
vegetables.

SHORTCUT CHEF

Cook your onions the night before or in the morning. Marinate the tomatoes while the kids are doing their homework. Wash and dry the arugula after breakfast. Cook the chicken a little ahead—the sandwiches are good hot or room temperature.

The chicken and onions can also be cooked under the broiler. Watch them carefully, turning the onions often.

If it's not tomato season, don't use tomatoes. Thin slices of avocado, mango, papaya, or grilled pineapple are delicious variations.

Green Bean and Fried Egg Sandwich

On those nights when it's too hot to cook or you're just plain too tired, this is a quick and tasty meal that doesn't take much thought or effort. No green beans on hand? Use mushrooms, peas, onions, or any other vegetable you've got. This is one of my favorite meals to eat when there's no one home but me.

4 SERVINGS

¾ pound green beans, trimmed

4 teaspoons butter

Coarse-grained salt and cracked black pepper

4 large eggs, lightly beaten

8 slices bread

SHORTCUT CHEF

Cook the veggies ahead and make sure you've got everything you need to pull off this dish. Use leftovers if you have them.

FROM MOM'S LIPS TO YOUR EARS

Little shops in Italy sell sandwiches like this and they are my favorite. When my husband and children have driven me to the point of needing a well-deserved vacation but sadly I can't leave the house, I make my little green bean sandwich and pretend I'm not related to any of them.

IN a small pot of boiling salted water over medium-high heat, blanch green beans until cooked through, 4 to 6 minutes. Drain. In a small nonstick skillet, melt 1 teaspoon of butter. Add one fourth of green beans to pan. Season with salt and pepper to taste. Cook beans until lightly golden brown. Lightly beat eggs in a medium bowl. Add one fourth of egg mixture to cooked beans. The eggs will set up quickly. Using a spatula, flip egg-bean mixture to uncooked side and immediately lay two slices of bread over cooked side. Finish cooking, about 2 minutes. This heats up and softens the bread. Remove bread slices to a serving plate. Tip egg onto a bread slice, folding it in half as you do. Make the next three sandwiches the very same way, or better, let each diner make his or her own.

Pan-Fried Mozzarella Sandwiches

My grandmother used to feed this to my father and his brother when they were children. It was served on Saturday afternoons or Sunday evenings when she was too tired from raising rambunctious boys to put much effort into the evening meal. A sandwich alone doesn't a dinner make, so serve this meal with a few veggie sides and a simple salad.

2 SERVINGS

2 large eggs

¼ cup low-fat milk

½ teaspoon coarse-grained salt

Cracked black pepper

2 ounces part-skim milk mozzarella cheese

4 slices square Italian or sourdough sandwich bread, crusts removed

Extra-virgin olive oil spray

IN a large shallow dish, whisk together eggs, milk, salt, and pepper until completely combined. Cut mozzarella into six slices. Set on a plate near stove. Quickly, so that one slice of bread doesn't soak up more than its fair share of egg batter, dredge slices of bread in egg mixture, coating both sides evenly. Set aside.

SPRAY a 12-inch nonstick skillet with oil spray. Set over medium-high heat. When oil is hot but not smoking, add bread to pan. Cook until golden, 2 to 3 minutes. Turn two bread slices over and place half of cheese on each cooked side. Place remaining two slices of bread, grilled side down, on top of cheese. Continue cooking until undersides are golden. Flip sandwiches over and cook last side until golden, 2 to 3 minutes.

SHORTCUT CHEF

Whisk the eggs with milk, salt, and pepper and keep refrigerated until you're ready to cook. Gather the kitchen tools you'll need. Set the table. This is a good meal to assign others to cook. If they can make grilled cheese, they can deal with this variation.

Yes, the recipe calls for cheese and eggs. Yes, the sandwiches are pan fried but there's no reason that they can't be part of a balanced diet. Cheese, eggs, and bread all have their rightful place in the food pyramid. Be portion wise and eat your veggies, too.

FROM MOM'S LIPS TO YOUR EARS

You heard my daughter. Eat your vegetables too, even if a tossed salad is the best you can do. Anything is better than nothing. I usually serve fruit for dessert with this meal. Try the Berries with Brown Sugar on page 376.

Italian Country Loaf Sandwich

Create enough leftovers throughout the week to build this sandwich on the weekend. This is no spur-of-the-moment meal but you don't have to follow the recipe if you've got ideas of your own. Try sliced cucumbers, grilled vegetables, cooked chicken, or salami instead of tuna and egg. ■ You've probably figured it out already but this sandwich is great for casual entertaining and picnics. When I know the weather is going to be unbearably hot, I plan out my no-cook menus for the week and this always makes the cut. It's nutritious, easy to deal with, and substantial enough to serve on its own, which means no side dishes are necessary.

6 TO 8 SERVINGS

SHORTCUT CHEF

Make the dressing in advance, make the tuna salad, blanch the beans, cook the eggs, slice the tomatoes, and chop the herbs. Tick even one of these tasks off your to-do list and you're ahead, which as you know is the key to healthy eating for good.

MORPH Make a double batch of the vinaigrette and turn it into Potato-Cucumber Salad (page 158) tomorrow. Make extra tuna salad and toss it with pasta, tomatoes, and blanched veggies later in the week. Cook extra green beans and turn them into a frittata (page 140) tomorrow.

1 round loaf crusty bread (1 to 1½ pounds)

FOR THE DRESSING

2 cloves garlic, minced

1 medium shallot, minced

¼ cup plus 2 tablespoons red wine vinegar

Coarse-grained salt and cracked black pepper

½ cup extra-virgin olive oil

FOR THE TUNA SALAD

Two 6-ounce cans white albacore tuna packed in water, drained

2 teaspoons capers, rinsed and roughly chopped

2 tablespoons roughly chopped herbs (parsley, basil, mint, or a combination)

¼ cup thinly sliced scallions (white part only; about 2)

FOR THE SANDWICH FILLING

½ pound green beans, trimmed and blanched

4 medium tomatoes, cut into ½-inch slices

½ cup loosely packed herbs (parsley, basil, mint, or a combination)

3 hard-boiled large eggs, peeled and sliced

SLICE loaf of bread in half horizontally. Remove some of the soft center to make a hollow in the loaf. Reserve bread center for another use.

PREPARE THE DRESSING: In a small mixing bowl, place garlic, shallot, and red wine vinegar. Let stand up to 30 minutes. Whisk in salt, pepper, and olive oil. Taste and adjust seasonings. Set dressing aside.

PREPARE THE TUNA SALAD: In a small bowl, combine tuna, capers, chopped herbs, and scallions. Pour roughly one fourth of dressing over tuna. Stir until combined. Set aside.

TOSS green beans with about one fourth dressing. Set aside.

ASSEMBLE THE SANDWICH: Drizzle approximately one fourth of dressing over bottom half of bread. Cover with a layer of tomato slices, followed by a layer of fresh herbs, a layer of tuna, a layer of egg slices, and finally a layer of green beans. Repeat until all ingredients are used up, finishing with a layer of tomatoes. Drizzle remaining dressing over inside top half of bread. Place top half of bread over sandwich. Press together and wrap tightly in plastic wrap. Place on rimmed cookie sheet (to catch any juices that may escape) and put another cookie sheet on top. Press the sandwich 2 hours or more by placing heavy cans on top. Turn sandwich over halfway through pressing process. Cut into equal wedges and serve.

Guyometer:
Fantastic sandwich.

Shallots have their own distinctive flavor and lend a wonderful characteristic to the dressing. Extra garlic or minced onions are not good substitutes for shallots, no matter what anyone tells you. Carry on without shallots if you can't get them. The dressing will still be good, just different. The next time you're at the market, look for shallots near the garlic and onions and buy some.

FROM MOM'S LIPS TO YOUR EARS

Don't skimp on the bread even if it means a special trip to the bakery. Get a good loaf of crusty Italian bread or tell the person behind the counter what you're doing and go with his recommendation if it sounds reasonable.

Easy Pizza Dough (for Easy Pizza)

If you've never made pizza dough before, or if you have and wish you hadn't, you'll be delightfully surprised at how simple this recipe is. It takes longer to read the recipe through than it does to prepare it (unless you've taken one of those speed-reading courses). The dough keeps marvelously well in the refrigerator overnight or in the freezer.

TWO 12-INCH THICK-CRUSTED PIZZAS OR

FOUR 10-INCH THIN-CRUSTED PIZZAS; 6 TO 8 SERVINGS

3 1/2 cups unbleached flour

2 packages active dry yeast

1 teaspoon coarse-grained salt

1/2 teaspoon sugar

1 1/2 cups lukewarm water

1/2 teaspoon olive oil

Cornmeal for dusting pizza peel or cookie sheet

PLACE flour, yeast, salt, and sugar in a mixer fitted with a dough hook. While mixer is running, gradually add water; knead on low speed until dough is firm and smooth, about 10 minutes. Turn mixer off. Pour oil down the side of bowl. Turn mixer on low once more for 15 seconds to coat inside of bowl and all surfaces of dough with the oil. *Alternatively, using a food processor fitted with a metal blade:* Place flour, yeast, salt, and sugar in bowl of a food processor and pulse to blend. Pour water through feed tube with machine running. Process until dough forms a ball. Place in oiled bowl. *By hand:* In a large bowl, whisk together flour, yeast, salt, and sugar. Stir in water until dough begins to form. Knead dough on a floured surface until smooth, about 10 minutes. Place in oiled bowl.

COVER bowl with plastic wrap. Let dough rise in a warm spot until doubled in bulk, about 2 hours.

CREATE your own pizza using the following directions as a guide or proceed using recipes on pages 126–133.

ROLLING OUT THE DOUGH AND BAKING THE PIZZA

PREHEAT oven to highest setting, 500° or 550°F. If using a pizza stone, place stone in oven on bottom rack and heat oven 1 hour. Punch dough down and cut in half or fourths. On a generously floured work surface, place one piece of dough.

BY hand, stretch dough into a circle. For thin pizza, roll dough into a large circle with a floured rolling pin until very thin. Don't worry if your circle isn't perfect, and if you get a hole just pinch edges back together. To prevent dough from sticking to counter, turn dough over; add flour to dough, counter, and rolling pin as needed. Sprinkle a pizza peel or rimless cookie sheet generously with cornmeal. Transfer dough to pizza peel or cookie sheet. Add toppings. Slide dough onto pizza stone or place cookie sheet with pizza on bottom rack. Bake 10 to 12 minutes, or until golden. Remove pizza from oven, using a pizza peel if you used a pizza stone, and serve immediately. Roll out remaining dough, top with desired toppings, and bake or freeze in freezer bags.

Make double batches of the dough and divide and freeze leftovers so you've never got an excuse to eat out. Place a bag of frozen dough on the counter before you leave for work. By the time you cruise in from your commute, the dough will be ready to roll, top, and bake.

If you don't have a pizza stone, put one on your wish list and get it as soon as you can—preferably one the size of your bottom oven rack, not a round one the size of a pizza, which is just too small. Keep it in your oven at all times. That's a great place to store it, and it'll never bother anyone. Lots of dishes love to be cooked on a stone, which provides extra-high heat.

If you are using a pizza stone, have the second pizza ready to go onto the stone immediately after the first pizza comes out. Just left sitting on the stone, the cornmeal burns.

BBQ Chicken Pizza

BBQ chicken pizza is part of a healthy lifestyle? You betcha. Living well for life means good, better, and best choices daily. Thin-crusted homemade pizza from scratch passes the napkin grease test every time. You know what I'm talking about here. Place a paper napkin over the top of carryout pizza and it will instantaneously become saturated with rust-colored grease. I can think of more palatable ways to spend fat calories. Make pizza from scratch—don't leave the fate of your waistline to somebody else.

TWO 10-INCH PIZZAS; 4 SERVINGS

8 ounces boneless, skinless chicken breast

¾ cup Jack's BBQ Sauce (page 242)

Easy Pizza Dough for two 10-inch thin-crusted pizzas (page 124)

Cornmeal for dusting pizza peel or cookie sheet

½ cup loosely packed, roughly chopped flat-leaf parsley or cilantro

1 cup loosely packed, freshly grated part-skim milk mozzarella cheese

PREPARE BBQ CHICKEN: In a small pot or skillet with straight sides, place chicken breast and enough water to cover. Poach chicken over medium-high heat until just cooked, 6 to 8 minutes. Pour off water. Don't wash pan just yet. When chicken is cool enough to handle, shred into thin pieces. Resist the urge to chop or dice chicken with a knife; it will look nicer torn. Place chicken back in same skillet or pot you cooked it in. Pour BBQ sauce over chicken; toss until well coated. Set aside.

PREHEAT oven to highest setting, 500° or 550°F. If using a pizza stone, place stone in oven on bottom rack and heat oven 1 hour.

ON a generously floured work surface, place half of dough. By hand, form dough loosely into a ball; stretch into a circle. Using a floured rolling pin, roll dough into a 10-inch circle until very thin. Don't worry if your circle isn't perfect, and if you get a hole just pinch edges back together.

TO prevent dough from sticking to counter, turn dough over; add flour to dough, counter, and rolling pin as needed. Sprinkle a pizza peel or cookie sheet generously with cornmeal. Transfer dough to pizza peel or cookie sheet. Working quickly, spread half of chicken with BBQ sauce over pizza. Sprinkle with half of herbs, and finally, half of cheese.

USING a peel, slide dough onto pizza stone or place cookie sheet with pizza on bottom rack. Bake 10 to 12 minutes, or until golden. Remove pizza from oven and serve immediately. While first pizza is cooking, roll out remaining dough and top with remaining toppings. Bake and serve immediately.

Guyometer:
Perfect Monday Night
Football *food.*

SHORTCUT CHEF

Buy the best BBQ sauce you can get your hands on. Read the labels. As always, watch calorie, sugar, sodium, and fat counts.

The recipe calls for a scant cup of grated part-skim milk mozzarella cheese, intended to be enough cheese to top two pizzas. You can bump up the amount of cheese if you want to, but if you're trying to lose weight anytime soon, try the pizza first with $1/2$ cup of cheese; then increase if you must.

Speaking of cheese, along with *ready-to-go* pizza dough in my freezer, I keep a giant bag of grated mozzarella and pizza-portioned batches of Microwave Tomato Sauce (page 247). You might say I've always got custom pizza kits on hand in my freezer.

Sandwiches, Pizzas, and Frittatas

Italian Sausage Pizza

Our minds shouldn't be consumed with thoughts of foods we wish we could eat.

Rather, our lives should be filled with foods we love to eat. Everything in moderation.

When you're craving Italian sausage pizza, make some.

TWO 10-INCH PIZZAS; 4 SERVINGS

Easy Pizza Dough for two 10-inch thin-crusted pizzas (page 124)

Cornmeal for dusting pizza peel or cookie sheet

1 ½ cups Microwave Tomato Sauce (page 247)

Coarse-grained salt and cracked black pepper

½ teaspoon red pepper flakes (more or less to taste)

2 tablespoons chopped or slivered garlic (optional)

8 ounces Italian sausage, cooked and crumbled (or see tip)

1 ½ cups loosely packed, roughly chopped fresh basil leaves

1 cup loosely packed, freshly grated part-skim milk mozzarella cheese

PREHEAT oven to highest setting, 500° or 550°F. If using a pizza stone, place stone in oven on bottom rack and heat oven 1 hour.

ON a generously floured work surface, place half of dough. By hand, form dough loosely into a ball; stretch into a circle. Using a floured rolling pin, roll dough into 10-inch circle until very thin. Don't worry if your circle isn't perfect, and if you get a hole just pinch edges back together.

TO prevent dough from sticking to counter, turn dough over; add flour to dough, counter, and rolling pin as needed. Sprinkle a pizza peel or cookie sheet generously with cornmeal. Transfer dough to pizza peel or cookie sheet. Using a rubber spatula, spread half of tomato sauce over dough. Season with salt, pepper, and red pepper flakes. Working quickly, spread half of garlic and Italian sausage over pizza. Scatter with half of herbs and finally, half of cheese.

USING a peel, slide dough onto pizza stone or place cookie sheet with pizza on bottom rack. Bake 10 to 12 minutes, or until golden. Remove pizza from oven and serve immediately. While first pizza is cooking, roll out remaining dough and top with remaining toppings. Bake and serve immediately.

Guyometer:
Fantastic. Why can't we
have this every night?

Instead of frying sausage in fat, save a few calories by poaching it in simmering water. Place sausage links in a small pot, cover with water, bring to a boil, immediately reduce to a simmer, and cook until firm. Drain and cool. Using a knife, slice sausage links into small coins.

You can get away with using less Italian sausage. I'm satisfied with the idea, the aroma, and small bursts of sausage on my pizza. If you've got hungry meat-loving diners on the guest list, use the full 8 ounces. Look for low-fat Italian sausage—it's out there. Do side-by-side tastes of regular versus low fat when you can.

FROM MOM'S LIPS TO YOUR EARS

Get the best Italian sausage you can find. I buy it in bulk and freeze it in 8-ounce packages. That way, no one gets more than he should eat. I do this with meat and chicken so I don't have to think about portion control.

Pizza with Tomato Sauce, Basil, and Cheese

Erin is my five-year-old niece. The child doesn't eat. Well, that's not entirely true. I think she had a hot dog last Thursday. And some movie candy on Saturday. I'm pretty sure she ate the middle of a "Big Girl grilled cheese sandwich with no grill (blackened crumbs) please" sometime Monday. But that's all the kid eats, except this pizza minus the green worms (basil). I'm going to try to sneak a few vegetables into the sauce next time. ■ The success of this pizza and all recipes lies in the quality of the ingredients. Make your own Microwave Tomato Sauce whenever you can. And for heaven's sake, use fresh basil.

TWO 10-INCH PIZZAS; 4 SERVINGS

Easy Pizza Dough for two 10-inch thin-crusted pizzas (page 124)

Cornmeal for dusting pizza peel or cookie sheet

1½ cups Microwave Tomato Sauce (page 247)

Coarse-grained salt and cracked black pepper

1 teaspoon red pepper flakes (optional)

1½ cups loosely packed, roughly chopped fresh basil leaves

1 cup loosely packed, freshly grated part-skim milk mozzarella cheese

PREHEAT oven to highest setting, 500° or 550°F. If using a pizza stone, place stone in oven on bottom rack and preheat oven 1 hour.

ON a generously floured work surface, place half of dough. By hand, form dough loosely into a ball; stretch into a circle. Using a floured rolling pin, roll dough into a 10-inch circle until very thin. Don't worry if your circle isn't perfect, and if you get a hole just pinch edges back together.

TO prevent dough from sticking to counter, turn dough over; add flour to dough, counter, and rolling pin as needed. Sprinkle a pizza peel or cookie sheet generously with cornmeal. Transfer dough to pizza peel or cookie sheet. Using a rubber spatula, spread half of tomato sauce over dough. Season with salt and cracked pepper and red pepper flakes (if using). Working quickly, scatter pizza with half of basil and finally, half of cheese.

USING a peel, slide dough onto pizza stone or place cookie sheet with pizza on bottom rack. Bake 10 to 12 minutes, or until golden. Remove pizza from oven and serve immediately. While first pizza is cooking, roll out remaining dough and top with remaining toppings. Bake and serve immediately.

If Erin's not joining you for dinner, shake crushed red pepper flakes or dried oregano over pizza sauce. But before you even think of sprinkling your pizza pie with spices or dried herbs, be sure they have a pungent aroma. If they don't, throw them out and get fresh ones. Spices and herbs don't have the shelf life of books.

Pesto Pizza

Okay, so it's not exactly the kind of pesto pizza that has 2 cups of pesto sauce smeared all over it, which for your information is upwards of 2,400 pesto calories alone, not to mention a million or more grams of fat per whiff. Try this slimmed-down version and see if it'll do for you. If not, have the real thing in small doses.

TWO 10-INCH PIZZAS; 4 SERVINGS

8 large cloves garlic, peeled and very thinly sliced

1 teaspoon olive oil

Easy Pizza Dough for two 10-inch thin-crusted pizzas (page 124)

Cornmeal for dusting pizza peel or cookie sheet

Coarse-grained salt and cracked black pepper

$\frac{1}{2}$ cup pine nuts

2 cups loosely packed, roughly chopped fresh basil leaves

$\frac{2}{3}$ cup loosely packed, freshly grated Parmesan cheese

1 cup loosely packed, freshly grated part-skim milk mozzarella cheese

PREHEAT oven to highest setting, 500° or 550°F. If using a pizza stone, place stone in oven on bottom rack and heat oven 1 hour.

PLACE garlic and olive oil in a small nonstick pan. Heat to medium and sauté until garlic is golden, 3 to 5 minutes. Set aside.

ON a generously floured work surface, place half of dough. By hand, form dough loosely into a ball; stretch into a circle. Using a floured rolling pin, roll dough into 10-inch circle until very thin. Don't worry if your circle isn't perfect, and if you get a hole just pinch edges back together.

TO prevent dough from sticking to counter, turn dough over; add flour to dough, counter, and rolling pin as needed. Sprinkle a pizza peel or cookie sheet generously with cornmeal. Transfer dough to pizza peel or cookie sheet. Sprinkle dough with salt and pepper. Working quickly, spread half of garlic and pine nuts over pizza. Scatter dough with half of basil and finally, half of cheeses.

USING a peel, slide dough onto pizza stone or place cookie sheet with pizza on bottom rack. Bake 10 to 12 minutes, or until golden. Remove pizza from oven and serve immediately. While first pizza is cooking, roll out remaining dough and top with remaining toppings. Bake and serve immediately.

Don't worry about the large quantity of garlic called for in the recipe (unless you're going on a first date). When it's toasted, it mellows out. Really.

Broccoli & Pasta Frittata

It's hard to get excited about a broccoli entrée. But whenever I whip up this broccoli pasta frittata topped with bubbly golden melted Parmesan cheese, hungry diners magically appear. It's a very hearty, quick-to-prepare supper and requires only a simple green salad to complete the meal.

4 TO 6 SERVINGS

1 tablespoon olive oil

6 ounces spaghetti, cooked

2 large eggs

8 large egg whites

½ teaspoon coarse-grained salt plus more to taste

¼ teaspoon cracked black pepper plus more to taste

1 pound broccoli, trimmed, cooked, and cut into bite-size pieces

3 scallions, thinly sliced (white part and some green)

2 tablespoons loosely packed, roughly chopped fresh oregano or 2 teaspoons dried

2 teaspoons finely grated lemon zest (about ½ lemon)

¼ cup loosely packed, finely grated Parmesan cheese (or curls—see tip)

IN a 10-inch nonstick skillet with an ovenproof handle, heat oil over low heat. Add pasta to pan and cook very slowly for 30 minutes (while you're prepping rest of dish), turning once so both sides are a little crunchy. You're making a delightful "crust" for your frittata.

IN a medium bowl, whisk eggs, egg whites, salt, and pepper. Set aside for a minute. In another bowl, toss together broccoli, scallions, oregano, and lemon zest. Season with salt and pepper to taste; add to pan with pasta. Pour eggs over broccoli and pasta. Increase heat to medium-low and cook, covered, until just set, about 20 minutes. While eggs are cooking, preheat broiler.

Cooking Thin with Chef Kathleen

TOP frittata with Parmesan cheese and place under broiler until cheese is completely melted and golden brown, 3 to 5 minutes. Slide frittata out of pan and onto serving plate. Serve immediately.

Guyometer:
It's okay. It's a hot meal.
I didn't have to cook it.
And my wife says it was
better for me than a
16-ounce porterhouse.

SHORTCUT CHEF
Plan ahead by cooking extra pasta on spaghetti night.

MORPH Cook extra pasta and broccoli, toss it with a quick vinaigrette, and you've got broccoli pasta salad for lunch tomorrow.

Drag a vegetable peeler over a block of Parmesan to create thin cheese curls. Let them fall directly over the almost-cooked frittata. Place under the broiler and voilà, a gorgeous frittata with all the glory of cheese. If you don't have a vegetable peeler, use the smallest side of a cheese grater to create thin shavings.

Frittata with Potatoes, Prosciutto, and Peas

This is a great supper to plan for because it's better with leftover potatoes—not because they have better flavor, but because you get to skip a step! By now, you should be pretty good at planning your meals for the week. Don't fall out of that habit. It's very important to plan ahead even if it's a rough plan. You'll have some direction and you'll naturally work toward getting the shopping and prep done.

4 TO 6 SERVINGS

1½ pounds potatoes (Yukon Gold or russets), peeled and cut into ½-inch slices

2 large eggs

8 large egg whites

½ teaspoon coarse-grained salt plus more to taste

¼ teaspoon cracked black pepper plus more to taste

1 teaspoon extra-virgin olive oil

1 cup peas (fresh or frozen)

1 ounce prosciutto or bacon, trimmed of fat and rind, cut into ¼-inch strips

¼ cup shaved Parmesan cheese (see tip)

PLACE potatoes in a medium saucepan. Cover with cold salted water. Bring to a boil. Reduce heat to a simmer and cook until potatoes are just fork-tender, about 20 minutes. Drain; set aside.

PREHEAT broiler. In a large bowl whisk eggs, egg whites, salt, and pepper. Set aside.

IN a 10-inch nonstick skillet with an ovenproof handle, heat the oil over medium-high heat. Add potatoes. Season with salt and pepper to taste. Cook, stirring often, until potatoes start to brown, about 5 minutes. Pour egg mixture and peas into pan. Using a heatproof spatula, slowly stir eggs in a figure-eight motion until just beginning to set on edges. Reduce heat to medium-low. Continue cooking, occasionally sliding spatula around edges of pan to let raw egg flow underneath, until frittata is set on bottom but not on top, about 4 minutes. Place prosciutto strips over frittata and scatter Parmesan over prosciutto. Place pan under broiler and cook just until top is set and cheese is melted and golden brown, 3 to 5 minutes.

SHORTCUT CHEF

Crack the eggs and cook the potatoes. Be sure you have all the other ingredients and the tools you'll need. Read the recipe through start to finish. These little steps go a long way toward cutting prep time in half.

My mom says use 2 eggs per person if this is all you're serving. I'm always Jonesing for dessert—trying to free up calories wherever I can—so I opt for mostly egg whites.

The prosciutto used in this recipe is a little fancier than bacon, but bacon or pancetta (an Italian-style bacon) will work just fine in this recipe. Keep bacon or pancetta in the freezer and cut what you need off the frozen block. You don't need to use it strip by strip.

Use a vegetable peeler to shave very thin slices of Parmesan off a wedge of cheese, as you would peel the skin off a carrot. Do not press down hard, or the slices will be too thick and you will use twice as much to cover the surface of the frittata, which will double the calories from the cheese.

Frittata with Tomatoes, Basil, and Parmesan

If you've got eggs, you've got dinner. If you're entertaining and you have eggs, you have the fixings for a chic enough supper to impress even the most savvy of diners. Frittatas never go out of culinary vogue, they look rich and rustic and elaborate, as if they took all day to make. But they're quick, light, and nutritious, so learn the 1-2-3 techniques of frittata-making and add this to your "help-I'm-in-a-dinner-jam" recipe file.

4 TO 6 SERVINGS

4 large eggs

6 large egg whites

Coarse-grained salt and cracked black pepper

4 teaspoons extra-virgin olive oil

4 cloves garlic, sliced paper thin

2 cups cherry tomatoes or any combination
  of small tomatoes

¾ cup loosely packed, roughly chopped basil leaves

¼ cup thinly shaved Parmesan cheese (see tip, page 137)

*Guyometer:
It's better than
cardiac-patient
food.*

PREHEAT broiler. Whisk eggs and egg whites together in a large bowl. Season with salt and pepper to taste. Set aside.

SHORTCUT CHEF

Plan ahead by cooking extra veggies earlier in the week so you've got frittata filling options. For this frittata recipe, crack the eggs, slice the tomatoes, or grate the cheese ahead if you've got a few spare minutes. It's a pretty quick way to prepare dinner so don't worry if you can't get any prep done ahead.

PLACE 2 teaspoons olive oil, garlic, and tomatoes in a 10-inch nonstick skillet with ovenproof handle. Turn heat to medium and cook until garlic is golden and tomatoes begin to soften and blister a little. Add remaining 2 teaspoons of oil and swirl to coat pan bottom; pour egg mixture into pan with tomatoes and garlic. Using a heatproof rubber spatula, slowly stir eggs in a figure-eight motion until just beginning to set on edges. Sprinkle with

Cooking Thin with Chef Kathleen

basil and continue cooking, occasionally sliding spatula around edges of pan to let raw egg flow underneath, until frittata is set on bottom but not all the way on top, 4 to 5 minutes.

SCATTER Parmesan cheese over frittata and place pan directly under broiler just until top is golden brown and set and cheese is melted, 1 to 2 minutes. Let frittata stand 5 to 10 minutes. To serve, slide frittata onto a serving platter and cut into wedges. Frittata may also be cooled to room temperature, then cut and served.

If the queen's coming for dinner: This is a lovely weekend entertaining kind of dish. It's great for brunches, lunches, light meals, or tapas (appetizers), too. It's perfectly acceptable to serve frittatas at room temperature.

The egg to egg white ratio is up to you and your nutrition goals. You can make the frittata with all egg whites or all whole eggs. I use a combo because I'm forever watching calories and like to have enough calories left over at the end of the day to spend on dessert if my sweet tooth is getting the best of me, so I scrimp and save wherever I won't notice.

If you can't get good tomatoes or basil, throw something else in the frittata instead. You can't mask inferior ingredients no matter how hard you try. Use frozen peas, green beans, leftover grilled vegetables, asparagus, mushrooms, whatever you have around or whatever you can easily get. You don't have to use all small tomatoes, either; use sliced or chunked tomatoes if you want. Just make sure you're using pick-of-the-crop quality ingredients.

Green Bean Frittata with Parmesan Cheese

Glamorous enough to serve guests, this speedy supper requires very little preparation, only 6 minutes to cook, and can be on the table quicker than you can blow your day's calories on a big burger deluxe with fries. If you don't have green beans on hand or just don't feel like cooking them, use what you've got. Leftover cooked potatoes, grilled, roasted, or frozen vegetables, caramelized onions, dried tomatoes, and fresh herbs make great frittata fillings.

4 TO 6 SERVINGS

2 large eggs

8 large egg whites

½ teaspoon coarse-grained salt

¼ teaspoon cracked black pepper

2 teaspoons extra-virgin olive oil

1 pound green beans, trimmed, cooked, and cut into 1-inch pieces

¾ cup loosely packed, coarsely chopped basil leaves

¼ cup thinly shaved Parmesan cheese (see tip, page 137)

If the queen's coming for dinner: Garnish with sprigs of basil, flat-leaf parsley, or thyme. Edible flowers and lightly dressed mixed garden greens are pretty, too.

PREHEAT broiler. In a large bowl, whisk eggs, egg whites, salt, and pepper.

IN a 10-inch nonstick skillet with an ovenproof handle, heat the oil over medium-high heat. Pour egg mixture into pan. Add green beans and basil. Using a heatproof spatula slowly stir eggs in a figure-eight motion until just beginning to set on edges. Reduce heat to medium-low. Continue cooking, occasionally sliding spatula around edges of pan to let raw egg flow underneath, until frittata is set on bottom and almost set on top, about 4 minutes.

LAY Parmesan over frittata, place pan under broiler, and cook just until top is set and cheese is golden brown, 3 to 5 minutes more.

Side Salads and
Savory Slaws

I USED TO COME UP with the nightly specials at my restaurants

by scouring the salad sections of my favorite cookbooks. Because I cooked in

warm-weather climates, customers looked forward to broiled and grilled

meats and fish with interesting side salads and slaws. When you think about it,

it's a great way to cook at home, too. What could be easier than tossing a

scrumptious salad to accompany broiled meat, baked fish, or grilled chicken?

Dinner just doesn't need to be "Thanksgiving" hard. This simple approach to cooking is heaven-sent relief from complicated five-part meals and multitask casseroles too cumbersome to prepare on-the-fly. You've got pages of easy inspirations in the palm of your hands, so you don't even have to think too hard.

No one wants hot-weather food in the dead of winter, so choose your sides accordingly. Warm Potato Salad (page 154) with Broiled Flank Steak and Salsa Verde (page 252) is a simple summer meal. Quick and Spicy Carrot Slaw (page 147) with Dee Dee's Quick Broiled Chicken (page 338) is a great frosty night feast.

Lots of these salads and slaws are great left over, so plan on making extra. Add a few slices of leftover chicken or beef, wrap everything in a tortilla, and you've got a healthy lunch that's definitely better than anything you could buy and you won't have to stand in line.

Homework assignment: Choose three recipes from this chapter and three different cuts of meat or fish. Pair them according to your tastes and you've got three easy home-cooked meals in the bag. All you have to do is make out your shopping list. Examples: Plain broiled salmon with Yogurt Cucumbers (page 149), pan-seared pork tenderloin with Fennel, Carrot, and Cranberry Salad (page 151), and grilled chicken with Napa Cabbage Salad with Spicy Peanut Sauce (page 153).

Apple and Raw Beet Salad

Darlings, these are virtually free calories, which means the portion-control police can't cite you for dining on huge portions. This salad is outrageously delicious, so don't pooh pooh it till you've tried it. Bust out of your culinary comfort zones. There's a world of deeply satisfying flavors out there.

6 TO 8 SERVINGS

1 teaspoon grated ginger

1 pound beets

1 large Granny Smith or similarly flavored and textured apple

3 tablespoons sherry vinegar or other vinegar you like

½ teaspoon coarse-grained salt

⅛ teaspoon cracked black pepper

1 to 2 tablespoons extra-virgin olive oil

USING a microplane grater (or smallest holes of a box grater), grate fresh ginger directly into a medium-size salad bowl. Using large-holed side of grater, grate beets and apple more coarsely into bowl with ginger. Toss until ginger is evenly distributed. Add sherry vinegar, salt, pepper, and oil to bowl and toss to coat evenly. Taste and adjust seasonings. Serve immediately or keep refrigerated.

Guyometer:
He ate every last bite and he hates beets.

MORPH Turn this salad into an entrée by serving it with perfectly roasted boneless, skinless chicken breast and another savory vegetable side, such as Green Beans with Fresh Corn (page 178).

If you haven't purchased a plastic mandoline, this is yet another inspiration to do so. Otherwise, grate the beets and apple pieces using a food processor or very sharp knife (cut beets and apples into thin slices, stack the slices directly on top of one another, and cut them into matchstick-size strips).

Remember the microplane grater I told you not to live a minute longer without? Did you get it yet? It's time. It's the fastest way I know to instantly grate fierce flavors (garlic, ginger, onions, and citrus peel, just to name a few) right into your favorite recipes or almost finished sauces.

Side Salads and Savory Slaws

Apple, Cucumber, and Tomato Salad

Want to turn this salad into supper? Pretend you're a California (or warm-climate) chef and serve it over or next to a piece of chicken or grilled fish. All you need is another simple veggie or some garden lettuces, and dinner is a done deal. Don't fool with this recipe if you can't get good ingredients, though—it's just not worth it. ▪ And one more thing: You need to get into the fresh herb mind-set if you haven't already. I'm not suggesting you start a nursery or anything, but try growing them in little pots on a sunny counter. They're not expensive and in fact it's cheaper to grow your own. When mine die, I replace them. Fresh herbs really do make just-okay food over-the-top great, and let's face it, when you reduce the oil and fat in foods you've got to make up the flavors somehow.

4 SERVINGS

1 medium cucumber, peeled, seeded, and thinly sliced

Coarse-grained salt

2 large tomatoes, cored, peeled, and cut into wedges

3 scallions, thinly sliced (white part only)

2 large apples, peeled, cored, and cut into wedges

½ jalapeño, seeded and minced (more or less to taste)

2 tablespoons roughly chopped mint leaves

1 tablespoon olive oil

Juice of 1 lime (or more to taste)

PLACE cucumber slices in a colander. Season generously with salt and toss until well coated. Place a 1-gallon plastic bag, filled with water and sealed, over cucumbers to weight them down and let stand in sink 1 hour. You can skip this step altogether but the salad won't have as intense a cucumber flavor.

PLACE cucumber, tomatoes, scallions, apples, jalapeño, and mint in a medium nonre-active bowl. Pour olive oil over salad and toss to coat evenly. Add lime juice and season with salt to taste. Serve immediately.

SHORTCUT CHEF

Prep the cucumbers ahead, squeeze the lime juice if you get a spare minute or two, slice the scallions, and prep the tomatoes.

If you've never skinned a tomato, here's how: Fill a medium pot with water and bring to a boil. Set the pot of hot water in a sink. Plunge tomatoes into the hot water for a minute and remove. Water that spills over will go down the drain instead of all over the stove. When the tomatoes are cool enough to handle, core and peel. However, if you don't mind the skins, skip the whole process.

Side Salads and Savory Slaws

Cabbage Salad with Lemon and Mint

Because this salad is so incredibly delicious, you will probably end up eating it in large quantities. The salad should be made well ahead of serving because the cabbage needs time to marinate in the dressing.

4 SERVINGS

4 cups shredded cabbage (about ½ small head)

1 lemon, sliced into very thin wheels and seeded

1 clove garlic, minced

½ teaspoon salt

Cracked black pepper

1 teaspoon sugar

Juice of 1 lemon (or more to taste)

½ cup loosely packed, roughly chopped dill, mint, and/or cilantro leaves

¼ cup dried raisins, currants, or pomegranate seeds

COMBINE ingredients. Mix well. Taste and adjust seasonings. Refrigerate 4 hours or more. Serve.

SHORTCUT CHEF
Use that precut cabbage available right in the produce section of your supermarket.

MORPH Pan-fry or broil some delicious white fish, heat up some corn tortillas, slice some tomatoes, and you've got yourself the makings for fish tacos.

Quick and Spicy Carrot Slaw

If you're a muncher, you need to keep a big bowl of this in the fridge. I'm not saying eat carrot salad instead of dessert. I'm just saying that when you're cruising the fridge in search of trouble it's better you're stopped dead in your tracks with stuff like this. It's sweet, hot, spicy, very satisfying, and filling. It'll give you a quick pick-me-up and keep you going till mealtime. Besides, it's really, really good.

6 TO 8 SERVINGS

½ cup raisins (optional)

2 tablespoons red wine vinegar

¼ cup fresh lemon juice (or more to taste)

¼ teaspoon paprika

¼ teaspoon ground cumin

¼ teaspoon cayenne pepper

2 tablespoons olive oil

One 10-ounce bag carrots, grated (about 4 cups)

½ cup loosely packed, roughly chopped cilantro leaves

*Guyometer:
Pretty good for a
vegetable salad.*

PLACE raisins in a small pot, cover with cold water, and bring to a boil over medium-high heat. Immediately turn heat off and let raisins sit while you prepare rest of salad, or until very plump.

IN a large nonreactive bowl, whisk together red wine vinegar, lemon juice, paprika, cumin, cayenne, and olive oil. Add carrots. Drain raisins, add to salad, and toss until thoroughly combined. Add cilantro, taste, and adjust seasonings. Serve immediately. It's really great left over, too.

SHORTCUT CHEF

If you're in a hurry, sick of cooking, lethargic, or plain old unmotivated, use pre-grated carrots and reward yourself for getting a veggie side dish on the table. It doesn't matter how you get the job done; it matters that you do it.

Side Salads and Savory Slaws

Carrot, Parsley, and Lemon Salad

No excuses for not getting in your five veggie sides a day with recipes this easy. Make a double batch and eat some for lunch tomorrow. Serve this with grilled, broiled, or roasted chicken or fish, another veggie side or two, and dinner is done. Remember, the name of the game is to keep things simple. Choose recipes you can deal with on the given day. Frozen vegetables count.

4 TO 6 SERVINGS

1½ pounds carrots, peeled, or two 10-ounce bags grated carrots

Juice of 2 lemons

1 tablespoon olive oil

Coarse-grained salt and cracked black pepper

½ cup loosely packed, roughly chopped flat-leaf parsley

GRATE carrots (or open bagged carrots) and place in a large serving bowl. Pour lemon juice and olive oil over carrots and toss to coat. Season with salt and pepper to taste. Add parsley. Refrigerate 1 hour or overnight.

MORPH Stuff the salad into a warm corn tortilla with salsa and thinly sliced chicken or steak or turn it into a turkey wrap with layers of thinly sliced tomatoes and fresh spinach leaves.

Go ahead and use ready-grated carrots. Carrots you shred yourself will taste better, but if it's the difference between getting vegetables or not, go for the bagged grated carrots.

Yogurt Cucumbers

Another quick veggie solution. By now I'm sure you're beginning to see why there are nights I skip the entrée altogether. With veggie sides and salads this quick and tasty, who needs to fuss with complicated entrées? All-veggie dinners are a great way to increase good calories and cut out a high-calorie meal during the week.

4 TO 6 SERVINGS

2 English cucumbers

1 teaspoon coarse-grained salt

½ to 1 cup plain low-fat yogurt

Juice of 1 lemon

Cracked black pepper

PEEL, seed, and slice cucumbers. Place in a colander; season with salt. Weight slices down by placing a 1-gallon plastic bag, filled with water and sealed, over them. Let drain 1 hour or longer. Discard water bag.

PLACE cucumbers in a serving bowl and add yogurt, lemon juice, and pepper. Stir until all ingredients are combined. Serve immediately.

MORPH Serve this salad with chicken or fish, one more veggie side, or a quick tossed salad, and dinner is done. Quickie on-the-go lunch: roll leftover chicken and yogurt salad into a flour tortilla and hit the road.

SHORTCUT CHEF
Prep the cucumbers the night before, up to the point of salting. Plan ahead, cook ahead, eat on time. Remember, you're building healthy habits. All your efforts will pay off in spades.

MORPH Serve this salad with Quick Broiled Fish and Perfect Microwave Rice (page 236) and you could win the jammy race. You know, jammies, as in PJ's. Whoever gets to bed first wins.

The recipe calls for you to weight the salted cucumbers. This process draws out the water, leaving you with highly flavored cucumber slices.

FROM MOM'S LIPS TO YOUR EARS
"Nobody asked you to eat the ice cubes, Kathleen. This recipe has been in my family for fifty years that I remember. My auntie Florence used to make it. She crushed her ice cubes by wrapping them in a towel and smashing them with a hammer."

Icy Cucumber Salad

This salad is a family favorite, and truthfully, I do enjoy the firm, crisp texture of the cucumbers and the sweet, tart nature of this quickest-ever salad.

4 SERVINGS

1 large or 2 small cucumbers, peeled, seeded, and sliced ¼ inch thick

Coarse-grained salt

⅓ cup white vinegar

½ teaspoon sugar

Cracked black pepper

½ cup crushed ice

PLACE cucumber slices in a colander. Season generously with salt and toss until well coated. Place a 1-gallon plastic bag, filled with water and sealed, over cucumbers and let stand 1 hour. You can skip this step altogether but the salad won't have as intense a cucumber flavor. It will still be quite good.

PLACE cucumbers in a serving dish. Add vinegar, sugar, and black pepper. Taste and adjust seasonings. Cover with ice and let stand 30 minutes, or until cucumber salad is icy cold.

Fennel, Carrot, and Cranberry Salad

I guarantee your family and friends will go berserk over this salad. My mother says that's a bit of an exaggeration, but it really is great. Broil a piece of chicken, steak, or fish, microwave a few green beans, and dinner is done. My dad loves this salad so much he usually has two helpings. Of course we don't mention that there's fennel in it.

4 SERVINGS

¼ cup red wine vinegar

2 tablespoons honey

2 tablespoons olive oil

I head fennel, cored and grated or cut into fine julienne

2 carrots, peeled and grated or cut into fine julienne

¼ cup dried cranberries, cherries, or raisins

Coarse-grained salt and cracked black pepper

IN a small bowl, whisk together red wine vinegar, honey, and olive oil. Place fennel, carrots, and cranberries in a medium bowl and toss with half of dressing. Let stand refrigerated for 4 hours. The fennel will throw a lot of water, so just before serving, drain off and discard all the liquid. Pour second half of dressing over salad. Season to taste. Serve immediately.

*Guyometer:
Off-the-chart good;
real guys eat fennel
salad. (They made
me say that.)*

SHORTCUT CHEF
You do have to refrigerate the salad for 4 hours, so plan ahead. Make the dressing early in the day and you can grate the carrots but don't grate the fennel—it will turn brown. I suppose you can buy and use pre-grated carrots.

You've got to cut the fennel and carrots slaw style. Use a mandoline or the grater attachment on a food processor or upright mixer.

To julienne any fruit or vegetable, peel, core, and remove root ends as necessary. Using a sharp knife, cut into thin slices. Stack slices neatly on top of one another, then cut slices into matchstick-thin strips. To mince or cut into fine cubes, neatly stack the matchsticks and cut crosswise.

FROM MOM'S LIPS TO YOUR EARS
You really should buy a cheap plastic mandoline (page 69). It takes the work out of prep like you wouldn't believe. And use the guard. But if you don't have one, follow the tip above.

Garden Lettuce Salad

I'll never forget the first time I tossed a salad for my culinary mentor and boss, Chef Judy Rodgers (owner of Zuni Café, San Francisco). It took me nearly thirty attempts to toss what I thought to be the perfect salad. When I finally set the salad before her at our six o'clock tasting she rejected it on sight, or on smell if you want to get technical. She detected a perfume of garlic. "I didn't use garlic," I said confidently. "Were you cutting raw garlic recently?" "Yes. I chopped garlic but I didn't let the greens touch my cutting board." "Smell your hands, Kathleen." The garlic had seeped into my skin. The salad is hand-tossed and Judy picked it up. ■ To this day I think of that incident to remind me how to really taste and smell food. I learned salad greens should be thoughtfully dressed and require just the smallest amount of oil, salt, and vinegar and perhaps a crack or two of fresh black pepper to bring out their best flavors.

4 SERVINGS

8 cups garden lettuces, washed and dried

2 tablespoons good-quality extra-virgin olive oil

$1/8$ teaspoon coarse-grained salt

1 tablespoon good-quality vinegar

Cracked black pepper (optional)

If Judy Rodgers is coming for dinner: Wash your hands before you toss the salad, and for heaven's sake, don't oversalt.

PLACE greens in a large tossing bowl. Drizzle with oil and, using your hands, gently toss until well coated. Sprinkle with salt and add vinegar a few drops at a time. Toss to coat well. Taste and adjust seasonings as necessary. Add pepper if you like. Serve immediately.

Don't skimp on the extra-virgin olive oil. Buy the best you can afford, in quantities you'll use, and don't keep it around for ages. Olive oil should be used within the year it's pressed. Store olive oil in a dark, cool location. Try different vinegars, such as sherry, champagne, and balsamic. Be sure there's nothing in the ingredients list except vinegar. A lot of vinegars are watered down, and with those you'll never get the dressing to taste right.

Buy the freshest and best-looking salad greens you can, locally grown if at all possible. The leaves should be whole and perky and have few blemishes. Some lettuces are so sandy they require two washings, but don't leave greens in the water too long or they'll become water-logged. Invest in a salad spinner, which is the quickest, most efficient way to dry greens. They're under $25. Budget it in when you can.

Napa Cabbage Salad with Spicy Peanut Sauce

"Honey, what's for dinner?" "Cabbage, dear." "Oh. I just called to tell you not to wait for me. I've got late meetings." Don't *tell* him napa cabbage slaw is on the menu, just serve it. This really is a fantastic salad, so don't knock it till you've tried it. Cook a piece of salmon or chicken breast and dinner is a done deal.

6 TO 8 SERVINGS

1 tablespoon sesame oil

3 tablespoons rice wine vinegar

¼ cup light soy sauce

2 tablespoons sugar

1 tablespoon freshly grated ginger

½ teaspoon red pepper flakes (more or less to taste)

8 cups thinly sliced napa cabbage (sometimes called Chinese cabbage)

1 cup loosely packed, roughly chopped cilantro leaves or whole cilantro leaves

3 scallions, thinly sliced (white and green parts)

1 medium carrot, grated

1 cup toasted (or not) peanuts, roughly chopped

PREPARE dressing in a small nonreactive bowl by whisking together sesame oil, rice wine vinegar, soy sauce, and sugar. Stir until sugar dissolves. Add ginger and pepper flakes. Set aside.

IN a large salad bowl, toss together cabbage, cilantro, scallions, and carrot. Toss in peanuts. Add dressing and toss until evenly distributed. Taste and adjust seasonings. Serve immediately.

SHORTCUT CHEF

Make the dressing ahead, toast the peanuts ahead, pick the cilantro leaves, and grate the carrot. Cheat and buy pregrated carrots or use the largest holes of your box grater. It's quick and adds another veggie to dinner.

Toast the nuts in a nonstick pan over medium-high heat, tossing often, until fragrant and crunchy, 3 to 5 minutes.

Warm Potato Salad

I can't imagine a Memorial Day spread without some variation of a great potato salad on the holiday table. People often equate potato salads with too many calories and too much fat (from eggs and mayonnaise) and therefore deny themselves the simple pleasure of dining on one of America's most revered comfort foods. This recipe takes the chubby out of that myth and puts the good chow back on the menu. I've tested this salad with many different varieties of potatoes, and while any potato will do, Idahos are particularly delicious.

4 TO 6 SERVINGS

2 shallots, finely minced

4 tablespoons white wine vinegar

2 tablespoons dry white wine

1½ pounds potatoes, peeled and quartered

Coarse-grained salt and cracked black pepper

2 tablespoons extra-virgin olive oil

¼ cup loosely packed, finely chopped herbs (parsley and/or chives)

PLACE shallots in a small shallow dish and cover with vinegar and white wine. Let stand as long as you can, up to 1 hour if possible. Place potatoes in a medium pot and cover with cold water. Bring to a boil over medium-high heat. Reduce to a simmer and cook until fork-tender, about 20 minutes. Drain. When cool enough to handle but not cold, cut potatoes into ½-inch cubes or even-size chunks. Place in serving bowl and season with salt and pepper.

WHISK olive oil into shallot mixture. Season with salt and pepper to taste. Add chopped herbs. Taste and adjust seasonings. While potatoes are still warm, toss them with dressing. Serve now or later.

SHORTCUT CHEF

The dressing can be made several hours in advance up to the point of adding the chopped herbs. Dice and marinate the shallots whenever you get a free moment throughout the day. If you don't mind room-temperature salad, cook the potatoes ahead but do try the salad warm when you have the time.

Shallots have their own distinctive flavors and lend wonderful qualities to any dish they adorn. Go ahead and delete or substitute onion for the shallots—just know that you'll have a decidedly different finished dish.

FROM MOM'S LIPS TO YOUR EARS

If you're not into the taste of raw onions, it really makes a difference if you marinate the shallots ahead of time.

Cooking Thin with Chef Kathleen

Roasted Pepper Salad with Basil and Mint

This salad is so great you should never ever take red peppers off the grocery list. I know that sounds a little obsessive. But this is just one of those good-for-you finds I could eat three times a week.

4 SERVINGS

2 pounds red bell peppers (4 to 5 large)

2 tablespoons olive oil

1 tablespoon balsamic vinegar

2 tablespoons fresh lemon juice

¼ cup loosely packed, roughly chopped basil and mint leaves

Coarse-grained salt and cracked black pepper

PREHEAT broiler to high. Core and cut peppers into quarters; remove seeds and membranes. Place skin side up on a baking sheet under broiler until skins blacken slightly. Place hot peppers in a plastic bag, seal, and let stand 15 minutes. When cool enough to handle, remove skin from peppers. Place peeled peppers in a serving dish.

IN a small bowl, whisk together oil, vinegar, lemon juice, herbs, salt, and pepper. Taste and adjust seasonings. Pour over peppers. Serve immediately or let stand at room temperature up to 4 hours.

Guyometer: Even better with steak, but pretty good as far as healthy goes.

SHORTCUT CHEF
You can use jarred roasted and peeled peppers. Rinse them thoroughly, though. But don't you dare use bottled lemon juice.

MORPH Grab a baguette, slice it in half lengthwise, load it up with a layer of this salad, some arugula or other salad greens, and thinly sliced skim-milk mozzarella cheese or leftover cooked chicken breast or steak.

Peppers are kind of square. When you're cutting them, cut off each of four sides around the core and stem. Reserve tops, bottoms and any scraps for soup stock.

You can certainly use orange or yellow bell peppers in this salad but the only reason to do so is to add color. They're usually more expensive than red peppers, but when they're on sale, by all means use them. Don't use green peppers, which lack the sweet nature of their red, yellow, and orange cousins.

Orange, Beet, and Goat Cheese Salad

This is not an everyday salad but I thought you could use a fancy-ish salad for week-end or holiday entertaining, so I stuck it in. Several components of this plated salad can be made days in advance.

4 TO 5 SERVINGS

2 to 3 medium beets

3 tablespoons roughly chopped walnuts

FOR THE VINAIGRETTE

1 tablespoon minced shallots

3 tablespoons fresh orange juice

1 tablespoon sherry vinegar

2 tablespoons balsamic vinegar

Coarse-grained salt

1 tablespoon extra-virgin olive oil

Cracked black pepper

½ ounce goat cheese

½ ounce low-fat cream cheese

4 to 5 oranges

4 to 5 gourmet crackers or melba toasts

8 ounces mixed salad greens

SHORTCUT CHEF

The longer the beets marinate, the better they taste, but don't keep them for more than three days. Roast them in advance, too. They'll hold in the refrigerator several days. The vinaigrette can be made on the morning you need it and the salad can be plated in advance up to the point of tossing the greens with the dressing.

MORPH Roast some salmon (page 302) and you won't have to prepare anything else but this salad.

PREHEAT oven to 400°F. Trim beets of leaves, stems, and any dangling roots. Wrap beets in aluminum foil and bake until tender or a fork goes through them easily, 60 to 75 minutes. Place walnuts on a cookie sheet and place in oven during last 5 minutes the beets are cooking. Toast until golden.

PREPARE THE VINAIGRETTE: While beets are cooking, place minced shallots in a nonreactive bowl with orange juice, sherry vinegar, balsamic vinegar, and salt. Let mixture stand 10 to 30 minutes. Whisk in olive oil and pepper. Taste and adjust seasonings. Set aside.

WHEN beets are cool enough to handle, rub off outer layer of skin by holding beets one at a time under cool running water, gently peeling back skin with a paring knife or your hands. Cut into quarters. Sprinkle with salt and let stand 15 minutes. Pour 1 tablespoon prepared vinaigrette over beets, toss to coat evenly, and set aside or refrigerate until ready to use.

WHISK goat cheese and cream cheese together in a small bowl and refrigerate until it's time to assemble the salad.

USING a sharp paring knife, trim off top and bottom of oranges, then slice away peel and pith, beginning at top and paring downward. Slice oranges crosswise into ¼-inch slices. Divide evenly among serving plates.

PLACE equal portions of marinated beets on each plate. Spread 1 teaspoonful of cheese mixture over each cracker. Do this at the last minute or the cheese dries out and crackers get soggy.

PLACE salad greens in a nonreactive bowl and toss to coat with half of remaining dressing. Correct seasonings. Set aside. Drizzle remaining dressing evenly over oranges and beets on each plate. Gently drop greens into center of each plate, distributing evenly. Garnish each salad with one goat cheese cracker and a sprinkling of walnuts.

The recipe calls for the goat cheese to be cut and mixed together with cream cheese, because a lot of people think they don't like goat cheese. But there are some really wonderful mild, spreadable varieties out there and if you find one you like on its own, use that. Alternatively, skip the goat cheese spread on toast altogether. Crumble a little goat cheese over the salad and move on. And if you're not into fussy presentations, place oranges, beets, and greens in a large salad bowl, toss with the dressing, and serve.

FROM MOM'S LIPS TO YOUR EARS

If you don't have a bottle of sherry vinegar, it's worth getting. Use this recipe as a guide and change it to suit your family and time constraints.

Potato-Cucumber Salad with Chive Mayonnaise

I know you're probably thinking, Does she think I have all day to cook one lousy side dish? Of course I don't. Prepare this salad ahead of time and cook a piece of salmon just before you're ready to eat. The salmon takes 15 to 20 minutes (page 300) unless you're feeding an army.

4 SERVINGS

2 medium cucumbers

½ teaspoon plus ¼ teaspoon coarse-grained salt

2 pounds small white or red potatoes, washed

2 tablespoons olive oil

2 tablespoons plus 2 tablespoons red wine vinegar

1 teaspoon celery seed

Cracked black pepper

½ cup low-fat mayonnaise

½ cup plain nonfat yogurt

¼ cup minced fresh chives

2 stalks celery, cut into ¼-inch slices

PEEL cucumbers, slice lengthwise, and using a spoon, scrape out seeds. Slice cucumbers into ½-inch slices. Place in a colander and sprinkle with ½ teaspoon salt. Place a 1-gallon plastic bag, filled with water and sealed, over cucumbers to weight them down. Let stand 30 minutes or as long as possible.

MEANWHILE, place potatoes in a large pot and cover with cold water. Over medium-high heat, bring to a boil. Cook until potatoes slide off a fork when pierced, about 12 minutes. Drain potatoes, cut into quarters, and place in a large bowl.

IN a small bowl, whisk together olive oil, 2 tablespoons vinegar, ¼ teaspoon salt, the celery seed, and cracked black pepper. Pour over hot potatoes; mix well. Using the same small oily bowl, whisk together mayonnaise, yogurt, remaining 2 tablespoons vinegar, and chives.

ADD cucumbers and celery to bowl with potatoes. Pour mayonnaise dressing over salad and toss until well combined. Serve immediately or keep refrigerated.

SHORTCUT CHEF

Cook potatoes or peel, slice, and seed cucumbers ahead of time. The potatoes don't have to be hot and the longer the cucumbers sit salted, the better. If you're going to prep the cucumbers hours and hours ahead, throw them in the fridge to drain. Place a plate under the colander to catch the cucumber water.

Side Salads and Savory Slaws

Tomato-Cucumber Salad with Lemon Yogurt Dressing

This salad should be made only when tomatoes are at their peak. So if they're not, skip to another recipe. A mediocre tomato isn't going to get better tasting no matter what you do to it. ■ If it's the dressing you're craving, and I don't blame you, make the salad without the tomatoes. Double up on the cucumbers. Bake a piece of any fish you love and call it dinner.

4 TO 6 SERVINGS

¼ cup fresh lemon juice

1 small or ½ large sweet onion, thinly sliced

1 medium English cucumber, peeled, seeded, and cut into ¼-inch slices

Coarse-grained salt

2 pints cherry tomatoes or 3 large or 4 medium tomatoes, cored and sliced

Cracked black pepper

FOR THE DRESSING

Reserved lemon juice from marinating onion slices

½ cup plain low-fat yogurt

2 cloves garlic, minced

½ cup loosely packed, roughly chopped assorted fresh herbs (any combination of basil, parsley, mint, oregano, thyme, marjoram, and chervil)

2 tablespoons extra-virgin olive oil

Coarse-grained salt and cracked black pepper

SHORTCUT CHEF

Slice the onions and/or the cucumbers ahead, and make the dressing a day in advance if you can find the time. If you're in a super hurry you could skip the garlic or use store-bought preminced, which is very different from fresh, but if it's the difference between using it or not, use it. It takes smarts to cheat and it's better than eating out.

MORPH Make extra dressing, set it aside, and use it later in the week. I've used it as a dressing for potato salad, green bean salad, and as a mayonnaise substitute on gyro-style sandwiches.

Cooking Thin with Chef Kathleen

IN a small shallow dish, pour lemon juice over onion slices. Make sure all slices are covered. Let stand 30 minutes or up to 2 hours, turning occasionally.

SEASON cucumber slices generously with salt and place in a colander. Place a 1-gallon plastic bag, filled with water and sealed, over cucumbers to weight them down. Let stand in sink while you prepare rest of salad. This process draws out their water.

PLACE sliced tomatoes on a serving platter and season with salt and pepper to taste. Let stand 30 minutes, turning occasionally.

PREPARE THE DRESSING: Strain lemon juice off onions directly into a small nonreactive bowl. Add yogurt, garlic, herbs, oil, and salt and pepper to taste. Whisk together. Taste and adjust seasonings. Set aside.

ARRANGE cucumbers and onions over tomatoes. Pour dressing over salad, toss to coat, and serve immediately.

Guyometer:
Didn't think
I'd like it but
I did.

If the queen's not coming for dinner: If the queen has phoned ahead that she'll not be able to attend your soiree, toss everything together in a bowl and skip the platter business.

If you have access to heirloom or different varieties of tomatoes, use them. The salad is fun with different colored small, medium, and large tomato slices polka dotted with cherry, teardrop, and pear tomatoes. The most important thing is that you use the sweetest tomatoes you can get, so go for taste over color and size when selecting them.

The recipe calls for you to marinate the onions in the lemon juice for 30 minutes or as long as you can. This pickling process calms down the peppery bite onions often have and calms down diners who "can't eat raw onions." Choose the sweetest onions you can get your hands on, though, because no amount of pickling can remove all the bitterness from an onion.

Tomato, Cucumber, and Roasted Pepper Salad with Jalapeño and Cumin

If you're thinking, Why should I waste my time making a complicated-sounding salad like this? read the morph box below. The only way to stick to a life of healthy eating is to stop resisting it. The only way to love good-for-you food is to keep it simple and keep it flavorful. Listen, we've done our homework—the recipes are quick and tasty, so cook already.

4 TO 6 SERVINGS

2 large ripe tomatoes, peeled and cubed

2 large red peppers, roasted, peeled, seeded, and diced

1 large cucumber, peeled, seeded, and cubed

1 tablespoon minced jalapeño

¼ cup loosely packed, roughly chopped flat-leaf parsley

¼ cup fresh lemon juice

½ teaspoon ground cumin

Coarse-grained salt and cracked black pepper

PLACE tomatoes, peppers, cucumber, jalapeño, parsley, and lemon juice in a serving bowl. Toss to combine. Add cumin and salt and pepper to taste. Refrigerate at least 1 hour. This is really delicious when it's cold.

SHORTCUT CHEF

Roast peppers and squeeze the lemon juice the night before. Don't peel the tomatoes. Use jarred roasted peppers but rinse them thoroughly. Too lazy to mince jalapeños? Use dried red chili flakes or Tabasco sauce to taste.

MORPH Serve this salad over a piece of grilled chicken or fish and call it dinner.

I don't like the texture of the skin of the tomatoes, so I usually plunge them in boiling water for 30 seconds and remove it.

Vegetable Sides

are limited to piles of unidentifiable floating vegetable-like objects served up in

the school cafeterias of your youth and second-rate overcooked restaurant

zucchini swimming in grease, do your best to block those memories out. It

will no doubt require effort on your part to overcome such trauma, especially if you have childhood mashed-pea syndrome to overcome too, but vegetables you prepare at home just don't compare.

Thoughtfully chosen, seasonal vegetables are movie star magical all on their own when properly cooked. High drama, lots of flavor, flair, and crunch, but not a lot of work, at least not these preparations. Put some energy into veggie sides; they're easy to deal with and wonderfully exciting to eat. Besides, if dinner plates aren't an entertaining myriad of colors, flavors, and textures, we leave the table dissatisfied and head straight to Ben & Jerry's for consolation. Great veggie sides are a surefire quick cure-all.

The sky's the limit, portion-wise, you know. I've never heard of anyone being cited for overeating green beans. How much fennel slaw is too much? So what if you eat all the squash? We're not talking burgers and fries here.

Plan the vegetables first and you'll find that sometimes you don't even need to fuss with an entrée. I'm not saying your family can make that kind of transition overnight but they'll come around eventually. All-vegetable meals once a week are a great way to increase good calories and cut down on the bad.

Baked Asparagus

This is one vegetable that I wouldn't eat canned or frozen. Fresh is best and it doesn't matter how thick or thin or what color. Asparagus is available in white, purple, and green varieties but most of us only come across green. Some people prefer thin asparagus, claiming fat asparagus is overgrown and bitter. This is just not so.

4 SERVINGS

2 bunches asparagus (see Mom tip)
1 to 2 tablespoons extra-virgin or good-quality olive oil
Coarse-grained salt and cracked black pepper

PREHEAT oven to 400°F. Place asparagus in a large plastic bag. Drizzle half of olive oil over asparagus, seal bag, and shake until asparagus is coated evenly with olive oil. (Depending on size of asparagus, 1 tablespoon oil may not be enough—add more if this seems to be the case.) Place asparagus in a single layer on a cookie sheet; season with salt and pepper. Bake 12 minutes for crunchy or up to 20 minutes, depending upon your preference. Crunchy is fantastic.

Guyometer: Asparagus! My mother made me eat it but hey, this doesn't taste like that.

If the queen's coming for dinner: Toss cooked asparagus with fresh lemon and garnish with thin curls of Parmesan cheese.

SHORTCUT CHEF
Toss asparagus with oil, salt, and pepper as directed and store in the refrigerator until you're ready to bake it. Get into the habit of prepping tonight's or tomorrow's dinner during the day and you'll be eating in more than out. The weight will come off quicker with healthful home-cooked meals and you know it.

MORPH Serve one other simple veggie side and a piece of oven-baked fish such as salmon and dinner is all done. Cook extra asparagus and throw it into a frittata, polenta, or pasta later in the week.

Asparagus starts losing its sweetness the minute it's cut; therefore, as always, look for the freshest stalks possible.

FROM MOM'S LIPS TO YOUR EARS
You forgot to tell them to snap off the woody bottoms of each stalk. Mother Nature saw to it that the asparagus breaks in just the right spot. Save the ends for stock.

Balsamic Roasted Beets

This is a great vegetable side dish, requiring very little prep time or attention, for that matter. Since you're reading the recipe, I'm assuming you like beets.

4 SERVINGS

½ **pound beets (about 6 small or 3 medium), trimmed of greens**

2 tablespoons balsamic vinegar (or more to taste)

Coarse-grained salt and cracked black pepper

SHORTCUT CHEF

Place beets in oven pan with water, cover with foil, place them in oven, and set the timer to start cooking the beets when it's convenient for you.

Roast extra beets, which are a great addition to salads, such as the Salad Niçoise on page 280 or the Chicken and Asian Noodle Salad on page 274. Stick 'em in your lunch box or snack on them when you're standing in front of the refrigerator contemplating calorie violations.

Purple and red beets taste wonderful with any darker vinegar, such as red wine, sherry, or even black currant cassis. Yellow beets are delicious with champagne or white wine vinegar. The truth of the matter is that you can use any vinegar on any beet variety. You'll know when you come up with a combination you like.

PREHEAT oven to 400°F. Place beets in a small baking dish. Add water to reach one quarter of the way up sides of beets. Cover tightly with foil. Bake 1 to 1½ hours, until fork-tender (nowhere near mushy). When beets are just cool enough to handle, using a small paring knife, trim off any funky remaining stem or root nodules (anything you don't want to eat) and, under running water, rub skins off. Cut beet into quarters (bite-size pieces) and place in a small bowl. Add vinegar, salt, and pepper to beets. Toss to coat evenly. Taste and adjust seasonings. These are especially delicious after marinating for a day or two and will keep up to a week in the refrigerator, tightly covered.

Little Grandma's Broccoli

If you avoid broccoli because you've only seen it shriveled, dried, and lined up next to cauliflower, celery, and carrots in a similar state on aluminum party trays lined with kale, give it another chance. We just love this dish. ■ Admittedly, our family eats broccoli only when it's prepared this way because according to our Little Grandma Helen this is how broccoli is fixed, period. I've never heard of another way she fixed it or of another way my father would eat it. Any other preparation was simply wrong. Who's gonna argue with a ninety-four-year-old lady?

6 SERVINGS

2 to 3 stalks fresh broccoli

¼ cup fresh lemon juice

1 tablespoon olive oil

1 teaspoon dried oregano

Coarse-grained salt and cracked black pepper

PEEL broccoli stalks to remove tough strings. Cut each stalk lengthwise into halves or quarters, depending on size. Put into a large glass baking dish with ½ cup water. Cover tightly with plastic wrap. Microwave on medium-high for 14 to 17 minutes, depending on size of your bunch of broccoli and how tender you like your vegetables. Drain. Add lemon juice, olive oil, oregano, and salt and pepper to taste. Mix well. Serve warm or cold.

SHORTCUT CHEF
Wash, trim, and peel broccoli and store in a bag in the refrigerator until you're ready to cook it.

MORPH Cook extra broccoli but don't dress it. Use it in the Broccoli Pasta Frittata (page 134). Add cooked broccoli to soups, pasta, polenta, or salad dishes.

Oven-Roasted Carrots and Parsnips

Block out any childhood post-parsnip-trauma distress disorders and proceed with this recipe at once. It's a lickety-split way to get in two servings of veggies and it's a really delicious combination. If you can peel and cook carrots, you can peel and cook parsnips. Don't knock 'em till you've tried 'em in your adult years.

6 TO 8 SERVINGS

1 pound carrots, peeled and cut into 1-inch chunks

1 pound parsnips, peeled and cut into 1-inch chunks

1 tablespoon extra-virgin olive oil

Coarse-grained salt and cracked black pepper

SHORTCUT CHEF

Peel carrots and parsnips ahead.

MORPH
Turn this simple veggie side dish into a roasted veggie extrava-ganza—throw tiny potatoes cut in half, peeled turnips cut into same-size chunks, cloves of garlic, and sprigs of thyme onto the cookie sheet with the carrots and parsnips. Mm mm good.

FROM MOM'S LIPS TO YOUR EARS

Believe it or not, even my veggie-hating son will eat this, which means it gets the highest guyometer reading ever.

PREHEAT oven to 400°F. Place vegetables in a plastic bag, add olive oil (using only enough to coat vegetables evenly). Shake until well coated. Pour vegetables onto a cookie sheet in a single layer, add salt and pepper to taste, and roast uncovered, turning once, until they are cooked through, 25 to 35 minutes.

*Guyometer:
Ding, ding, ding,
off-the-charts
great—for a
vegetable.*

Cooking Thin with Chef Kathleen

Carrots with Paprika and Parsley

On super-hectic days, I count on super-quick recipes like this to keep me from giving in to fast-food urges. I usually ask someone to toss a salad while I prepare these and broil a piece of fish. With a little teamwork you can get dinner on the table in 20 minutes, tops.

4 TO 6 SERVINGS

1 teaspoon olive oil

3 cloves garlic, minced

¼ cup water

1 teaspoon sugar

1 pound carrots (about 6 medium), peeled and cut into ½-inch coins

1 to 2 tablespoons vinegar

Coarse-grained salt and cracked black pepper

1 teaspoon paprika

¼ cup loosely packed, roughly chopped flat-leaf parsley

Guyometer:
Mm mm good.
"Mom, Dad did not say that."
"If he'd bothered to try them he would have."

PLACE oil and garlic in a 2-quart saucepan. Set on stove, turn heat to medium, and sauté until garlic bubbles a bit. Immediately add water and sugar. Stir and add carrots. Cook, covered, until carrots are just tender, 5 to 7 minutes. Remove from heat; add vinegar, salt and pepper to taste, paprika, and parsley. Taste and adjust seasonings.

SHORTCUT CHEF

Prep carrots ahead or cheat and get those little snack-size baby carrots—the recipe will work just fine.

Whatever you do, don't buy carrots with roots coming out all over the place. Try to buy them with their tops on during carrot season, late summer through early winter, but bagged carrots are quite good too. Look Mom carrots are one of the best brands out there, consistently good and sweet.

Vegetable Sides

Cauliflower with Lemon and Red Pepper Flakes

If you have to eat vegetables you might as well make them taste good. Cauliflower is one of my least favorite vegetables. "Kathleen, stop bad-mouthing everything you hate. Just because you don't like it doesn't mean we want to know about it." "Mom, other people might hate it, too, so I'm telling them that with a few key flavor ingredients they'll like it, too."

4 SERVINGS

1 medium head cauliflower, trimmed of green parts, cored, broken into florets

½ cup water

Juice of 1 to 2 lemons

1 tablespoon olive oil

¼ teaspoon red pepper flakes (or more to taste)

Coarse-grained salt

SHORTCUT CHEF

Trim cauliflower ahead and store in a plastic bag, refrigerated. Squeeze the lemon juice in advance. Any tiny step toward dinner cuts kitchen labor significantly.

Remove the outer leaves from the head, scrape or carve off any dark spots, and slice out the core. Using your hands, break the head into florets. Technically, you can cook the head whole, but why? It will take longer and you're going to have to break it up sooner or later.

PLACE cauliflower in a microwave-proof dish with the water and cover tightly with plastic. Microwave on high 12 to 14 minutes or until just tender. Don't cook it too long. If you overcook it, it really smells bad. Drain and season with lemon juice, olive oil, red pepper flakes, and salt. Taste and adjust seasonings. Serve immediately, at room temperature, or refrigerate until cold.

Guyometer:
It's great.

Corn on the Cob

I can't tell you how many times I've gone to a restaurant and ordered plain old corn on the cob, only to have a dishwater-gray cob with sea-bearing corklike texture plopped down before me. Sometimes the easiest dishes are hard to make, but if you cook corn on the cob this way it will always be great.

4 SERVINGS

4 ears fresh sweet corn, husked and broken in half
2 tablespoons butter (optional)
Coarse-grained salt and cracked black pepper (optional)

BRING a large pot of water to a boil, add corn, and boil 2 to 3 minutes, or until corn is just cooked. You'll really only learn corn doneness by trial and error. Cook it 3 minutes today, 2½ minutes next time. Size of the kernels will determine cook times too. Thank goodness it's not brain surgery. Experiment until you're happy. Eat the corn plain and simple or add butter, salt, or pepper as desired.

Guyometer: One of the few times I can turn down butter.

SHORTCUT CHEF

Get your spouse to cook dinner. Able diners who don't take their turn at the foot of the stove should miss as many meals as they don't participate in.

The fresher the corn, the better. Stop by farm stands, visit the farmers' markets, or buy your corn from a reputable specialty market that moves its produce quickly. Fresh-cut corn looks the part. The stem end appears fresh cut, not dried out and chalky. The husks are green, almost wet; the kernels are plump and lively.

If corn's on our menu, it's because it's sweet and delicious. Therefore I don't waste fat calories on butter. A little salt is all I need but I even skip that when the corn is really, really sweet. Try it without butter once. You'll be converted too.

Sweet Corn and Pattypan Squash with Butter

I thought butter in the title would get your attention. A little bit of the real thing is okay in moderation. And by now we're all well aware of the need for fat in our diets. This is a wonderful veggie side dish that takes very little effort. Serve it with baked fish, grilled chicken or steak, and a green salad and you've got an easy-as-pie dinner menu. This dish can easily be made with cusa, that pale green squash that shows up in the summertime, or use green zucchini and yellow squash.

4 TO 6 SERVINGS

2 teaspoons butter

2 tablespoons water

2 cups cubed pattypan squash, zucchini, or other summer squash

1 cup fresh corn kernels (about 2 ears)

Coarse-grained salt and cracked black pepper

1 tablespoon fresh lime juice

IN a medium-size skillet over medium-high heat, melt butter with the water. Reduce heat to medium, add squash, cover, and cook 10 minutes. Uncover, add corn, and season with salt and pepper to taste. Stir to combine all ingredients, taste, and adjust seasonings as necessary. Cook 2 minutes more, add lime juice, and serve immediately. See, I told you it was easy.

SHORTCUT CHEF
Use frozen corn if you can't get your hands on fresh or you're just feeling too lazy to drag your knife down a cob of corn (come on, you can do it—it's the difference between just okay and truly great).

MORPH Make extra and throw it into a frittata with some fresh basil the next night.

Try the butter, water, salt, and pepper method of cooking veggies as presented in this recipe and apply it to other veggie combinations—peas, green beans, cut carrots, and so on.

Cooking Thin with Chef Kathleen

Sweet Corn with Butter and Chives

That's right—buttuh. Surely you didn't think for one single second that I'd cook *without* butter. There's no reason on earth why one cannot enjoy discretionary doses of sweet cream butter. Discretionary use defined: when nothing else will enrich and enhance the finished dish as well.

6 SERVINGS

4 cups fresh corn kernels (6 to 8 ears)

1 tablespoon butter

¼ cup water

Coarse-grained salt and cracked black pepper

2 tablespoons thinly sliced chives

BREAK corn cobs in half. Using a sharp knife, starting at the top of each cob, slice the kernels from the cob. They'll fly everywhere, so do it in the sink. If you cut slowly, they won't leave the room.

PLACE butter, water, and corn in a 10-inch nonstick skillet over medium-high heat, bring to a boil, and cook until water is reduced by half. Season with salt and pepper. Toss in chives; mix thoroughly. Serve immediately.

Guyometer:
It's a vegetable.
What do you
want me to say?

SHORTCUT CHEF

I suppose you can cheat and use frozen corn.

If you can't get your hands on fresh chives, go ahead and use thinly sliced green onions.

Vegetable Sides

Mock Fried Eggplant

Except for my older brother, Paul, who possesses the discriminating palate typical of most seven-year-olds (eww, ick, I'm not eating that), this has become a family favorite. That Paul still hasn't developed a taste for vegetables wouldn't be so troublesome except for the fact that he's not seven or eight or even nine. He's forty. He loves parsnips and corn, so there's hope for him yet.

4 SERVINGS

1 medium to large eggplant, cut crosswise into ¼-inch slices

Olive oil spray or 2 tablespoons olive oil

Coarse-grained salt and cracked black pepper

3 to 4 tablespoons balsamic vinegar (or more to taste)

Guyometer:

Quadruple yuck until I actually tried it. It's pretty good but if I let on, my wife will make it more often. I'm still hoping French fries will show up if I complain loudly enough.

LAYER all eggplant slices on a microwave-proof plate; cover tightly with plastic wrap. Microwave on high for 5 minutes.

HEAVILY spray or add a small amount of oil to a large nonstick skillet, turn heat to medium-high, and place one layer of eggplant in pan. You won't be able to cook all eggplant slices at once because entire surface of each slice must make contact with pan bottom, so you'll be cooking them in batches. Season with salt and pepper and spray or brush eggplant slices again with olive oil. Cook until golden brown, turning once, 3 to 5 minutes per side. Spray eggplant slices with oil as needed; some slices will require additional oil and some won't.

AS eggplant slices finish cooking, transfer to a plate with a lip or a shallow bowl. Drizzle each layer of eggplant generously with balsamic vinegar. Serve at room temperature.

MORPH This is something we always make in big batches. It's just as great left over and even better piled into a baguette with tomato slices and basil. Try it in a frittata, pasta salad, or lasagne (minus the balsamic vinegar).

FROM MOM'S LIPS TO YOUR EARS

Try everything at least once.

Paul's Parsnip or Beet Chips

My brother Paul called one night, boasting about the delicious deep-fried parsnip chips he was making. "They're really great fried in peanut oil. All you need is a sprinkle of salt. We can't stop eating them. They'd be great for your book." "Paul, they're deep-fried." "Yeah, so? They're a vegetable, aren't they? Last I heard, they were healthy." ■ Leave it to a guy to think that because the fat's on a vegetable, it doesn't count. But I knew he was on to something. It just so happened that my mom and I were trying to perfect our baked beet chip recipe at the time. We combined Paul's idea, the parsnips, and the beets to come up with this great "potato-chip fix."

4 SERVINGS

1 pound parsnips, peeled and sliced paper thin, or 1 pound beets, peeled and sliced ⅛ inch thick

1 tablespoon olive or peanut oil

Coarse-grained salt and cracked black pepper

PREHEAT oven to 425°F. Spray a cookie sheet with cooking spray and set aside. Place parsnips or beets in a plastic bag, add oil, sprinkle with salt and pepper, seal bag, and shake until evenly coated. Spread on cookie sheet. Bake 1 hour, turning every 15 minutes (beets only need to be turned once). Remove any darkened ones early, since a few will cook faster. Serve immediately. They're best hot.

Guyometer: Chips? And they're healthy? Hmm. Pretty good.

SHORTCUT CHEF

If you've got a plastic mandoline you can have these in the oven in 5 minutes. If you don't, you'll have to cut them by hand using a very sharp knife. Consider buying a mandoline—put it on your wish list. They're really great to have around for quick slaws, homemade chips, scalloped potatoes, pickles, you name it.

FROM MOM'S LIPS TO YOUR EARS

It's food. It's not a beauty contest, Kathleen. Tell them how to make the beets. They're not so ugly and the combination of the beets and parsnips is cute. Besides, you can bake them at the same time.

Broiled Fennel with Lime and Parmesan

Just because you've never tried fennel doesn't mean you should stay living on the dark side of the moon. I once fed this to a finicky, fussy, too-hip-for-her-own-good twenty-four-year-old urbanite who swore she'd hate it. Well, guess what: "Kathleen, that fennel is to die for." Even my dad likes this. If it's good enough for Miss Big-City-Chic and my pop, it's good enough for you.

4 SERVINGS

3 tablespoons good-quality olive oil

2 large fennel bulbs, trimmed top and bottom, cut lengthwise into generous
    ¼-inch slices

Coarse-grained salt and cracked black pepper

Juice of 2 limes

6 tablespoons grated Parmesan cheese

PREHEAT broiler. Pour only enough olive oil on two cookie sheets to prevent fennel from sticking (about 1½ tablespoons each). Place fennel in a single layer on cookie sheets and, without adding any more oil, coat both sides of fennel by turning it over on pan. If you have one, a pastry brush works well, but so do your fingers. Season fennel slices with salt and pepper on both sides. Squeeze juice of 1 lime over fennel slices and place under broiler.

MORPH Love it on a baguette with grilled chicken. Bake a piece of fish, toss a salad, and you don't have to put any more energy into dinner.

BROIL for 5 minutes. Some edges may blacken slightly. Remove fennel from the oven and, using tongs or a spatula, turn over each slice. Top with Parmesan, making sure all surfaces of fennel are coated with cheese. Place back under broiler for 1½ to 3 minutes, or until cheese starts to brown.

Cooking Thin with Chef Kathleen

ALLOW fennel to remain on cookie sheets until ready to serve. Do not refrigerate. This is wonderful served at room temperature. Just before serving, squeeze remaining lime over fennel slices.

Guyometer:
It's good.

I know, fennel looks a little Dr. Seuss–esque when you first lay eyes on it, with those big feathery frond-topped hollow stalks attached to pearly white softball-size bulbs. It's the bulb you're after, so lop off the greens and stalks. Trim the bulb of any brown or yucky-looking spots. Cut in half and remove some of the core, which is cone shaped. For this recipe, cut fennel lengthwise into $1/4$-inch-thick slices.

FROM MOM'S LIPS TO YOUR EARS

You heard her, my husband likes it. He's the biggest skeptic there is. Besides, you shouldn't miss out on something this good and this easy to cook.

Green Beans with Fresh Corn

Butterfat calories aren't hidden, disguised, buried, or wasted. The butter's sweet aroma and flavor are front and center for you to taste, savor, and enjoy. Remember: moderate, don't eliminate. If you're too restrictive you'll be back on the yo-yo-go-round before you know what hit you.

4 SERVINGS

1 pound green beans, trimmed

2 cups fresh corn kernels (about 4 ears)

1 tablespoon butter (optional)

Coarse-grained salt and cracked black pepper

½ cup roughly chopped, loosely packed fresh basil leaves

BRING a pot of water to a rolling boil, add beans, and cook 5 minutes. When they're just about done, add corn. Cook 1 to 2 minutes more and drain. Place vegetables in a bowl with butter and toss while still warm to melt butter. Add salt and pepper to taste. Add basil and toss once more. Serve immediately.

SHORTCUT CHEF

Prep the green beans and cut the corn off the cob when you get a free few minutes.

Very good-quality olive oil instead of butter is a fine swap. If you've got access to farmers'-market-quality beans and corn you may choose to skip the added fat. It's up to you.

If you use a wire mesh strainer to plunge the vegetables in and out of the boiling water, you won't have to chase green beans or corn kernels around in boiling hot water. A metal colander you can dip into and out of the pot will work too.

*Guyometer:
Mm. My two
favorite vegetables.*

Cooking Thin with Chef Kathleen

Green Beans with Lemon and Parmesan

My friend Brady's life was devoted to food and wine. He had a wonderful sense of taste and took great pleasure in savoring simple clean flavors. He loved to eat this dish right out of the tossing bowl. The hot beans heat the oil slightly and warm the cheese. The recipe calls for extra-virgin olive oil, so be sure to use a very pleasant-tasting olive oil. Vegetable or canola oil won't do, so if you don't have good oil on hand, put it on your shopping list and make this another time. ■ The truth of the matter is that you can serve it hot, warm, or room temperature. It's another dish that doesn't have to be prepared at the last minute.

4 TO 6 SERVINGS

1 pound green beans, trimmed

2 teaspoons extra-virgin olive oil

Coarse-grained salt and cracked black pepper

1 to 2 tablespoons fresh lemon juice

1 ounce Parmesan cheese

BRING 8 cups of salted water to a boil. Add green beans and cook to desired degree of doneness, 6 to 8 minutes. Strain beans and place back in pot. Drizzle olive oil over beans and stir to coat. Season with salt and pepper; stir once more. Taste and adjust seasonings. Gradually add lemon juice to your liking. Adjust seasonings. Divide beans among serving plates. Hold block of Parmesan over each plate and gently drag vegetable peeler over it, letting paper-thin cheese curls fall where they may, three to five per serving.

SHORTCUT CHEF
Trim the beans while you're watching TV.

Use a vegetable peeler to shave very thin slices off a wedge of Parmesan as you would peel the skin off a carrot. Do not press down hard or the slices will be too thick, and you will use twice as much, doubling the calories from the cheese.

Green Beans with Toasted Almonds

Serve this recipe hot or cold—it's great either way. If you're super starving and you're trying to prep dinner and not eat yourself into the next pant size, prepare a double batch of these green beans and snack on them while you cook the main dish. Use it as a Thanksgiving side dish and you can prepare it the morning of the big feast when things are less hectic in the kitchen.

4 SERVINGS

¼ cup sliced almonds

1 pound green beans, trimmed, cut into 1-inch pieces

Coarse-grained salt

2 teaspoons sherry vinegar (or more to taste)

1 tablespoon extra-virgin olive oil

Cracked black pepper

If the queen's coming for dinner: She'll be absolutely smitten. Refer to the dish as string beans with toasted almonds; it sounds fancier and besides, when she was a child, green beans hadn't been developed yet—string beans were it. That's right, green beans are stringless string beans. Cool, huh?

You can also toast almonds in a nonstick pan over medium-high heat (with no oil), stirring and shaking often until golden, about 5 minutes. Transfer them from the hot pan immediately to a plate so they cool quicker.

I just know you've got sherry vinegar in your pantry by now or, at the very least, it's on your shopping list. It's a lip-smacking-good, no-fat way to make food taste great, a real culinary secret weapon. Get with the program, people.

PREHEAT oven to 350°F. Spread sliced almonds on a cookie sheet in a single layer. Toast just until golden, 5 to 10 minutes. Set aside.

IN a large pot, bring generously salted water to a rolling boil. Add beans to pot, return water to a boil, and cook uncovered over high heat until beans are fork-tender, 6 to 8 minutes. Drain beans. Season with salt to taste. Place in a serving dish. Add vinegar, oil, more salt if needed, and pepper to taste. Toss to combine. Just before serving, add almonds and toss once more.

Peas with Pancetta

Sweet peas are sweetest when cooked immediately, as in a few hours after picking. However, since most of us don't live on farms, frozen peas are an excellent stand-in. Don't feel guilty if you opt for frozen peas. They're quite good, and eating any vegetable is better than not eating vegetables at all. I actually prefer frozen peas to fresh grocery store peas for the simple reason that most often the peas we get were harvested long ago, well past their peak of flavor.

4 SERVINGS

1 ounce pancetta or bacon, diced (I like country-style bacon—thick cut)

One 10-ounce package frozen baby peas, thawed

2 tablespoons water

Coarse-grained salt and cracked black pepper

IN a 10-inch nonstick skillet over medium-low heat, cook pancetta or bacon, stirring often, until golden brown and cooked through, about 2 minutes. If using bacon, remove pan from heat, drain bacon on paper towel, and wipe pan of grease. Return bacon to pan, set over low heat, and add peas and water. Toss to combine. Cook until peas are heated through, about 5 minutes. Taste. Season with salt if needed and pepper to taste. Serve immediately.

Keep pancetta and bacon in the freezer and cut what you need off the frozen block. So what if you cut through the bacon stack instead of using it up a piece at a time.

Buttermilk-Battered Baked Onion Rings

Baking these onion rings lets you indulge in the savory, salty crunch of delicious onion rings without the fatty horrors of deep-frying. The buttermilk keeps the flavors rich and intense. The key to this recipe is in choosing the onions. Don't accept that an onion is just an onion. Buy the absolute sweetest you can get your hands on. Walla Walla, Granex, Texas Sugar Babies, Maui, and Vidalia are just a few of the popular sweet varieties. Ask the produce people at your market for the best they've got.

4 SERVINGS

2 large sweet onions, peeled

½ cup buttermilk

2 tablespoons olive oil

I large egg white

⅔ cup flour

½ teaspoon coarse-grained salt

¼ teaspoon cracked black pepper

¼ teaspoon paprika

FOR DIPPING AND DREDGING

I cup buttermilk for dipping

I cup flour for dredging

Coarse-grained salt (optional)

PREHEAT oven to 450°F. Oil a baking sheet. Cut onions crosswise into ¾-inch-thick slices and separate into rings. Use largest rings, reserving smaller pieces for another recipe. Prepare batter in a small bowl by whisking together buttermilk, olive oil, egg white, flour, salt, pepper, and paprika. Stir until completely combined.

FOR DIPPING AND DREDGING: Pour buttermilk into a shallow dish. Place flour in a separate shallow dish. Dredge onion rings one at a time, first in buttermilk, then in flour, and finally in batter. Place onion rings on nonstick baking sheet and bake 8 minutes, turning once at halfway point. Season with coarse-grained salt (if necessary). Serve immediately.

SHORTCUT CHEF

Peel and slice the onions ahead and make the batter in advance too. At the very least, read the recipe through start to finish and lay out ingredients not requiring refrigeration, along with all your tools.

When the onion rings are done, eat them. Don't wait. They're not good cold. If you're serving them as a side dish for dinner, the entrée should be done before the onions come out. I suggest serving these tasty rings with a simple-to-get-on-the-table entrée such as grilled chicken, baked fish, or broiled steak and a tossed salad of mixed greens.

Potatoes and Corn with Butter and Chives

The nutrition police might try to give you a double-starch citation, but look them straight in the eyes and tell them, as part of a balanced diet, you've chosen potatoes and corn over Ben & Jerry's. It works every time.

4 SERVINGS

1¼ pounds tiny potatoes, scrubbed but not peeled

2 cups fresh corn kernels (about 4 ears)

2 tablespoons chopped chives or sliced scallions

1 tablespoon butter

Coarse-grained salt and cracked black pepper

PLACE potatoes in a large pot and cover with cold water. Bring to a boil, reduce heat to a simmer, and cook until fork-tender, 18 to 20 minutes. While potatoes are cooking, place corn in microwave-proof dish with 1 tablespoon water. Cook, covered, on high until just done, about 3 minutes. Drain potatoes and place back in pot. Add corn, chives, butter, and salt and pepper to taste. Smash with a potato masher or fork until coarse and very chunky. Serve immediately.

MORPH Serve this over an oven-baked salmon or pan-seared boneless, skinless chicken breast and call it dinner.

Choose the sweetest corn you can get your hands on or sweeten the corn with a teensy pinch of sugar.

Cooking Thin with Chef Kathleen

Buttery Mashed Potatoes

Achieving perfect mashed potatoes requires a little extra effort but the results are sublime. You cannot use a food processor, blender, or any other motorized apparatus to mash the potatoes. They get gluey. Processing potatoes by hand using a ricer, food mill, potato masher, or even just a wooden spoon yields perfect potatoes every time. Russet and Yukon Gold potatoes make the best mashed potatoes. Choose firm potatoes without a hint of green and no soft or discolored spots. Do not refrigerate your potatoes or the potato starch will gradually change into sugar, causing unpleasantly sweet potatoes that will not cook up well.

4 TO 6 SERVINGS

2 pounds Yukon Gold potatoes, peeled, cut into even-size, large chunks

¾ cup buttermilk

1 tablespoon butter (optional)

¼ cup chopped chives or sliced scallions

Coarse-grained salt and cracked black pepper

PLACE potatoes in a medium saucepan and cover with cold water. Bring to a boil, reduce heat to a simmer, and cook until fork-tender, 12 to 16 minutes. Drain in a colander. Immediately place potatoes back in pot you cooked them in and place on same burner that has been turned off. Stir occasionally over next 5 minutes to let potatoes dry out.

IN a small saucepan, warm buttermilk over medium-low heat. Do not boil. Pass potatoes through a ricer or food mill. Alternatively, leave potatoes in pot and mash by hand using a potato masher or wooden spoon. Stir in enough warmed buttermilk to obtain desired consistency. Add butter a teaspoon at a time, tasting after each addition—you may not use it all. Add chives or scallions. Add salt and pepper to taste; stir until combined.

SHORTCUT CHEF

Peel the potatoes the night before or when you get a few minutes. Keep refrigerated and covered in water until you're ready to get cooking.

If you've got some around, add a little roasted garlic puree (page 256). Or add roughly chopped fresh herbs (such as chives, basil, parsley, or thyme) to your just mashed spuds.

Grainy Mustard Smashed Potatoes

Mom's my secret ingredient. She comes up with all the truly great stuff. I guess when you're deep into raising four kids and a husband, inventing on-the-spot shortcuts and quick culinary solutions starts to happen in your sleep.

4 TO 5 SERVINGS

1 ¼ pounds small potatoes

1 tablespoon butter

2 tablespoons grainy mustard

Coarse-grained salt and cracked black pepper

PLACE potatoes in a large pot and cover with cold water. Bring to a boil, reduce heat to a simmer, and cook until fork-tender, 12 to 16 minutes. Drain potatoes and place back in pot you cooked them in. Add butter and mustard. Using a potato masher, smash until coarse and very chunky. Season with salt and pepper; taste and adjust seasonings. Serve immediately.

Guyometer:
These are good.
Is that butter I
taste?

SHORTCUT CHEF
Buy tiny potatoes in little plastic boxes at the market. They're practically clean enough to use as is.

Cooking Thin with Chef Kathleen

Quick Oven-Roasted Potatoes with Rosemary

This is my answer to the rosemary roasted potatoes served at Zuni Café in San Francisco. Hands down, Chef Judy Rodgers's are much better because they're lovingly made in wonderful baking ovens with just-out-of-the-ground potatoes, just-picked rosemary, fresh imported oils, and magical sea salts brought in from Lord knows where. But since I can't jet to Judy's, afford those calories very often, or afford those ingredients at home, I had to come up with a way to re-create a tide-me-over version.

4 TO 6 SERVINGS

2 pounds potatoes, peeled, trimmed, and cut into even-size, large chunks

2 tablespoons olive oil

Coarse-grained salt and cracked black pepper

2 to 4 tablespoons chopped fresh rosemary

PREHEAT oven to 400°F. Place potatoes in a pot, cover with cold water, and bring to a boil. Reduce to a simmer and cook until almost overdone, 20 to 23 minutes. Drain, place in a large bowl, and gently toss with olive oil and with salt, pepper, and rosemary to taste. Tip onto a cookie sheet that has been lightly coated or sprayed with just enough oil to cover it. Bake until potatoes are fork-tender and golden brown, 20 to 25 minutes, turning once at halfway point.

Guyometer:
Great.

Parboiling the potatoes first gives them a soft interior and a crispy edge.

Make use of summer's abundant bounty of fresh herbs; use rosemary or try a combination of your favorites—thyme, lemon thyme, sage, and oregano work very well.

When you need dinner in a dash, choose tiny new potatoes, leave their skins on, and don't bother boiling them. Bake 35 to 45 minutes.

Vegetable Sides

Pan-Smashed Potatoes with Hot Pepper

When no one's home I cut the recipe in half and have it for supper with a poached egg and maybe some salad greens lightly tossed with vinegar, oil, salt, and pepper. A nourishing comforting meal for nights when you'd prefer not to cook. You can hardly call this cooking, it's so simple.

4 SERVINGS

1 ½ pounds tiny new potatoes, scrubbed

2 tablespoons extra-virgin olive oil

2 cloves garlic, minced

¼ teaspoon red pepper flakes

Coarse-grained salt

PLACE potatoes in a large pot and cover with cold water. Bring to a boil, reduce heat to a simmer, and cook until fork-tender, 18 to 20 minutes. While potatoes are cooking, place olive oil, garlic, and red pepper flakes in a medium-size nonstick pan over medium heat. Sauté until garlic is golden, about 3 minutes. Turn off heat. Drain potatoes, add to pan with garlic, and smash with a potato masher or spoon until coarse and very chunky. Season with salt to taste.

Fast Baked Sweet Potato Home Fries

You won't miss Mc-You-Know-Who's fries a bit once you make this delicious alternative. These are so quick to prepare and so deeply satisfying, you'll be surprised at how simple it is to add another side dish to the evening meal.

4 TO 6 SERVINGS

2 medium sweet potatoes, peeled

Extra-virgin olive oil or nonstick vegetable spray

Coarse-grained salt and cracked black pepper

2 tablespoons coarsely chopped flat-leaf parsley

I clove garlic, minced

I teaspoon freshly grated lemon zest

PREHEAT oven to 400°F. Cut sweet potatoes crosswise into ¼-inch-thick slices. Place only enough olive oil on a cookie sheet to prevent sweet potatoes from sticking.

ARRANGE sweet potatoes in a single layer on cookie sheet. Turn them over once before baking to ensure that both sides are coated with oil. Season with salt and pepper to taste. Bake until golden, turning once and seasoning undersides with salt and pepper at halfway point, about 25 minutes total.

WHILE the potatoes are in the oven, in a small bowl toss together parsley, garlic, lemon zest, and a bit more salt and pepper. Taste. Adjust seasonings.

TRANSFER cooked potatoes to a large bowl; add parsley mix. Working quickly, toss potatoes to coat evenly; place back on cookie sheet in a single layer. Bake for an additional 2 minutes, which will take peppery bite out of the garlic.

SHORTCUT CHEF

Peel and slice the sweet potatoes, place in a plastic bag, drizzle with olive oil, seal the bag, and then shake and turn to coat with oil. Keep refrigerated. Make the parsley, garlic, and lemon zest mix ahead, too.

If you drizzle the olive oil a teaspoon at a time onto the cookie sheet and use a paper towel to distribute it, you'll find that you use considerably less oil.

If you don't feel like fussing with the parsley, garlic, and lemon zest part of the recipe, don't. The sweet potatoes are fantastic with or without the seasonings.

Vegetable Sides

Sweet potatoes tend to leak
and make a sugary mess. To
avoid scrubbing, use a nonstick pan, or line a pan or baking dish with parchment
paper or foil. The mess is a
sign they're done, but they
don't always leak, so check
with a fork for tenderness.

Sweet potatoes can cook at
just about any temperature
between 325° and 425°F. If
you're cooking something
else, leave the oven at the
setting it's on. Just remember
to keep an eye on them.
Cooking times will vary
greatly, depending upon the
size of the potatoes and the
temperature of the oven.
They're done when they're
very soft and mushy all over.
If there's a hard spot when
you touch it, that same hard
spot will be there when you
try to eat it, so leave it in a
little longer.

FROM MOM'S LIPS
TO YOUR EARS

Eat sweet potatoes at least
once a week if you're not in
the veggie side dish cooking
groove yet. They're easy
and take little thought.
Okay, so start with once a
month.

Sweet Potatoes with Cilantro and Lime

I don't know what it is about sweet potatoes but when I think about them, I get that same feeling of excitement I do about warm baked goods. I think it's their sugary sweet nature combined with their savory undertones and creamy texture that I find so down-home comforting. This is a look-ma-no-hands preparation. You'll have plenty of time for main-dish preparation. Sometimes this is my dinner when it's just me. I'm sure I'm missing some essential vitamin or mineral, but it's better than my old pizza-by-the-slice days.

4 TO 6 SERVINGS

2 pounds sweet potatoes (about 3 medium)

Coarse-grained salt

¼ cup fresh lime juice (or more to taste)

½ cup loosely packed, roughly chopped cilantro leaves

4 to 6 tablespoons plain low-fat yogurt

4 to 6 lime wedges

PREHEAT oven to 400°F. Scrub sweet potatoes and pierce with a fork a few times. Place on a cookie sheet lined with parchment or in a glass baking dish. Bake them until completely soft and fork-tender, 25 to 35 minutes.

WHEN potatoes are hot but cool enough to handle, slice open lengthwise. Scoop flesh into a serving dish. Season with salt, lime juice, and chopped cilantro. Stir until combined. Taste and adjust seasonings. Garnish each serving with a dollop of yogurt, no more than a tablespoon unless you're crazy about the stuff, and a wedge of lime.

Rainy's Sweet Potatoes

My friend Rainy is a self-proclaimed "huge fan of sweet potato fries"—the baked variety of course (page 189). "In the summer, I make a mean roasted sweet potato on the grill. Slice each sweet potato you plan to cook in three or four places, not all the way through. Take thin slices of peeled Vidalia onion and insert them directly into the cuts you made. Sprinkle with salt and pepper, wrap them tightly in aluminum foil, and throw on the grill for an hour. Turn frequently. The onions caramelize and the combination is just delicious. Sometimes I even precook the sweet potato in the microwave for 2 to 3 minutes so it doesn't need to be on the grill as long." ■ Because it was the dead of winter when we finally got around to testing this recipe, and because my mom kept cutting all the way through the sweet potatoes instead of making three-quarter (of the way through) cuts, we came up with this easy oven-bake version for the culinarily impaired.

4 SERVINGS

1 large sweet potato, peeled and cut into ¼-inch slices
Coarse-grained salt and cracked black pepper
1 large apple, peeled, cored, and cut into ½-inch slices
½ small onion, thinly sliced

PREHEAT oven to 400°F. In an 8 × 8-inch nonreactive baking dish, place a single layer of sweet potatoes. Season with salt and pepper to taste. Place a single layer of apples over sweet potatoes and sprinkle with salt and pepper. Add a layer of onions and continue layering ingredients, ending with a layer of sweet potatoes. Be sure to season each potato layer with salt and pepper. Place a piece of parchment paper directly over top layer. Cover dish tightly with aluminum foil and bake 60 to 70 minutes, or until sweet potatoes are fork-tender and cooked through. In summer, do it Rainy's way, foil-wrapped on the grill. They're great that way and there's nothing to clean up.

Guyometer: It's not steak but as far as vegetables go, this is pretty good.

You don't have to cook this dish at 400°F. If you've got something else in the oven throw these in, too. They'll cook to perfect doneness sooner or later. Just check them every 15 minutes or so. If they overcook a little, so what? Pretend you wanted to end up with mashed-apple-and-onion sweet potatoes.

FROM MOM'S LIPS TO YOUR EARS

I'm not such a big fan of onions, so I used some apple slices instead of onion slices in Rainy's recipe.

Winter Squash

Even for chefs, shopping for squash can be a bit intimidating. How do you choose a good squash? Which varieties are tasty? Which ones are good for baking? ▪ Rely on your instincts and hope that your grocer is stocking palatable varieties. There are many to choose from, each with its own distinctive flavor characteristics. Some are nutty, others are sweet and savory. The best way to learn about squash and which ones you'll like best is to try them all. When purchasing squash, buy two varieties at a time and cook them together. Conduct your own side-by-side taste comparison, analyzing flavor differences, textures, and cook times. You'll soon discover which varieties your family likes best. Sweet Dumpling, butternut, acorn, delicata, hubbard, and sugar pumpkins are some of my personal favorites. ▪ Choose squash with no bruises, brown spots, or blemishes of any kind. The skin should be smooth and firm. Store whole squash in a cool, dark place. The countertop works fine, too, for a day or two. Just don't refrigerate them.

4 SERVINGS PER 2-POUND SQUASH

Okay, so you bought it, now what? Winter squash can be baked, roasted, diced and sautéed, microwaved, and mashed. It can be turned into soup and baked into gratins, pies, breads, muffins, and cakes. The natural flavor of squash can be enhanced with simple additions. Try bacon, onions, garlic, cheeses like Parmesan or Gruyère, sweeteners like maple syrup or brown sugar, fresh herbs such as sage or thyme, ground spices such as cardamom, cinnamon, nutmeg, or curry powder (but not all together).

To peel or not to peel is entirely up to you. Just know that you don't have to peel squash. I don't know who started that but you can eat the peels. Even in the fanciest restaurants they serve it with the skin on and expect you to eat it.

Of course there are times you wouldn't want to eat the peels; when a recipe calls for diced squash, you need to peel it. When you're using squash "meat" for soups you'll be instructed to scoop the flesh out of the skin. Follow recipe directions and keep in mind that you can enjoy squash without a lot of fussy peeling and preparation.

Hi-yuh! How to cut squash without losing a limb. Before you leave the store take your pick of the day over to the nearest produce person and ask him or her to cut it in half for you. Cook cut squash the day you bring it home.

If your produce person went on strike and you have to cut it yourself, it can be downright hard but it's not impossible. Before you get started, place a wet towel under a cutting board larger than the squash (the towel helps anchor the cutting board to the counter). Using a very sharp cleaver or chef's knife, cut the squash in half lengthwise. Whatever you do, don't try to cut through the stem—you won't be able to. And remember, there's no reward for squash cut exactly in half.

I really love how pretty squash rings look but it's just not worth risking your life for. It's better to cut the squash in half lengthwise first and then cut slices. You'll have crescent moons instead of full moons. So what? Go slow, pay attention to what you're doing, don't let anything distract you, and you'll get the job done safely. Scoop out the seeds and carry on.

PREHEAT oven to 400°F. Cut squash lengthwise and scoop out seeds as if you were cleaning cantaloupe. Sprinkle squash cavities with salt and pepper and brush with olive oil. Don't glop it on—a thin coat that doesn't drip is all you need. Or spray with nonstick olive oil spray. Lay squash cut side down on a cookie sheet and bake 35 to 45 minutes, or until tender to the touch and golden on cut side. Using a spoon, scoop cooked squash from skin and place in a serving bowl. Taste and adjust seasonings with salt and pepper. Serve immediately.

IF no one's home but me, I don't bother scooping the squash from the skin. No one's looking and why should I get an extra bowl dirty?

Squash and Potato Puree

This is a little fancier than Monday through Friday food but if you have the time, it's quite good and a dish we eat throughout fall and winter. It's great for weekend or holiday entertaining, too, because it's just a little fancier than plain old mashed potatoes. It's quite palatable to children because of the sweet nature of the squash. Just don't tick off the ingredients list to the little darlings before they taste it.

6 TO 8 SERVINGS

1 pound butternut squash (1 medium)

1 teaspoon olive oil

Coarse-grained salt and cracked black pepper

4 to 6 cloves garlic, peeled and cut in half lengthwise, sprouts removed

2 sprigs thyme

1 pound Yukon Gold potatoes (3 or 4 potatoes)

½ cup buttermilk

2 tablespoons minced chives

PREHEAT oven to 375°F. Cut squash in half lengthwise. (Follow procedure on pages 192–193.) Remove seeds. Brush cut surfaces with olive oil. Season with salt and pepper to taste. Place garlic and 1 sprig of thyme in cavity of each half. Place cut side down on a cookie sheet and bake 25 to 35 minutes, or until completely soft and tender.

MEANWHILE, peel potatoes and cut into uniform chunks. Place cut potatoes in a saucepan large enough to hold them and cover with cold salted water. Bring potatoes to a boil, reduce heat, and simmer until a fork goes through them easily, about 20 minutes. Don't overcook potatoes or they will become waterlogged.

WHEN the squash is just cool enough to handle, scrape meat from skin and pass through a ricer or food mill along with

SHORTCUT CHEF

Make the whole dish the night before you're going to serve it. No one has to know you made this the day before. Butternut squash tastes great in this dish but other winter squash will work just as well.

Cooking Thin with Chef Kathleen

cooked garlic, discarding thyme sprigs. Do the same with cooked potatoes. If you are serving this right away, gently heat buttermilk in a small saucepan over medium-low heat. Add enough buttermilk to combined puree to get consistency you prefer. Season to taste with salt and pepper. Stir in chives just before serving.

MORPH You can easily turn this into soup by thinning it with chicken stock. You might serve it with a salad of winter garden lettuces and pan-fried mushrooms. You know when I say fried I'm talking non-stick pan with a teensy bit of oil.

We call for a ricer, which really does make a lovely mashed potato product—perfect in fact. But if you don't have one, pretend your preference is for a country-style chunky puree and use a handheld potato masher or fork.

Microwave Squash

What kind of squash, Kathleen? Any hard winter squash will do. I usually ask the nearest produce person for his or her recommendation and then I choose one that looks sufficient enough to feed the number of hungry diners showing up. I make it a policy, though, to try different varieties every time I shop. No repeats until I've sampled every variety available. They're all richly flavored and deeply satisfying to eat.

4 TO 6 SERVINGS

One 2-to-3-pound winter squash, cut in half lengthwise and seeded
Coarse-grained salt and cracked black pepper

PLACE halved squash cut side down in a shallow microwave-proof baking dish. Cover with plastic wrap and microwave on high for 15 minutes. Remove from microwave, pierce with fork to test doneness, keep wrapped, and let rest 10 minutes. If the queen won't be joining you for dinner, serve squash right in the skins; otherwise, using a spoon, scrape squash from skins into a serving dish. Season with salt and pepper to taste. Serve immediately.

If the only reason you're not eating squash is because it's too scary to cut, get over it. Take the squash over to the produce person and ask him or her to cut it in half for you. Otherwise, place a wet towel under a cutting board to anchor it to the counter. Using a sharp knife, cut the squash in half lengthwise. Go slow, pay attention to what you're doing, don't let anything distract you, and you'll get the job done.

Sugar Snap Peas with Fresh Oregano

Unlike sweet peas, snap peas require little preparation and no shucking before cooking. You need only break off the stem ends and remove the string that runs the length of their top side. Buy snap peas that are crisp, firm to the touch, unblemished, and deep green. Eat them the day you buy them or the next day at the latest. Store them longer and you'll miss out on their sweet nature and firm bite.

4 SERVINGS

2 teaspoons extra-virgin olive oil or butter

¾ pound sugar snap peas, stem ends and strings removed

Coarse-grained salt and cracked black pepper

1 tablespoon loosely packed, coarsely chopped oregano

IN a 10-inch nonstick skillet, heat the oil over medium-high heat until hot but not smoking. Add snap peas and cook, tossing often, until just done, 3 to 4 minutes. Sprinkle with salt and pepper to taste. Add oregano, toss a few times more, and serve immediately.

Guyometer:
He won't say, but we know he snacks on them before dinner, too.

They're really great just plain. Drop them in salted boiling water for 2 to 3 minutes, or until they're bright green and still crunchy. They never take longer than 3 minutes to cook, so don't get distracted. Taste one. You'll know when they're done.

If you compulsively snack while you cook (and I do), cook snap peas before the entrée, set them on the counter, and munch on them while you prep the rest of supper. You might want to do a double batch so there are some left over for dinner.

FROM MOM'S LIPS TO YOUR EARS

Listen, I don't want to scare you but they're really easy to overcook. I do it at least half the time, which makes me really appreciate the times I don't.

MORPH Chard, like
spinach, is good tossed into
pasta, served over polenta,
and baked into savory pies
and tarts.

Remove the stems from the
Swiss chard by tearing the
leaves off the stem or cutting
the stem out of each leaf using
a sharp knife. Tear or chop the
leaves into large pieces. Next,
wash the chard the same way
you wash spinach but don't
dry it; let the water cling to
the leaves. The water helps
the chard steam. If you want
to eat the stems, cut them
into 1/2-inch pieces, wash
them, and put them in the
pan a minute or two before
the leaves.

I love a little anchovy in my
sautéed Swiss chard. It adds
an intense salty flavor. Mash
one or two anchovy fillets and
add to the pan with the oil.
No one will know.

FROM MOM'S LIPS TO YOUR EARS

My daughter forgot to tell
you that there are several
varieties of chard: red,
white, and green—thick or
thin stemmed. All varieties
have their virtues. When
buying chard, choose
bunches with firm, bright
green leaves and healthy
stems void of bruises. Try a
different variety each week.
It's so easy to prepare, you
can add it to the weekly
meal plan.

Sautéed Swiss Chard

Some people are unsure about Swiss chard and frankly have to be
tricked or at least talked into eating it. You may wish to mix the
chard with more familiar greens, such as spinach, until you win the
crowd over. Not that anyone's ever going to say, "Hey, Mom, can we
have Swiss chard again?" But they might. It's not bitter, it's really
quite good, and sometimes it's the only decent-looking fresh vegetable in the market.

4 SERVINGS

3 cloves garlic, thinly sliced

1 medium onion, thinly sliced

1 tablespoon olive oil

1 1/2 pounds Swiss chard, chopped or sliced
    and washed (see sidebar for instructions)

Coarse-grained salt and cracked
    black pepper

1/4 teaspoon red pepper flakes

PLACE garlic, onion, and oil in largest nonstick pan you have.
Cook, stirring often, over medium heat until onion has completely softened and garlic is golden, 15 to 20 minutes. Add
Swiss chard to pan and cook, stirring often, until leaves are tender, 2 to 4 minutes. Season with salt, pepper, and red pepper
flakes. Stir until evenly distributed. Taste and adjust seasonings.
Serve immediately.

Slow-Roasted Tomatoes with Garlic and Thyme

A simple side dish you can prepare ahead. These tomatoes are delicious served room temperature with a few drops of your favorite vinegar and a drizzle of extra-virgin olive oil.

4 TO 6 SERVINGS

8 ripe, firm Roma tomatoes or any small ripe and sweet tomato

½ teaspoon coarse-grained salt

Cracked black pepper

8 small sprigs thyme

1 clove garlic, thinly sliced

1 tablespoon vinegar (any kind)

2 tablespoons olive oil

PREHEAT oven to 300°F. Core tomatoes and then cut a ¾-inch-deep X into core end of each tomato. Sprinkle insides of tomatoes with salt and pepper. Stuff a thyme sprig and a slice of garlic into each tomato.

PLACE tomatoes in a shallow baking dish in neat little rows. Okay, so they don't have to be neat. Bake tomatoes 1½ to 2 hours, or until shriveled but not dried out. When ready to serve, drizzle a bit of vinegar and oil to taste over the tomatoes.

SHORTCUT CHEF If all you have time to do is set out the ingredients and tools, then so be it. If you've got more time, prep the tomatoes, place them in your oven, and set the timer to sound 1½ hours prior to dinner. They reheat nicely, so cook them completely ahead if you've got the time.

MORPH Turn these tomatoes into a heartier cheesy side dish to serve with a lean supper. Just before you're ready to eat, shave a little Parmesan cheese over each tomato and run them under the broiler until the cheese is melted, 3 to 5 minutes.

These tomatoes are also great smashed between slices of toasted garlic-rubbed bread, making the beginnings of a great sandwich; you fill in the rest. They're great in frittatas, pasta salads, or warm pasta dishes, for that matter.

Pasta, Polenta, Beans, and Rice

MOST OF US HAVE MASTERED boiling water and opening jars of sauce. Branching out won't be hard. Pasta suppers add great variety to your diet. If you use a light sauce, you'll get a quick, nutritious, low-calorie, one-dish meal. Even using heavier sauces made with high-calorie items such as sausage is okay because you'll be distributing the calories among all the portions and thus use less than you would if sausage were the entrée.

Polenta is a stylish supper; it's delicious, it has fewer calories per serving than pasta, it's just as quick, and you can easily morph the leftovers into another meal. In your honor, we've come up with a self-bake just-add-water (and a pat of butter) recipe for polenta. Just about any pasta topping is great spooned over polenta, so give it a try. Eaten plain or with a shaving or two of Parmesan cheese, it's one of my all-time favorite comfort foods.

A word about beans: Don't post the menu in advance when you're serving them as the entrée for the first time, and start with Spicy Black Bean Chili (page 232). Everyone loves chili, especially if you serve it with Quick Corn Bread (page 231). Once you've earned your family's trust, you can progress from there. Sandwich a bean dinner in between two more popular dinners. Remember, if you need to change your diet, you have to be willing to try some of these things. All these recipes are Dad-tested. I'm not saying my dad loved every dish, but if he complained too loudly, we didn't put it in the book.

Pasta with Fast Tomato Sauce

If all you've got in the house is a pound of pasta and two cans of tomatoes, you've got the makings of a great dinner. This quick, homemade alternative to high-sugar, high-fat, high-priced, jarred pasta sauces is simple to prepare and something you can proudly serve. The vegetarian sauce stands on its own or is wonderful enhanced with the addition of Italian sausage, ground beef, or homemade meatballs.

6 SERVINGS

¼ cup extra-virgin olive oil

4 medium cloves garlic, minced

Two 28-ounce cans crushed or diced tomatoes with juice

1 teaspoon coarse-grained salt

Cracked black pepper

¼ cup coarsely chopped basil leaves (about 20 leaves)

1 pound uncooked pasta, such as penne or ziti

PLACE olive oil and garlic in a large sauté pan and turn heat to medium. Cook until garlic is fragrant but do not brown. Stir in tomatoes, salt, and pepper to taste. Reduce heat to medium-low and simmer until sauce has slightly thickened, stirring occasionally, 10 to 15 minutes. Taste and adjust seasonings. Add basil and simmer for 1 minute more. Meanwhile, cook pasta according to package directions in plenty of rapidly boiling water until al dente. Drain pasta and season with salt. Serve sauce over cooked pasta and stash leftover sauce in the freezer for another meal.

SHORTCUT CHEF
It's already a shortcut meal but gather all the ingredients, mince the garlic, and assemble the tools you'll need. Cook the pasta if that will free up some time for you later.

MORPH
Make this sauce in batches —it freezes well. But the beauty of this sauce is that it is so quick. Use it on a meatball sandwich, as a base for ratatouille, or to invigorate your favorite beef stew. Embellish the vegetarian version with rinsed, chopped capers; a few anchovies; chopped fresh oregano, parsley, or thyme; or ripe olives.

If you've got leftover pasta hanging around, place it in an ovenproof dish, toss to coat well with tomato sauce, and top with a slice or two of provolone, Parmesan, or part-skim milk mozzarella cheese for a quick baked pasta supper. Heat in a 375°F oven until pasta is heated through and cheese is bubbly, about 30 minutes.

FROM MOM'S LIPS TO YOUR EARS
Use good canned tomatoes. I like Muir Glen and Progresso.

Spaghetti and Meatballs

Of course we have a recipe for spaghetti and meatballs. This isn't the do-without, make-your-family-miserable, have-no-fun, weight-loss cookbook! If you're going to take the time to make these super-delicious, super-moist meatballs, make at least a quadruple batch. They freeze well. Then next time you're craving spaghetti and meatballs, all you'll have to do is boil noodles if you also have ready-to-go Microwave Tomato Sauce (page 247) in your freezer.

6 SERVINGS

FOR THE MEATBALLS

2 slices bread, crusts removed

6 tablespoons plain low-fat yogurt

I teaspoon plus I tablespoon olive oil

I teaspoon water

I teaspoon minced garlic (about I clove)

2 tablespoons chopped flat-leaf parsley leaves

Coarse-grained salt and cracked black pepper

2 large egg whites, lightly beaten

¾ pound lean ground sirloin

FOR THE PASTA SAUCE

I tablespoon minced garlic (about 3 cloves)

One 28-ounce can crushed or diced tomatoes with juice

I teaspoon coarse-grained salt

Cracked black pepper

¾ pound uncooked spaghetti

¼ cup coarsely chopped basil leaves (about 20 leaves)

PREPARE MEATBALLS: Combine bread and yogurt in bowl you'll make meatballs in. Let stand 10 minutes to soften. In a medium sauté pan, heat 1 teaspoon olive oil, 1 teaspoon water, and all the garlic (about 4 cloves, for both meatballs and sauce) over medium heat until the garlic is fragrant but not browned, about 2 minutes. Turn off heat and set aside. Mash bread and yogurt together. Add 1 teaspoon cooked garlic (reserving rest for sauce), egg whites, parsley, and salt and pepper to taste; mix until well combined. Add ground sirloin. Mix thoroughly. Shape into meatballs.

PREPARE SAUCE: In a medium saucepan over medium heat, combine remaining cooked garlic with tomatoes and their juice. Bring to a simmer. Stir in salt and pepper. Reduce heat to medium-low and simmer until sauce has slightly thickened, 5 to 7 minutes or longer, depending on how thick tomatoes were to begin with. Taste and adjust seasonings.

COOK MEATBALLS AND BOIL PASTA: In a large nonstick skillet, heat 1 tablespoon olive oil over medium-high heat. Add meatballs and cook, turning often, until golden brown on all sides, about 10 minutes.

WHILE meatballs are browning and sauce is reducing, cook pasta according to package directions in plenty of boiling water until al dente. Drain pasta and season with salt. When meatballs are browned, drain on a plate lined with paper towels to remove excess fat. Add meatballs to pot with sauce. Cook until meatballs are completely cooked through, 7 to 10 minutes more. Add fresh basil and cook 1 minute more. Pour sauce and meatballs over cooked spaghetti and serve immediately. Ideally, the spaghetti should not sit around—it should be cooked at the last minute and served right away.

Guyometer: Real spaghetti and meatballs— now we're talking!

SHORTCUT CHEF

If you don't have pasta sauce in your freezer by now, I'm sure you have frozen meatballs from the last time you made this. Right? I'm trying to make your life easy—work with me, people.

Sauté the garlic for the meatballs and spaghetti sauce at the same time using the pot you'll prepare the sauce in. Make the sauce ahead, make the meatballs ahead, and cook the noodles a little earlier if it will make things easier.

Spaghetti with Baby Back Rib Sauce

You know those rich meat sauces you get in fancy Italian restaurants, the kind you'd never make at home, the kind you almost never order because you know you're asking for cardiac trouble? This reduced-calorie, velvety rich, deeply flavored sauce possesses an almost smoky quality and rivals the best of them.

4 SERVINGS

½ slab baby back ribs (8 ribs), separated

Coarse-grained salt and cracked black pepper

1 teaspoon minced garlic

¼ teaspoon red pepper flakes

One 28-ounce can crushed or diced tomatoes with
   juice or whole tomatoes in puree

1 pound uncooked spaghetti

*Guyometer:
Don't be late
for dinner.*

HEAT a large nonstick skillet over medium-high heat and place ribs in skillet. Season with salt and pepper to taste. Cook, turning occasionally, until ribs are golden brown (discard any excess fat). Reduce heat to medium-low, add garlic and crushed red pepper flakes to pan, and cook for 1 minute. Add tomatoes (crush in pan with a fork; for whole tomatoes, use your hands) and their juice or puree to pan, and adjust heat to a steady simmer. Taste for seasoning. Cover and cook, stirring occasionally, until rib meat is falling off the bone and very tender, about 1 hour.

SHORTCUT CHEF
This is one of those sauces that freeze well. Make a double or triple batch and freeze in family-size batches. It won't take you any more time and there will be something good to defrost next week.

MORPH This is excellent served over Creamy Baked Polenta (page 227).

MEANWHILE, cook pasta in plenty of boiling water according to package directions. Drain pasta, return to pot, and season with salt. Pour rib sauce over pasta, tossing to coat evenly, and serve. You might want to take the meat off the bones and tear it up so you don't hear, "I only get one or two tiny ribs? I'll starve."

Linguine with Zucchini

If you find yourself with only a few minutes to prepare supper, try this recipe. Chances are you'll have most of the ingredients on hand. Turn this light supper into a hearty meal with the addition of sautéed shrimp or chicken. Pump up the flavors with red pepper flakes, capers, anchovies, or crumbled feta cheese.

4 TO 6 SERVINGS

1 pound uncooked linguine

1 tablespoon extra-virgin olive oil or butter

2 cloves garlic, minced

3 scallions, thinly sliced

3 medium zucchini or yellow squash, cut into cubes

1/4 cup basil leaves

2 tablespoons minced mint leaves

1 cup soft bread crumbs, toasted

Coarse-grained salt and cracked black pepper

4 teaspoons grated Parmesan cheese

*Guyometer:
Well, it wasn't steak but it was pretty good for healthy stuff.*

COOK pasta in plenty of boiling water according to package directions until al dente. Drain pasta, return to pot, and season with salt.

MEANWHILE, heat olive oil or butter in a large sauté pan over medium heat. Add garlic and cook for a minute or so. Add scallions and zucchini or yellow squash. Cook, stirring occasionally, over medium-low heat just until squash is cooked through. Add basil, mint, cooked pasta, and bread crumbs to pan. Toss until well combined and pasta is heated through. Season generously with salt and pepper to taste. Divide among serving plates. Top with Parmesan cheese.

SHORTCUT CHEF

Slice the zucchini and scallions in advance. Cook the bread crumbs ahead, and if car-pool duties are particularly crazy, cook the pasta ahead, too. It reheats okay in the microwave.

Pasta with Sausage and Broccoli Rabe

For goodness' sake, you can't eat the same thing all the time or you'll go mad with boredom. This is a palatable way to try broccoli rabe (also called rapini). Heck, anything combined with real sausage has got to be good, no? If you positively can't make yourself try broccoli rabe, use regular broccoli or Swiss chard or even beet greens.

4 TO 6 SERVINGS

1 pound broccoli rabe, trimmed of damaged leaves

1 pound pasta (orecchiette is particularly good)

2 tablespoons water

4 cloves garlic, very thinly sliced

½ pound Italian sausage, cut into ¼-inch slices

CUT broccoli rabe into 3- to 4-inch pieces, discarding stems. Place in a large soup pot and cover with cold water. Turn heat to high and bring just to a simmer. Immediately turn off heat and drain, reserving 1 cup of cooking liquid. Rinse broccoli rabe with cold water until it has cooled off or spread it out on a towel to cool.

MEANWHILE, cook pasta in a large pot of boiling water according to package directions until al dente. While pasta is cooking, place 2 tablespoons water in a cold skillet with garlic and sausage and then turn heat to medium-low. Cook, stirring occasionally, until garlic is golden and sausage is cooked through, 5 to 7 minutes. Pour reserved broccoli water into pan with sausage.

SHORTCUT CHEF

Cook the broccoli rabe the night before and you'll be way ahead. Whatever you do, read the recipe through start to finish before you get started. It's a little out of the ordinary but relatively painless.

Cooking Thin with Chef Kathleen

WHEN pasta is cooked, drain it, place it right back in pot you cooked it in, and season with salt. My mom says you could use a real serving dish but I say why bother getting one dirty? You'll just have to wash it and the pot's already headed for the dishwasher. Anyway, do what you want and when you figure it out, pour sausage sauce over pasta and stir in cooked broccoli rabe. Taste and adjust seasonings. Serve immediately.

Guyometer: Now this is real food.

This is a great dish to make for company, especially if you cook the broccoli rabe early. Garnish it with toasted fresh bread crumbs and/or freshly grated pecorino Romano or Parmesan cheese.

Linguine with Tomato and Shrimp Sauce

If I told you that it was possible to make pasta sauce from start to finish in the microwave, would you make it? Chances are you have most of the ingredients on hand. One-stop shopping at a reputable fish market to pick up the shrimp is probably all the foraging necessary to get this fit, fast feast on the table.

4 SERVINGS

3 cloves garlic, minced

½ cup diced sweet onion (such as Vidalia, Walla Walla, Granex, or Maui)

1 tablespoon extra-virgin olive oil

One 28-ounce can crushed tomatoes with juice

2 small bay leaves, broken in half

⅛ teaspoon red pepper flakes or to taste

Coarse-grained salt

1 pound uncooked pasta, such as linguine or spaghetti

1 pound medium shrimp, peeled and deveined

¼ cup coarsely chopped flat-leaf parsley

IN an 8-cup Pyrex measuring cup or large microwave-proof bowl, place garlic, onion, and olive oil. Toss thoroughly to coat. Microwave on medium-high for 5 minutes. Add tomatoes and their juice, bay leaves, and red pepper flakes to garlic and onion; stir to combine. Microwave uncovered on medium-high for 20 minutes, or until thickened. Season with salt to taste. Adjust consistency by adding water if sauce is too thick. Cook a bit longer if it's too thin.

MEANWHILE, cook pasta in plenty of rapidly boiling water according to package directions until al dente. Drain pasta and season with salt.

ONCE tomato sauce is proper consistency, immediately add shrimp. Make sure all shrimp are covered with sauce. Let stand 5 minutes—the heat of the sauce cooks the shrimp. Check shrimp for doneness. Remove bay leaves. If shrimp isn't cooked through, microwave uncovered on medium-low in 1-minute increments until done. Add parsley, stir, taste, and adjust seasonings. Pour shrimp sauce over cooked pasta, toss, and serve immediately.

Guyometer:
I love shrimp.

SHORTCUT CHEF
If you have time to get ahead, mince the garlic, dice the onions, clean the shrimp, and/or chop the parsley. Buy the shrimp peeled and deveined if it's the difference between cooking at home or eating out. It will cost you a little more but not more than eating out. Cook the pasta in advance if you're really in a time pinch. Get in the habit of prepping ahead. Ten focused minutes in the kitchen devoted toward dinner prep is all the edge you need sometimes. If you're really in a jam, you can leave out the garlic or onions or use prechopped jarred garlic and frozen chopped onions.

MORPH Make a double batch up to the point of adding the shrimp and freeze it. Pack it in a nice microwave-proof container clearly labeled. You can thank me later.

Pasta with Baked Tomatoes, Bread Crumbs, and Cheese

I really have to portion my serving when I make this supper. It's so unbelievably good that I can hardly control myself. The pungent aroma of baking garlic and herbs wafting through the house as the tomatoes cook sends danger-Will-Robinson-she's-going-to-overeat-again signals to my brain. To stop myself from eating the whole batch in a single sitting, I make only enough for the number of people coming to the table, not even a half portion more.

4 TO 6 SERVINGS

4 cups coarse bread crumbs (preferably homemade)

2 ounces pecorino Romano, freshly grated and loosely packed

2 tablespoons olive oil

2 cloves garlic, minced

¼ cup loosely packed, roughly chopped oregano leaves

Coarse-grained salt and cracked black pepper

One 28-ounce can whole tomatoes with juice

1 pound uncooked pasta, such as penne

SHORTCUT CHEF

Make the cheesy herb bread crumbs ahead, prep the tomatoes, and cook the pasta if you want to. Naturally, precooked pasta isn't quite as good as just cooked, but if you're sure the *New York Times* won't be reviewing you this evening, pre-cook it, especially if it's the difference between a home-cooked meal and Yellow Pages call-in cuisine.

PREHEAT oven to 425°F. In a small bowl, combine bread crumbs, cheese, olive oil, garlic, oregano, and salt and pepper to taste. Taste and adjust seasonings. Set aside. Drain tomatoes directly into a microwave-proof measuring cup or glass dish. Squish (but don't break apart) the tomatoes as you're draining them and set juices aside for a minute. Place tomatoes in a single layer in a glass baking dish large enough to hold them. Distribute bread crumb mixture evenly over tomatoes. Try to keep crumbs on top of tomatoes, letting as little as possible fall between them, but don't drive yourself crazy if the crumbs fall all over the place.

Cooking Thin with Chef Kathleen

It's just food. Place tomatoes in oven and bake until crumbs are golden and you can't stand to wait another minute longer to eat, about 40 minutes.

WHILE tomatoes are baking, cook pasta in a large pot of boiling water according to package directions until al dente. Microwave reserved juices from tomatoes on high for 15 minutes, until thickened.

WHEN pasta is cooked, drain, place in a large serving bowl, and season with salt. Pour reduced tomato juice and baked tomatoes over pasta. Stir until ingredients are evenly distributed. Serve immediately, while crumbs are still crunchy.

Guyometer:
Really great.
It's pasta.

Prep the dish up to the point of putting it in the oven. Place the tomatoes in the oven and set your oven timer to start baking so the dish will time perfectly with your preferred dinner hour. Throw the pasta in the pot when you walk in the door, toss with the reserved tomato liquid, and voilà, you're done, another healthy dinner.

I know you've got bread crumbs in your freezer because you completely understand the importance of this time-saving tip and the significant role this simple savory ingredient plays in food. Keep them in your freezer with all the other get-dinner-on-the-table-in-a-hurry supplies you've got stashed in there. Work with me.

Don't panic when you get to pecorino Romano cheese. Yes, it's my policy not to send you on ingredient wild-goose chases and yes, you can use a good-quality Parmesan instead, but pecorino Romano is a pungent, dry, aged sheep's milk cheese particularly useful in the healthful kitchen because a little goes a long, long way. Buy a small amount and you won't have wasted a lot of money if you hate it.

Pasta with Eggplant

Don't you dare turn the page because you "hate eggplant." Have you ever had my mom's eggplant pasta? I thought not. It's really, really great. You're probably sick of hearing me say that about every recipe, but we did put all our favorites in this book.

4 TO 6 SERVINGS

2 tablespoons olive oil

1½ pounds eggplant (about 1 large), peeled and cut into ¾-inch cubes

1 pound uncooked pasta, such as penne

3 cloves garlic, minced

½ cup diced onion

One 28-ounce can whole tomatoes with juice

12 kalamata olives, pitted and chopped

Coarse-grained salt

¼ teaspoon red pepper flakes

¼ cup roughly chopped basil leaves

PLACE 1 tablespoon of olive oil in a 10-inch nonstick skillet over medium heat. Add eggplant and cook, stirring often, until golden brown on all sides, about 20 minutes.

MEANWHILE, cook pasta in boiling water according to package directions until al dente. While pasta is cooking, prepare sauce.

PLACE remaining 1 tablespoon olive oil, garlic, and onion in a 3-quart saucepan and turn heat to medium. Sauté a few minutes and then add tomatoes with their juice, crushing them with your

SHORTCUT CHEF

Prep as many of the ingredients as you can anytime you get a window of even 10 minutes throughout the day or the night before. Peel and dice the eggplant, chop the onions and garlic, crush the tomatoes, and cook the pasta ahead if it makes your life easier.

MORPH

If cooking at home is new, I can't urge you enough to make big batches of every recipe you can. Freeze extras in dinner-size portions for those days you're just too tired to cook. It takes a little while to get into a good cook-at-home groove, and if you give yourself a night off here and there, it's easier to stick with it.

fingers as you add them to the pot. Add cooked eggplant and olives to the pot and cook until sauce has thickened and reduced a little, about 20 minutes. Season with salt, red pepper flakes, and basil. Cook for 1 minute more. Taste and adjust seasonings. When pasta is al dente, drain and season with salt. Add pasta to sauce, stirring to combine. Serve immediately.

You're going to have to get two pans dirty for this recipe but stay with it. It's worth it. When you sauté the eggplant don't panic when three of the cubes soak up all the oil in the first 10 seconds. Whatever you do, resist the urge to add more oil to the pan because eggplant is sponge-like. It will soak up every drop you add, certainly more than you'd ever want to consume. The eggplant will brown on all sides eventually. You just have to watch it the whole time. Don't walk away from the stove during this part, and reduce the heat if you need to.

FROM MOM'S LIPS TO YOUR EARS

Just because you've never tasted it doesn't mean it's not good. I guess you've heard that before.

Pasta with Tomato Sauce and Chickpeas

I wouldn't exactly call my father's reaction to this particular dish ecstatic. He complained rather loudly that he got too many chickpeas and not enough noodles. And he did threaten to kill me for making him suffer through the testing of all this "healthy food." ■ My mom sees things a little differently: "He ate it. That's all that matters. He didn't eat steak with béarnaise sauce. He ate chickpea pasta. So he complained a little. What's new?"

4 SERVINGS

1 tablespoon olive oil

2 cloves garlic

1 medium onion, diced

8 ounces uncooked pasta, such as penne

One 15½-ounce can crushed tomatoes with juice

2 red bell peppers, roasted, peeled, seeded, and diced

¼ teaspoon cracked black pepper

½ teaspoon coarse-grained salt

1 cup Chicken Stock (page 95), canned broth, or water

One 15-ounce can chickpeas (also called ceci or garbanzo beans), drained and rinsed

¼ cup roughly chopped basil leaves

Guyometer:
Not my favorite but
better than most
of the stuff the
nutritionist tells
you to eat.

PLACE olive oil, garlic, and onion in a 3-quart saucepan. Turn heat to medium and cook, stirring occasionally, until onion begins to soften, 8 to 10 minutes. Meanwhile, cook pasta in plenty of boiling water according to package directions until al dente. Drain pasta and season with salt.

ADD tomatoes with juice, red peppers, pepper, and salt. Reduce heat to a simmer and cook 10 minutes. Add chicken stock or water if necessary to thin out sauce. Add chickpeas and basil to sauce and cook 5 minutes more. Taste and adjust seasonings. Add cooked, drained pasta to sauce and serve immediately.

SHORTCUT CHEF
Use jarred roasted peppers in place of fresh, use a microplane grater to grate the garlic quickly, and cook the noodles ahead.

MORPH Cook extra chickpeas (or buy an extra can) and dress them with your favorite salad dressing. They're good that way.

FROM MOM'S LIPS TO YOUR EARS
The recipe calls for canned chickpeas because we knew you probably wouldn't want to cook your own. But if you have the time, cook them from dried. There is a taste difference, but mostly cooking your own beans is no harder than cooking pasta noodles and it's a good habit to get into.

Pasta with Fava Beans

This is not the quickest dinner to get on the table, but with a little advance planning and prep, it's pretty straightforward. This is a great dish for weekend entertaining, especially if you want to show off a little. It's simple yet very elegant. ▪ It's true, fava beans require a few extra minutes in the kitchen, but it would be a culinary sin to let spring go by without celebrating this wonderful shelling bean in all its glory.

4 TO 6 SERVINGS

2 pounds fresh fava beans

I pound uncooked orecchiette pasta

2 tablespoons extra-virgin olive oil

2 large shallots, minced

I tablespoon water

One 28-ounce can whole plum tomatoes, drained

Coarse-grained salt and cracked black pepper

2 tablespoons thinly sliced scallions (white part only)

2 tablespoons coarsely chopped mint leaves

2 tablespoons coarsely chopped basil leaves

2 ounces feta cheese, finely crumbled

BRING a large pot of water to a boil. Shell fava beans from their large pods. Add beans to rapidly boiling water and simmer 45 seconds. Using a basket, skimmer, or slotted spoon, transfer immediately to an ice bath to cool. Remove beans from ice bath and peel or squeeze outer green skin off each bean. Set aside.

RETURN water to a boil, add pasta, and cook according to package directions until al dente. While pasta is cooking, in a large non-stick skillet, heat oil over medium heat. Add shallots and 1 table-

SHORTCUT CHEF

Prep the favas a day ahead or enlist the aid of a few after-school helpers and this pasta supper won't be too tough to master. Gather all the ingredients, mince the shallots, and cook the pasta if it's just for family—although Italians say every-one should be sitting down before the pasta is drained.

Cooking Thin with Chef Kathleen

spoon water; stir until shallots are evenly coated with oil and water. Reduce heat to low, cover, and cook until completely softened and translucent, about 5 minutes. Increase heat to medium-high; add tomatoes and salt and pepper to taste. Using a wooden spoon or spatula, break down or chop tomatoes right in the pan. Simmer tomatoes 2 minutes or so; add fava beans, scallions, mint, and basil. Cook another 5 minutes and taste and adjust seasonings.

WHEN pasta is done, drain, season with salt, and add to sauce. Add cheese and stir until just incorporated. Taste, adjust seasonings, and serve immediately.

If you want to impress Mr. Right: I don't think this would do it for him, but if you want to bowl over one of your girlfriends, this would be the dish to serve.

I can hear a few of you from here. Fava beans, what on earth? Now is as good a time as any for a little out-of-the-box cooking. Go get some fava beans. They're pods 5 to 7 inches in length and should be firm and bright green. Don't buy shriveled pods or pods blemished with black spots. Fava beans require two peelings. You remove the beans from the pods, then after the quick-cool method described in the recipe, you peel the thin, mostly bitter outer skin off the actual fava bean. So plan ahead and don't skip over this recipe. Fresh fava beans are a wonderful treat.

FROM MOM'S LIPS TO YOUR EARS

Don't think you can substitute onions or garlic for the shallots and expect the same results. You can substitute them okay and the sauce will be good, but you really should have shallots on your shopping list by now. I'm a mother. You don't listen. I nag.

Lazy Man's Lasagne

Leftover vegetables are lovely layered throughout lasagne—a perfect way to increase the good calories in a dish usually thought of as off limits for the health-minded. Sliced eggplant, zucchini, yellow squash, portobello mushrooms, tomatoes, and roasted peppers have made appearances in Daelemans family lasagne. Sautéed, pressed, and chopped leafy greens are easy to sneak in too. Spinach, beet greens, turnip greens, chard, or arugula can be added to the tomato sauce or folded into the herbed ricotta cheese. ■ Lasagne is a perfect dish to make on a lazy afternoon. Make a double batch; it won't take you any more time, and it *will* give you a night off next week.

10 TO 12 SERVINGS

¾ pound uncooked lasagne noodles

FOR THE MUSHROOM-TOMATO SAUCE

1 tablespoon olive oil

¾ pound mushrooms, cleaned and diced into ¼-inch cubes

½ teaspoon coarse-grained salt

Cracked black pepper

1 batch Microwave Tomato Sauce (page 247)

¼ teaspoon red pepper flakes

¼ to ½ cup loosely packed, roughly chopped basil leaves

FOR THE HERBED RICOTTA CHEESE

1 pound ricotta cheese

1 pound spinach, cooked, squeezed dry, and chopped

Mixed herbs, roughly chopped (any combination of oregano, mint, basil, parsley, and rosemary)

¼ teaspoon coarse-grained salt

¼ teaspoon cracked black pepper

½ pound part-skim milk mozzarella, grated

Cooking Thin with Chef Kathleen

PREHEAT oven to 350°F. In a large pot of boiling water, cook lasagne noodles according to package directions until al dente. Drain, lay noodles side by side on towels or a cookie sheet lined with parchment so they don't stick together, and set aside.

MEANWHILE, PREPARE MUSHROOM-TOMATO SAUCE: Place olive oil and mushrooms in a 3-quart saucepan over high heat. Season with salt and pepper and cook, stirring often, until mushrooms give up their water and dry out, 5 to 7 minutes. Add tomato sauce and red pepper flakes and simmer for 10 minutes; add basil and simmer 5 minutes more. Taste and adjust seasonings with salt and black pepper as necessary.

PREPARE HERBED RICOTTA CHEESE: Place cheese in a small mixing bowl. Add spinach, fresh herbs, salt, and pepper; stir to combine. Taste and adjust seasonings.

ASSEMBLE LASAGNE: In a 9 × 13-inch nonreactive baking dish, pour just enough sauce to barely cover the pan bottom so the noodles don't stick. Arrange one layer of cooked lasagne noodles over sauce. Cut them to fit. Drop small spoonfuls (dollops) of herbed ricotta cheese evenly over noodles, roughly 6 tablespoons of ricotta cheese per layer. Next, sprinkle 2 to 3 tablespoons of grated mozzarella cheese and then ¼ to ½ cup of sauce over this layer. Add second layer of noodles and, using a large spoon or spatula, press to compact layers. Continue to layer ingredients until you run out or the pan gets full. End with a layer of sauce and mozzarella cheese. There's a prize if you come out even but no one ever has. Bake 1 hour, or until lasagne is brown and bubbly and you can't wait another minute.

*Guyometer:
Why don't we
have this more
often?*

SHORTCUT CHEF

Cook the spinach and make the herbed ricotta cheese ahead of time. Make the tomato sauce ahead and cook the noodles in advance if you have the time. Start after breakfast.

FROM MOM'S LIPS TO YOUR EARS

This is not dinner in an instant, so make it on a day you have extra time. I suppose you can cheat and use good-quality store-bought tomato sauce, but I hope some of this book has sunk in by now and you've got a freezer full of Microwave Tomato Sauce and grated mozzarella cheese. If you do, the preparations will be quick.

Haight Family (Thanksgiving) Noodles

Try this when you have a lot of time. When my sister-in-law, Renie, announced she was going to bring her famous chicken and noodles to Thanksgiving dinner, I couldn't understand why. Renie says, "The savory perfume of the simmering broth wafting through the house brings back wonderful memories, inspiring me to get busy with all the other holiday preparations." ■ Part of the ritual of this dish is making pasta noodles from scratch. If you've got the time, make your own. Otherwise, choose a very good-quality dried noodle.

6 TO 8 SERVINGS AS A MAIN COURSE; 8 TO 10 AS A SIDE DISH

FOR THE CHICKEN AND BROTH

One 3-to-3½-pound whole chicken

Coarse-grained salt and cracked black pepper

1 medium onion, peeled and cut in half

1 handful baby carrots or 2 large carrots, peeled and cut in half

5 parsley stems with leaves still attached

5 cloves garlic, peeled, cut in half, and sprout removed (use less if you're not a fan of garlic)

FOR THE NOODLES

3 cups flour

½ teaspoon coarse-grained salt

3 large eggs, beaten

If the queen's coming for dinner: Serve this anyway. It's a rather homey dish and she can't get home cooking very often in the castle.

PREPARE CHICKEN AND BROTH: Season chicken inside and out with salt and pepper the night before or at least 1 hour ahead and refrigerate. In a large stockpot, place chicken, onion, carrots, parsley, and garlic. Add water just to cover chicken. Bring to a boil, then immediately reduce heat to a steady simmer. Skim off any foam and discard. Cook until meat is falling off the bone, 1½ to 2 hours. Remove chicken from pot. Reduce stock until you have 6 cups more or less. Taste stock and correct seasonings;

strain and reserve. Let chicken cool and remove the meat from the bones. Discard skin and bones and shred the chicken meat into bite-size pieces. This can be done the day before.

PREPARE NOODLES: Stir flour and salt together in a large mixing bowl and make a well in the center. Add eggs and, using a fork or your hands and working from the center out, gradually mix flour and eggs together until crumbly. You may have to add a few drops of water to bring dough together. Place dough on a counter and knead by hand until it forms a firm, smooth ball, 10 to 12 minutes. Cover with plastic wrap and let stand 45 minutes before rolling and cutting.

ROLL AND CUT NOODLES: If you have a pasta machine, roll dough according to machine instructions. To roll dough by hand, cut dough into quarters. Place one fourth of dough on lightly floured work surface. Roll from the center out with a rolling pin, turning dough in quarter turns as it gets larger. Pat and stretch dough using the palm of your hand every now and then until it is the thickness of fettuccine. Cut into ¼-inch-wide strips and place on a cookie sheet lined with parchment and dusted with a little flour. Spread out noodles so they don't gum up. Continue rolling and cutting until you've used up all the dough. Let pasta dry 30 minutes or overnight.

FINISH NOODLES: Pour chicken meat and chicken broth into a large soup pot and bring to a rolling boil. Add pasta noodles and cook on high 2 to 3 minutes, or until noodles are done. Taste and correct seasonings. Serve immediately in wide soup bowls.

Guyometer:
Fantastic.

SHORTCUT CHEF
Renie cooks the chicken, strains the broth, and separates the meat from the bones two days before Thanksgiving. When cooled in the refrigerator the fat rises to the top and hardens, making it easy to spoon off and discard. She prepares the homemade noodles on Thanksgiving eve and finishes the dish just before the bird is carved for Thanksgiving dinner. The noodles were traditionally served over mashed potatoes, so a small portion is fine.

FROM MOM'S LIPS TO YOUR EARS
Any day but Thanksgiving this is a complete dinner when served with a salad.

Carol's Tuna Pasta Salad

When it's just too hot to cook, try this hassle-free one-dish dinner. It's cool, light, and satisfying. Plain yogurt is whisked into the lemony dressing, eliminating unnecessary calories without compromising flavor. ■ Just for the record, I usually hate pasta salads. They're always dried out and bland. The noodles suck up all the dressing and require so much more dressing I might as well have had a quarter pounder with cheese and super-size fries. ■ I love this one and make excuses to go over to Carol's for dinner. It's really, really good and very, very simple. Pasta salads are Carol's specialty; try her Cold Pasta Salad with Roasted Peppers, Mozzarella, and Mango (next recipe).

6 TO 7 SERVINGS

I pound uncooked pasta, such as fusilli

¼ cup plain low-fat yogurt

¼ cup low-fat mayonnaise

⅓ cup fresh lemon juice (about I lemon) or more to taste

¼ teaspoon Tabasco sauce (or more to taste)

¼ cup loosely packed, coarsely chopped flat-leaf parsley

Coarse-grained salt and cracked black pepper

½ red bell pepper, roasted, peeled, seeded, and diced

⅓ cup loosely packed, thinly sliced scallions (white and green parts)

I tablespoon small capers, rinsed and coarsely chopped

One to two 6-ounce cans white albacore tuna packed in water, drained

BRING a large pot of water to a boil over high heat and cook pasta according to package directions until al dente. Drain, season with salt, and place in a large serving bowl; set aside.

PREPARE dressing in a small nonreactive bowl by whisking together yogurt, mayonnaise, lemon juice, Tabasco, and parsley. Taste and adjust seasonings with salt and pepper. Refrigerate until you're ready to dress the salad.

ADD red pepper, scallions, capers, and tuna to bowl with pasta. Break up tuna with a fork, leaving as many large chunks as you like. Toss until all ingredients are combined. Add dressing to pasta and toss until evenly distributed. Serve at room temperature or refrigerate a few hours.

Guyometer:
Is there more of
this stuff?

SHORTCUT CHEF
Make the pasta the night before, or the whole dish if you've got the time. It's great leftover.

Cold Pasta Salad with Roasted Peppers, Mozzarella, and Mango

My sister, Carol, usually serves this in the summer when it's too hot to cook. But she does make it in the winter when Chilean mangos show up in the markets. It's great served in smaller portions over a bed of mixed greens and topped with slices of seared, boneless, skinless chicken breast.

4 TO 6 SERVINGS (OR MORE AS A SIDE DISH)

1 pound uncooked pasta such as fusilli

Coarse-grained salt

½ cup balsamic vinegar

1 to 2 tablespoons olive oil

Cracked black pepper

1 ripe mango, peeled, seeded, and cut into thin strips

3 tomatoes, cut into chunks

1 red or yellow bell pepper, roasted, peeled, seeded, and cut into thin strips

1 to 2 balls fresh mozzarella (about ½ pound), cut into small chunks

½ cup loosely packed, roughly chopped basil leaves

COOK pasta in boiling water according to package directions until al dente. Drain and season with salt. In a large serving bowl, whisk together vinegar, oil, and salt and pepper to taste. Add mango, tomatoes, roasted peppers, and cheese. Stir to coat evenly with dressing. Add pasta and basil; stir to combine. Taste and adjust seasonings. Serve or keep refrigerated until serving time.

SHORTCUT CHEF
Cheat and use jarred roasted peppers, cook the pasta earlier, and whisk the dressing together ahead of time.

Guyometer:
It's better with
the chicken.

Creamy Baked Polenta

To me, a native Floridian, a former Maui resident, and a total California devotee, there are few good things about winter. Creamy baked polenta is one of them. It tastes so rich you feel as though you're committing cardinal culinary sins, but you're not. Polenta can be served simply with butter or cheese (oh, just a teensy bit) or topped with any sauce you'd serve over pasta. Leftovers can be spread on a cookie sheet and refrigerated overnight to become what's known as hard polenta. Hard polenta can be sliced into cubes, squares, triangles, or cookie cutter shapes and then baked or grilled and topped with savory sauces. Believe it or not, little cubes of leftover hard polenta can become unusually delicious croutons in your salad.

4 TO 6 SERVINGS

I quart water

I teaspoon coarse-grained salt

¼ teaspoon cracked black pepper

I cup coarse-ground polenta

I tablespoon butter

PREHEAT oven to 350°F. Pour water into a 1½-quart nonreactive baking dish. Add salt, pepper, and polenta; stir. Add butter. Place dish on center oven rack and bake uncovered 40 to 50 minutes, stirring at the halfway point. Polenta is done when practically all the liquid has been absorbed. Taste it. If it's creamy and good, it's done. If it's granular and unpleasant, let it cook a little longer.

> **MORPH** Make extra, turn it into hard polenta, and make Polenta with Blue Cheese and Walnuts (page 230).
>
> **FROM MOM'S LIPS TO YOUR EARS**
> Don't use instant polenta. It won't work in this recipe, and coarse-ground polenta just plain tastes better.

Meat Sauce for Polenta or Noodles

SHORTCUT CHEF
Prep your veggies the night before or throw the veggies in a mini chopper (separately) instead of mincing them perfectly by hand.

MORPH Make oodles and oodles of this stuff—it freezes quite well. Second time around serve it over lightly buttered fettuccine. Did I say buttuh? Moderate, don't eliminate. Balance your calories over the day and week. Skip the butter if you've been devilish this week. The meat sauce is delicious served over broiled leftover hard polenta, with or without a poached egg. Don't knock it until you've tried it.

If you can't get your hands on fresh porcini mushrooms, use 1/4 ounce dried porcini mushrooms. Place them in a small bowl with hot water from the tap for 30 minutes. Remove them from the liquid, rinse them to remove any sand, squeeze dry, and finely chop. Strain the mushroom soaking water through a fine-mesh strainer or cheesecloth and use it in the sauce.

This dish is a faint reminder of the wonderful ragùs featured on San Francisco's Zuni Café menu. If you're ever in the neighborhood, pray Chef Judy Rogers is serving ragù on the night you visit. You'll surely think you've died and gone to gastronomic heaven. But if San Francisco's not on your itinerary, try this recipe. It's very satisfying.

4 SERVINGS WITH 2 1/2 CUPS LEFT OVER

1 tablespoon olive oil

1 onion, peeled, cored, and finely diced

1 carrot, peeled and finely diced

1 stalk celery, finely diced

1/2 pound fresh porcini mushrooms, cleaned and finely diced, or 1/4 ounce dried porcini, soaked (see sidebar)

3/4 pound lean ground beef or a mixture of beef, veal, and pork

2 tablespoons tomato paste

1/2 cup good-quality red wine

One 28-ounce can peeled plum tomatoes, chopped (reserve juice)

1/4 cup loosely packed, roughly chopped herbs, such as parsley, basil, oregano, and/or sage

Coarse-grained salt and cracked black pepper

IN a 3-quart or similar-size saucepan, heat oil over medium-low heat. Add onion, carrot, celery, and mushrooms and cook until softened, about 15 minutes. Add meat to pan, breaking it up with a spoon, and cook, stirring often, 6 to 8 minutes (you'll still see pink). Add tomato paste (and strained mushroom liquid, if you used dried porcini), wine, tomatoes, and their juice. Bring to a simmer and cook until thickened, about 25 minutes. Add herbs and cook 5 minutes more. Season to taste with salt and pepper.

FROM MOM'S LIPS TO YOUR EARS

I suppose this is a good time to mention that if you scrape tomato paste from its can, place it in a small freezer bag, squish it into a log, and freeze it. You can then cut off the small amounts recipes call for next time.

Polenta with Blue Cheese and Walnuts

If you're new to this healthy lifestyle stuff I wouldn't necessarily announce this side dish ahead of time. Just let it show up one night and don't say a word. Serve it and they will come, trust me. This is a perfect way to use up leftover Creamy Baked Polenta.

4 SERVINGS

½ recipe Creamy Baked Polenta (page 227)

Olive oil or spray

2 ounces best-quality blue cheese (Maytag if available)

¼ cup walnut pieces

TO turn creamy polenta into hard polenta, pour onto a baking sheet with sides. Cover with plastic wrap and place in refrigerator overnight.

PREHEAT broiler to highest setting. Coat a cookie sheet with a fine mist of cooking spray or olive oil or use a nonstick baking pan. Cut hard polenta into 4 or 8 pieces and place on cookie sheet. Spray polenta tops with a fine mist of olive oil or use a pastry brush to brush lightly with oil.

PLACE polenta under broiler and cook until top just starts to brown, 5 to 8 minutes. Remove from oven, crumble cheese and walnuts over top of polenta, then place back under broiler until cheese melts and walnuts are golden, about 2 minutes more. Serve immediately.

SHORTCUT CHEF
If you're not using leftover polenta, make the polenta the night before.

MORPH Turn this into a divine Saturday afternoon lunch by serving two pieces per person with a tossed salad of mixed garden lettuces dressed with sherry vinegar, olive oil, salt, and pepper.

Quick Corn Bread

Don't put butter or honey on the table. If it's not there, you won't be tempted. This corn bread is really, really good straight from the oven. Besides, you can spend those calories someplace else if you want to. We serve this delicious corn bread with Spicy Black Bean Chili (next recipe), Chili Pork Stew (page 325), and light soup dinners.

9 TO 12 SERVINGS

- 1 cup flour
- 1 cup yellow cornmeal
- 3 tablespoons sugar
- 1 ½ teaspoons baking powder
- ½ teaspoon coarse-grained salt
- 1 cup skim milk
- ¼ cup canola or vegetable oil
- 1 large egg or 2 large egg whites, lightly beaten

HEAT oven to 400°F. Spray a 9-inch square baking pan with nonstick cooking spray. Combine flour, cornmeal, sugar, baking powder, and salt in a large bowl. Set aside.

IN a separate smaller bowl, whisk together milk, oil, and egg or egg whites. Pour wet ingredients over dry and, using a fork, stir until just combined. Do not overmix. Spread batter evenly in pan and bake 20 to 25 minutes, or until a toothpick inserted in the center comes out clean. Cut into squares or triangles and serve immediately.

Guyometer: Great, great, great.

SHORTCUT CHEF
The best you can do is to lay out all your ingredients and read the recipe start to finish so when you get in the kitchen you can move through the recipe confidently and quickly.

MORPH Doll it up by adding ½ cup sweet corn kernels, minced jalapeño, and/or some fresh chopped herbs to the batter.

Spicy Black Bean Chili

A batch of this and a slice of **Quick Corn Bread** (previous recipe) and you can have dinner on the table in no time, especially if you cheat and use canned black beans. Cooked dried beans, in my opinion, are better tasting and don't take a lot of time to cook, even if you forgot to soak them. Soaking shaves off only a half hour or so of cooking time anyway. If using canned beans means you'll make the chili and skip less nutritious carry-out, that's victory enough. Use the canned beans and don't give it a second thought.

4 TO 6 SERVINGS

½ pound black beans, soaked overnight, or two 19-ounce cans black beans, rinsed and drained

3 cups water, Vegetable Stock (page 96), Chicken Stock (page 95), or canned broth

1 carrot, peeled and quartered

1 stalk celery, quartered

½ large onion, cut in half

1 bay leaf

1 pinch red pepper flakes

FOR THE CHILI

1 cup finely diced sweet onion

1 tablespoon olive oil

One 15-ounce can tomatoes with juice, chopped or whole

1 teaspoon hot chili powder

½ teaspoon ground cumin

⅛ teaspoon ground cayenne

¼ teaspoon salt

PREPARE DRIED BEANS: Place beans in a 3-quart soup pot with water or stock, carrot, celery, onion, bay leaf, and red pepper flakes. Bring to a boil and immediately reduce to a steady simmer. Cook until beans are tender yet firm and still holding their shape, 25 to 35 minutes. Remove from heat and cool in their liquid. Don't overcook.

PREPARE CHILI: While beans are cooking, in a large pot place diced onion and olive oil and cook, covered tightly, stirring occasionally, over medium-low heat until translucent and completely cooked through, 10 to 12 minutes. Be careful not to burn onions—add a teaspoon or two of water if needed.

DRAIN beans in a colander, discarding cooking liquid. Remove and discard the vegetables from beans and transfer beans to pot with cooked onions. Add tomatoes with juice, chili powder, cumin, cayenne, and salt. Simmer chili over medium heat for 10 to 20 minutes, or until flavors are well combined. This is better served the next day but I can never wait that long.

*Guyometer:
Fantastic.
I love chili.*

MORPH Turn this into a meat lover's meal by adding 1/2 pound of cubed sirloin to the pot with the onion. Leftover black bean chili is a great take-to-work meal. Spoon leftover chili over a warm corn tortilla and top with a poached egg for a huevos rancheros takeoff.

You already know what I'm going to say; make a double batch and freeze it. The goal is to eat in at least five nights a week without working too hard at it. This lifestyle requires commitment, planning, and follow-through—not slave labor.

If you used canned beans, choose a good-quality bean—sometimes they're all smashed up already. You don't have to use black beans, either. Pinto beans, red beans, or any other type of bean will work.

Black and White Bean Salad with Cumin Vinaigrette

This is a snappy little salad, bright in color and flavor. Sometimes I call it "salsa" and dump it on things like grilled chicken or fish. When preparing this salad, make extra—it keeps well. I recommend you cook the beans in vegetable or chicken stock, but if you don't have either on hand, use water. You'll still end up with a delicious salad.

SHORTCUT CHEF

Use canned beans but rinse them thoroughly and get good canned beans. Sometimes they're all broken up and not pretty. Use jarred roasted peppers, rinsed well, if you must.

The black and the white colors look pretty but are not necessary (unless you're trying to keep a restaurant dining room full of guests coming back for more). If you do use two beans, cook them in separate pots. The black beans will color the white ones if they are cooked together.

This is one of those times you can reach into your freezer and pull out a bag of individually portioned snack-size bags of peppers you roasted and peeled on a day you had time. Don't even tell me you haven't done that yet. Shame on you.

4 SERVINGS

¹⁄₃ cup dried black beans, soaked overnight

¹⁄₃ cup dried white beans, soaked overnight

2 cups Chicken Stock (page 95), Vegetable Stock (page 96), or canned broth

2 carrots, peeled and cut in half

2 stalks celery, cut in half

1 medium onion, peeled and cut in half

FOR THE CUMIN VINAIGRETTE

¹⁄₄ cup apple cider vinegar

2 tablespoons olive oil

Juice of 1 orange

1 clove garlic, minced

¹⁄₂ teaspoon ground cumin

Coarse-grained salt and cracked black pepper

¹⁄₂ cup fresh corn kernels (about 1 ear)

¹⁄₂ cup diced roasted red bell pepper

2 tablespoons coarsely chopped cilantro or flat-leaf parsley

PLACE beans in separate pots and divide stock, carrots, celery, and onion equally between pots. Bring beans to a boil and immediately reduce to a steady simmer. Cook until tender, yet firm and still holding their shape, about 25 minutes. Remove from heat and cool in their cooking liquid. Don't overcook.

PREPARE VINAIGRETTE: While beans are cooking, whisk together vinegar, oil, orange juice, garlic, cumin, salt, and pepper. Taste and adjust seasonings. Set aside.

WHEN beans have cooled completely, drain and discard carrots, celery, and onion. Transfer beans to a large bowl and add corn, red pepper, and cilantro or parsley. Pour vinaigrette over salad. Mix well. Serve at room temperature or chilled.

Guyometer:
Well, I didn't think
I'd like it but it's
not bad.

IF IT'S UNBEARABLY HOT AND YOU CAN'T BEAR THE THOUGHT OF FIXING AN ENTRÉE

Turn this into a quick entrée by adding a can of drained tuna packed in water and serve the salad on a bed of garden lettuces tossed with some of the dressing. Garnish with cherry tomatoes cut in half; papaya, mango, and avocado; blanched snap peas, green beans, or carrots—whatever appeals to you.

Perfect Microwave Rice

My mom perfected this method of cooking rice and frankly she deserves a culinary Olympic gold. No time to cook? For a quick and savory meal in minutes, throw a chicken breast on the grill, toss a salad, and cook up a batch of this rice.

6 TO 8 SERVINGS

2 cups long-grain rice

3 ½ cups water, homemade stock (pages 95–97), or canned broth

1 ½ teaspoons butter or olive oil

Coarse-grained salt

MORPH Add leftover veggies to the rice during the last 2 minutes of cooking. Stir in fresh herbs, grated Parmesan cheese, or spices just after it comes out of the microwave. Be careful not to overmix cooked rice—it likes to be fluffed with a fork rather than stirred.

For more flavorful rice, use homemade chicken, vegetable, or beef stock or canned broth instead of water. If you go with canned broth, pay close attention to sodium levels—read the labels; opt for the low-sodium varieties because flavors intensify during cooking.

Most newer microwaves have a rice setting, so follow their directions, but if you're not satisfied, try this procedure. It works every time.

PLACE all ingredients except salt in an 8-cup glass measuring cup or a microwave-safe bowl. Rice doubles in size during cooking, so choose a container large enough to accommodate final product. Microwave uncovered on high for 10 minutes. Microwave uncovered on medium-low for 15 minutes. Do not stir rice at any time during cooking process. Season with salt and fluff with a fork just before serving.

Rice with Lemon and Parsley

So little time to cook; done in mere minutes. The nutrition police are always telling us to taste and savor, but this rice is wolf-down good. I'm sure you can hear my mother in your kitchen repeating that old saying "It should take at least as long to eat it as it does to cook it." Thanks, Mom. Can you imagine if we lived by that? We'd all be skinny sticks late for work.

6 TO 8 SERVINGS

2 cups long-grain rice

3 ½ cups water, homemade stock (pages 95–97), or canned broth

½ cup loosely packed, roughly chopped flat-leaf parsley

Juice of 3 lemons

1 ½ teaspoons butter or olive oil

Coarse-grained salt to taste

PLACE rice and water in an 8-cup glass measuring cup or a microwave-safe bowl. Rice expands a lot during cooking, so choose a container large enough to accommodate final product. Microwave uncovered on high for 10 minutes. Then microwave uncovered on medium-low for 15 minutes, or use the rice setting on your microwave. Season with parsley, lemon juice, butter or oil, and salt. Fluff with a fork as you incorporate each ingredient.

Do not stir the rice at any time during the cooking process. Rice is very temperamental and can become an unpalatable gluey ball within minutes, so be gentle. Fluff with a fork, never stir.

Microwave Tomato Rice

Culinary laziness is for everyone's greater good. It forces us to come up with quick and tasty meals. This recipe is just such an example, although it's really a myth that rice cooks faster in the microwave than on the stovetop. I do tend to favor microwave rice because it greatly reduces the chances of my burning down the house.

4 TO 6 SERVINGS

One 28-ounce can whole tomatoes with juice

2½ to 3 cups Chicken Stock (page 95) or water

2 cups long-grain rice

½ teaspoon coarse-grained salt

Cracked black pepper

1 tablespoon butter (optional)

Guyometer:
Great, especially if
she serves steak
with it.

DRAIN tomato juices directly into an 8-cup glass measuring cup or a microwave-safe bowl. Rice expands a lot during cooking, so choose a container large enough to accommodate final product. Squeeze tomatoes with your hands to release their juices into bowl and set tomatoes aside for now. Add enough chicken stock or water to tomato juice to total 3½ cups of liquid. Add rice to liquid and microwave uncovered on high for 10 minutes. Microwave uncovered on medium-low for 15 minutes or use rice setting on your microwave.

WHILE rice is cooking, roughly chop tomatoes or just squeeze them a little harder to shred them when you're juicing them. When rice is done, add tomatoes, salt, pepper, and butter (if using). Fluff with a fork as you incorporate ingredients. Serve immediately.

MORPH Add any seasonings you like to the rice once it's cooked. Try cumin, cayenne, and chili for Mexican-style rice or add a broken bay leaf to this recipe.

I usually cook my rice directly in an 8-cup glass measuring cup because I can measure the ingredients and cook in the same vessel, thereby getting away with as little cleanup as possible, but the truth of the matter is you can use any microwave-proof container.

Sauces, Condiments, and Other Really Cool Things You Ought to Make

A PRESENT WITH A BOW is always preferable to one without. These recipes for yummy condiments, cool salsas, and sauces are the big bows on the packages and the ribbons attached to the balloons. You don't have to eat airline-bland meals just because you've made the commitment to eat lean. And you're not dieting. Think of this as reorganizing your eating habits—a little culinary housecleaning. There's no reason to suffer, so don't. Cook. The recipes require little extra effort and no more thinking than pan-frying a pork chop.

Plain broiled steak is okay, but you might as well spend 10 minutes and make it outrageous. Besides, you need to replace the high-calorie fatty fun you're doing without with something even better. There's nothing hard about spooning Salsa Verde (page 252) over baked fish, tossing a salad, and baking a sweet potato. Dinner should never be more complicated than that unless you're in the mood to cook.

And speaking of festive cooking and lazy Saturdays spent experimenting in the kitchen, try it sometime. Cooking can be home-baked chocolate-chip-cookie fun and really relaxing when you don't have to get a meal on the table and when there are no time constraints.

And you should know by now, none of our recipes takes long, and lots of these toppings keep for days and weeks when properly stored.

Tomato Relish

It's not really a relish, but my thesaurus was stumped. I could hardly call this tomato ketchup or condiment or gravy. It's jammy and like marmalade but marmalade is orange, lemon, or grapefruit in my house. It's like chutney in that it's thick, yet it's a sauce, and it keeps well refrigerated. Use it on warm bread rubbed with garlic, spooned over Chicken Burgers (page 328), slathered on Meat Loaf (page 322), or served next to Pan-Fried Paprika Sole (page 304). It's great on hot dogs (you bet I love a good dog every now and then) and wonderful on hamburgers. Mostly, it's delicious and doesn't leave you craving butter- and cream-based sauces or mayonnaise.

10 SERVINGS

One 15-ounce can chopped tomatoes in puree

1 clove garlic, grated or minced

1 tablespoon grated fresh ginger

1 tablespoon apple cider vinegar or white or rice vinegar

2 teaspoons sugar

PLACE all ingredients in a 10-inch nonstick skillet over medium heat and cook, stirring occasionally, until thickened and jamlike, about 20 minutes. Taste and adjust seasonings.

Guyometer:
If she won't let you
have steak seven
nights a week, this
makes fish taste
better, that's
for sure.

SHORTCUT CHEF

Prep time will fly by if you've got a microplane grater. If you don't, this is another excuse to go out and get one. Grating garlic and ginger into soups, dressings, and sauces heightens and intensifies the simplest dishes with very little effort. If you love the fit food you eat, you won't be so quick to reach for the boys (Ben & Jerry).

If you're into cilantro, roughly chop some and add to the relish just before serving, unless you plan on using it the next day or next week. The fresh herbs will look positively awful after a few hours.

Jack's BBQ Sauce

Don't let the length of the ingredients list put you off. First, you should know by now that I hate long lists as much as you do and, second, you're sure to have most of this stuff on hand. The recipe is really a shake of this with a dash of that and requires just a teensy bit of chopping.

My friend Jack has traveled back and forth across the country a half-dozen times tasting and sampling closely guarded heirloom family recipes for his favorite sauce. He's charmed top-secret ingredients lists from chefs all over the place, combined the best of Memphis mom-and-pop BBQ shops with island secrets, and added a few flavors of his own to come up with this make-at-home version. Jack's sauce is the culmination of years of boot-stomping backyard research. He loves to eat and cook great food but he loves sharing it more. So from Jack to you, the world's best BBQ.

1½ CUPS

1 teaspoon olive oil

6 tablespoons finely chopped onion (about 1 small)

1 clove garlic, peeled and minced

1 bay leaf

2 tablespoons fresh lemon juice

1 cup ketchup

¼ cup water

2 tablespoons Worcestershire sauce

2 tablespoons brown sugar

½ teaspoon Tabasco sauce

¼ teaspoon cracked black pepper

¼ teaspoon celery seeds

¼ teaspoon ground allspice

IN a small saucepan, heat olive oil over medium-high heat until hot but not smoking. Add onion, garlic, and bay leaf. Reduce heat to low and cook covered until onion softens, 6 to 8 minutes. Add a little water if needed to keep onions from burning. Whisk in remaining ingredients. Bring to a boil, immediately reduce heat to a simmer, and cook 10 minutes, or until onion has softened completely and sauce has thickened to desired consistency. Remove bay leaf before serving.

Guyometer:
Great. Great.
Great.

Cucumber Yogurt Sauce

The key to making Monday-through-Friday cooking a reality is keeping things simple. The key to liking what you cook is keeping things flavorful and interesting. This sauce fits the bill. While you're preparing it, bake a piece of chicken or fish and serve this with Perfect Microwave Rice (page 236), a baked potato, or something else just as easy.

4 SERVINGS

I cup plain low-fat yogurt

I English cucumber or 2 regular cucumbers, peeled and seeded

Coarse-grained salt

I teaspoon minced jalapeño pepper

I tablespoon chopped chives

DRAIN yogurt through a fine sieve lined with cheesecloth or a paper towel. Let stand for 1 hour or overnight. Cut cucumber into ⅛-inch slices. Place in a colander set in your sink. Season with salt and place a 1-gallon plastic bag, filled with water and sealed, over cucumber slices to press and draw out their water. This will concentrate the flavor. Let stand 1 to 3 hours. Combine cucumber with yogurt, jalapeño, and chives. Serve over chicken or fish or eat it plain.

SHORTCUT CHEF
Set the yogurt in cheese-cloth, slice and drain cucumbers ahead, mince the jalapeños, too, if you've got the time.

MORPH Make enough to stuff in your lunch box tomorrow.

If you're not up to the task of mincing jalapeños, use Tabasco instead or try ¼ teaspoon red pepper flakes. Spicy is nice. A little cumin takes the salad in another direction altogether.

Guyometer:
Since when do we
get to eat sour
cream dressing?
Guess we fooled
him.

Horseradish Sauce

I feel a little guilty calling this a recipe because it's so simple. But since the whole point of the book is quick and simple, I figured you'd love a quickie. Keep some in your fridge all the time. It's a great low-fat spread or sauce for meat. Especially delicious on roast beef sandwiches or fish.

4 SERVINGS

½ cup plain low-fat yogurt

2 teaspoons prepared horseradish

PLACE yogurt and horseradish in a serving bowl and whisk until combined. Kept refrigerated, the sauce lasts up to one week.

Guyometer:
Better on meat
than fish, unless
you like spicy things
on your fish.

Quick Roasted Red Pepper Sauce

This *trompe l'oeil* (fool the eye) sauce was originally developed to accompany the Pan-Fried Potato Fish Cakes on page 306. Velvety smooth, unctuous, and rich tasting, this quick-to-make sauce seems like it should be forbidden, yet it just so happens to be totally fat-free. It's a great condiment for sandwiches, baked or broiled fish, char-grilled steak, or roasted chicken; I bet you can come up with half a dozen uses for it, too.

ABOUT 1 CUP

2 large red bell peppers, roasted, cored, peeled, and seeded

1 clove garlic, peeled and smashed

2 tablespoons Dijon mustard

2 tablespoons red wine vinegar

1 tablespoon roughly chopped basil leaves

¼ teaspoon red pepper flakes

Coarse-grained salt and cracked black pepper

PLACE peppers, garlic, mustard, vinegar, basil, and red pepper flakes in a blender. Pulse until smooth. Add salt and pepper to taste. Serve immediately or refrigerate tightly covered for 2 to 3 days.

SHORTCUT CHEF

You can cheat and use jarred roasted red peppers but it's easy and cheaper to roast peppers yourself. Check out the technique on page 257.

When red peppers are cheap, buy a dozen or so and roast them all at once. Core, peel, and seed them. Freeze in snack-size freezer bags, one to a bag. When a recipe calls for 1 tablespoon chopped roasted peppers, take out a bag, slice off what you need, and return the unused portion to freezer. Peppers are great to have around. You can throw them in soups, sauces, and salads, or use them on a baguette sandwich.

Microwave Tomato Sauce

This isn't so much a recipe as it is a technique, but it's important—too important to be lost in a tip box. I couldn't be sure you'd see it there and you really need to know it. This base sauce can be transformed into full-fledged pizza or pasta sauce. I make it in batches and freeze it in dinner-size and pizza-size portions. You don't have to cook every element of every meal from scratch, especially with recipes like this.

8 OR MORE SERVINGS

Two 28-ounce cans whole peeled tomatoes

POUR tomatoes into a strainer that has been fitted over a microwave-proof bowl. Using your hands, crush tomatoes. Press all juices into bowl. Set crushed tomatoes aside. Place bowl with juice in microwave and cook on high until thickened to almost the consistency of ketchup, 20 to 25 minutes. Add crushed tomatoes to sauce. Cool to room temperature.

Guyometer:
My mom used to
make this.

MORPH Flavor the sauce any way you like and use it on pizza, pasta, or to thicken soups and sauces.

The sauce is perfect as is for pizza topping. If you want to quickly turn it into pasta sauce, just after you add the crushed tomatoes to the cooked sauce, stir in 2 table-spoons olive oil, 1 teaspoon salt, 1/4 teaspoon black pepper, and 1/4 cup loosely packed, roughly chopped basil. You don't even need to reheat it.

FROM MOM'S LIPS TO YOUR EARS

All canned tomatoes are not created equal. Buy two different brands at a time and do side-by-side comparisons. Keep taste testing until you've come across one you love. I think Muir Glen and Progresso brands are consistently good but you be the judge.

Tomato Mushroom Sauce

My mom made me come up with this sauce because she thought the book needed another sauce recipe. "People like sauce, Kathleen; give the people what they want." Who wants to argue with her mother? The truth is she came up with the tomato mushroom sauce idea when we were testing the Chicken Burgers (page 328). She was sure my father would never go for burgers without a bun, and if he couldn't have a bun he'd surely never touch them without sauce. So we had to come up with a sauce and this is it. In the end he preferred them plain—they're just that good. If you haven't tried the Chicken Burgers (page 328) yet, make it a priority.

ABOUT 2 CUPS

1 tablespoon butter

1 clove garlic, grated or finely minced

½ cup thinly sliced white mushrooms

One 15-ounce can chopped tomatoes in puree

1 bay leaf

2 teaspoons thyme, oregano, or marjoram leaves

Coarse-grained salt and cracked black pepper

*Guyometer:
I think they should
add a little meat—
then I'd give it two
thumbs-up.*

IN a 10-inch nonstick skillet over medium-high heat, melt butter with garlic. Cook for a minute or so, stirring often, making sure not to brown garlic. Add mushrooms to pan and cook, stirring every now and then, until they give up their water. Add tomatoes, bay leaf, and thyme. Stir until combined. Add salt and pepper to taste. Reduce heat to a simmer and cook, stirring occasionally, until sauce is thickened, 15 to 18 minutes. Remove bay leaf.

SHORTCUT CHEF
Slice the mushrooms the night before; peel and mince the garlic.

Make batches of this and freeze them in dinner-size portions, clearly labeled—no mystery foil balls. This sauce is great over pasta, polenta, chicken, meat loaf, Italian sausage sandwiches, and on pizza.

Fast Tomato Cilantro Salsa

My sister, Carol (wife and mother of an ambitious five-year-old), came up with this quick salsa when she found herself hosting an impromptu parenting group party for twenty people. Keep the ingredients in your pantry and this recipe can be whipped up in no time at all. ■ Remember, just because you're making salsa doesn't mean you get to eat a whole bag of chips. Salsa is great on many, many things. So get a *small* bag of baked chips and limit your portion, even if it means sending the bag home with a friend or giving it to the squirrels.

ABOUT 3 CUPS

Two 14½-ounce cans diced tomatoes with green chilies

½ cup chopped cilantro leaves

Juice of 1 lime (or more to taste)

COMBINE tomatoes and cilantro in dish you will be serving it in. Season to taste with lime juice.

Guyometer:
Great!

MORPH This salsa is great over eggs—think huevos rancheros—rolled into tortillas with grilled chicken or steak and beans, or spooned over cooked rice.

You may wish to drain some of the juices out of your canned tomato product if you like your salsa chunkier.

Muir Glen is my brand of choice for tomatoes with green chilies. But use the best product you can get your hands on.

FROM MOM'S LIPS TO YOUR EARS
Much better than any salsa you can buy.

Pesto

The only difference between this pesto and a traditional pesto is what we leave out—the pine nuts and a whole lot of the olive oil. The pine nuts do add wonderful flavor and texture, but we're trying to cut calories any way we can without sacrificing our favorite foods altogether. I think this is a wonderful compromise. We use only ¼ cup of oil, which makes for a thick pesto. If you like your pesto thinner, add more oil, but server beware: watch your portion sizes. Pesto is very flavorful, so a little goes a long way. Don't get too heavy-handed or you could end up eating zillions of pesto calories.

¾ CUP

1 cup tightly packed basil leaves

1 to 2 cloves garlic, peeled (more or less to taste)

¼ cup very good quality olive oil

¼ cup freshly grated Parmesan cheese

Guyometer: Tasty. What do you call this green stuff?

COMBINE all ingredients in bowl of a food processor or blender. Blend until smooth. Store in freezer in usable amounts.

If basil is out of season or just too expensive, substitute flat-leaf parsley for the basil leaves. It's not the same but it's very good.

Make gobs and gobs of the stuff when basil is at its seasonal peak. Freeze pesto in snack-size freezer bags. Slice small portions off the frozen pesto popsicles and add to soups, pastas, and sandwiches throughout the year.

As in all cooking, the end result will be as good or bad as the quality of the ingredients you select. Because there are so few ingredients in this recipe, it's very important that you choose the very best you can get your hands on. Choose a nicely flavored imported Parmesan, such as Reggiano or Grana. The stuff in the green cans will not do.

FROM MOM'S LIPS TO YOUR EARS

If you don't like the taste of raw garlic, don't use so much. I make pesto without garlic all the time. I don't miss it and my husband doesn't keep me up with garlic heartburn.

If the queen's coming for dinner: By all means throw in a few nuts and go easy on the garlic. No one wants garlic breath at a time like this. Toast 2 tablespoons pine nuts in a dry nonstick pan over medium heat, stirring continuously, until golden, about 5 minutes. Combine with the rest of ingredients before pulsing or blending.

Cooking Thin with Chef Kathleen

Mango Papaya Salsa

I wasn't going to put this recipe in the book but everyone kept asking me if I would. It's an excellent salsa served throughout the tropics, but the fact is lots of us can't get delicious mangos and papayas and the chances of them both showing up in the market in usable form at the same time are zilch. Of course, you can make the recipe with all mango or all papaya, and I sometimes add pineapple, chopped grilled onions, or avocados.

ABOUT 6 CUPS

I medium papaya, peeled, seeded, and cut into cubes

I medium mango, peeled, pitted, and cut into cubes

I medium vine-ripened tomato, peeled and diced

$\frac{1}{2}$ cup coarsely chopped cilantro or flat-leaf parsley leaves

2 tablespoons rice vinegar

$\frac{1}{2}$ teaspoon Vietnamese chili paste (also called hot chili paste), or more to taste

$\frac{1}{2}$ jalapeño pepper, seeded and minced, or to taste

PLACE all ingredients in a nonreactive bowl, toss to combine, and let stand 10 minutes. Taste and adjust seasonings and serve immediately.

MORPH I love this salsa on black bean chili topped with a dollop of nonfat yogurt or sour cream. It's also great with chicken or fish. The salsa is best eaten the day you prepare it, but it will keep for approximately 3 days in the refrigerator.

The recipe isn't the same with parsley, but if you hate cilantro I suppose parsley will have to do. Vietnamese chili paste is relatively easy to find now. We have it here, so I'm betting you can get it, too. It's usually in the Asian foods section. If you absolutely can't find it, use red pepper flakes to taste.

Salsa Verde (Green Sauce for Chicken, Fish, or Meat)

Wash the parsley (and cilantro if you're using it) and thoroughly dry it before you get started. Don't wash the other herbs or you'll have wet, soggy salsa. Most herbs don't like to be washed, and while we're at it, neither do mushrooms. If you have to wash your herbs, be sure to dry them completely.

Take the salsa in any flavor direction you want. If I've got the time, I add either chopped garlic or shallots and a few pounded anchovy fillets. If you're going to use shallots, let them macerate in the lemon juice for a half hour to take away their bite. Try red wine vinegar instead of, or in addition to, the lemon juice. Orange juice is nice, too.

FROM MOM'S LIPS TO YOUR EARS

You don't need to spend $20 on fresh herbs. Use flat-leaf parsley as the base herb, up to 1½ cups if you want. Make up the other ½ cup with whatever appeals to you but the truth is the recipe works just fine if all you can get is parsley.

This is a wonderful sauce for just about anything. Not only do I use it for chicken, fish, and meat (see Flank Steak, Grilled Onion, and Tomato Sandwiches on page 314), but I've been known to toss it with leftover grilled vegetables or to dress up plain boiled potatoes. It's an olive-oil-based sauce, so don't be too heavy-handed. Use 1 tablespoon per serving. Thankfully, a little bit of this salsa goes a long way. ■ It can be thrown together in minutes and can be composed of just about any combination of fresh herbs you have on hand, including flat-leaf parsley, basil, oregano, cilantro, marjoram, thyme, chives, or chervil.

2 CUPS

2 cups coarsely chopped, loosely packed fresh herbs (see above)

1 tablespoon chopped capers, rinsed

Zest of 1 lemon, minced

1 tablespoon fresh lemon juice (or more to taste)

½ cup extra-virgin olive oil

Coarse-grained salt and cracked black pepper

IN a small nonreactive bowl, place herbs, capers, lemon zest, and lemon juice. Add olive oil; stir to combine. Add salt and pepper to taste. Serve immediately.

If the queen's coming for dinner: A few nasturtium petals added just before serving give the sauce a delicious peppery bite. She'll think she's in the French countryside.

Cooking Thin with Chef Kathleen

Watermelon Papaya Salsa

"Somebody must sell papayas, Kathleen. I guess people like them but they're blech if you ask me." "Mom, you tested this recipe—it says right here in your writing that it's great on chicken and fish." "Kathleen, you wanted watermelon salsa, it's watermelon salsa. You've been harping about it for weeks and I couldn't imagine what else you could put watermelon salsa on so that's what I wrote." ■ My Hawaii Café Kula customers loved my watermelon salsa. We served it on chicken and fish, spooned it into tacos, and topped black bean chili with it. "Well goody, goody for the California nuts-and-raisins crowd. Your father will never go for it."

ABOUT 3 CUPS

1 cup seeded and diced watermelon

1 small papaya, peeled, seeded, and diced

1/2 avocado, peeled and cut into large chunks

Juice of 1/2 to 1 lime

Salt

1/2 teaspoon Vietnamese chili paste (also called hot chili paste)

1 tablespoon chopped fresh mint leaves

COMBINE all ingredients together in a small nonreactive bowl. Taste and adjust seasonings. Serve immediately. It really won't keep for more than a day.

Guyometer:
Huh? Watermelon
salsa? Tell your
mother I've got
a dinner meeting
and I'll be home
around ten.

If you positively can't get your hands on Vietnamese chili paste (also called sambal oelek), use minced jalapeño pepper or 1/4 teaspoon red pepper flakes. When you finally do come across a jar of chili paste, throw it in your cart and start adding it to things. It's a wonderful fat-free flavor booster and it keeps forever.

You can make the salsa without the papaya or with mango if you like. Sometimes I add plump little cherry tomatoes and a bit of leftover grilled sweet onions.

Blue Cheese Dressing

None of the rich and creamy elements of the original version of this recipe are compromised by using these lower-calorie ingredients. After all, why bother making something if it isn't going to satisfy you? And since we're on the subject, the recipe calls for a measly ¼ cup of plain low-fat yogurt, so by all means use real sour cream if you want. Just don't eat the whole batch yourself.

8 SERVINGS

¼ **cup crumbled blue cheese (finest quality, such as Maytag)**

¼ **cup buttermilk**

¼ **cup plain low-fat yogurt**

2 teaspoons white vinegar

½ **teaspoon sugar**

2 tablespoons roughly chopped flat-leaf parsley leaves (optional)

Coarse-grained salt and cracked black pepper

IN a small nonreactive mixing bowl, combine blue cheese, buttermilk, and yogurt. Using a fork, mix and mash until cheese is pea size. Stir in vinegar, sugar, and parsley. Mix until thoroughly combined. Add salt and pepper to taste.

*Guyometer:
How can you go
wrong? It's blue
cheese dip.*

SHORTCUT CHEF

Make it a day ahead. It keeps very well and tastes even better the next day anyway.

MORPH I don't believe anyone in the United States of America needs me to point out ways to utilize blue cheese dressing, but if you're fresh out of inspiration, use it as an accompaniment (notice I didn't say side dish) to spicy Buffalo Chicken Wings (page 334).

FROM MOM'S LIPS TO YOUR EARS

Go on an ingredient goose chase if that's what it takes to get Maytag blue cheese. It's the best. It's produced smack dab in the middle of Iowa by the Maytag family, who have been making it since 1941. The cheese is creamy, crumbly, perfectly balanced, and consistent. Sure, it's a little more expensive, but why bother using bland or inferior blue cheese in blue cheese dressing?

Cooking Thin with Chef Kathleen

World's Best Vinaigrette

This is delicious tossed with lettuces or blanched green beans, spooned over tomato slices, drizzled over steamed veggies or potato-vegetable salads, or served as a chicken sauce. I'm sure you can think of a dozen good uses, too. ■ If you can get your hands on good-quality sherry vinegar (available in gourmet grocery sections and specialty markets or by mail order), the dressing will be all the more wonderful. Otherwise, use the absolute best-quality vinegar and oil you can afford. If you use red wine vinegar, choose one with an acidity level of 6 or 7 percent (usually indicated right on the front of the label) that hasn't been diluted with water. You'll end up with a pleasantly pungent dressing.

8 TO 10 SERVINGS

2 cloves garlic, minced
  (or less to taste)

1 small shallot, minced

3 tablespoons sherry vinegar,
  red wine vinegar, or balsamic
  vinegar

½ teaspoon coarse-grained salt

1 tablespoon Dijon mustard

4 to 5 tablespoons olive oil

3 tablespoons roughly chopped flat-leaf parsley or mixed
  herbs

Cracked black pepper

*Guyometer:
They're right
about this one—
it's really good.*

> Don't use salad, vegetable, or canola oil. They won't add anything to the finished dressing; they're tasteless fats, and who wants tasteless calories? There's just no point. Use a good olive oil or extra-virgin olive oil.
>
> The recipe calls for parsley but use any fresh herbs you want. I've used different combinations, depending upon the dish the dressing is ultimately bound for. I've used thyme, chervil, chives, oregano, and rosemary.

FROM MOM'S LIPS TO YOUR EARS

If you haven't got the right ingredients, don't make the dressing. It won't be right. Make an effort to get the ingredients you need and try the recipe. It's really great, it's easy, and it dresses up a lot of dinners in our house.

PLACE garlic, shallot, vinegar, and salt in a small bowl and let stand at least 30 minutes. This will take the peppery bite out of the garlic and shallot. Whisk in mustard, oil, and herbs. Add pepper to taste.

Microwave "Roasted" Garlic

This instant method has saved me on more than a few occasions when I didn't have the time for slow roasting or, admittedly, I was just plain lazy. If you have the time, I recommend you stick with the traditional method of slow-roasting garlic in a hot oven. You'll end up with sweet and deliciously caramelized garlic.

LEISURELY CHEF

Slow-roasted garlic is called superior by some. To make it, preheat oven to 375°F. Place 1 or 2 whole heads of garlic in a baking dish just large enough to hold them (the smallest one you have) with 2 tablespoons water. Cover tightly with aluminum foil and bake about 30 minutes, or until garlic is soft and smooshy all over.

MORPH This is a magical tip. Roasted garlic puree is an intensely flavorful fat-free way to thicken up sauces. A little reduced chicken stock with a bit of roasted garlic puree makes an excellent sauce in and of itself. Add sautéed mushrooms and herbs, spoon it over chicken, serve it with Buttery Mashed Potatoes (page 185), and you've got dinner.

1 TO 2 SERVINGS (BUT PUT IT IN SOMETHING)

2 large cloves garlic, unpeeled

MICROWAVE garlic on high for 1 minute, or until you begin to smell it. Peel away outer skin and remove sprout and stem end; discard. Use cooked garlic as you would raw garlic. By "roasting" you are softening the flavor. Even avowed garlic haters find this taste bearable.

*Guyometer:
The garlic is good,
not sharp. Is this a
different kind?*

Roasted Peppers

I wasn't sure how many of you had actually roasted peppers, so I thought I should include this quick "how-to" someplace other than buried deep in a recipe tip box.

▪ You can call me a full-fledged roasted pepper advocate because I firmly believe everyone should have them in the freezer. Roasted peppers are so meaty and flavorful. They're just fantastic on sandwiches, in pasta, in salads, or as a salad on their own (see Roasted Pepper Salad with Basil and Mint, page 155). When something needs a little color, just cut a few strips of your frozen peppers and voilà, color and flavor.

However many peppers you want to roast: red, yellow, orange—but not green

PREHEAT broiler to high. Core and cut peppers into quarters; remove seeds and membranes. Place on a nonstick baking sheet and broil until skins blacken slightly. Place hot peppers in a plastic bag, seal, and let stand 15 minutes. When peppers are cool enough to handle, remove skins. Place peeled peppers in a serving dish, use in a recipe, or freeze for later.

SHORTCUT CHEF
Designate a pepper-roasting time and roast a whole bunch. Freeze them in little plastic bags, two-packs or family-size packs, whatever makes you happy.

A good time to roast a bunch of peppers is when you've got the outdoor grill on for something else.

Balsamic Onion Marmalade

This is another heavenly condiment you can make for half the price of tasteless gourmet versions. I can't tell you how many times I've fallen for those gorgeously labeled gourmet goodies that cost seven dollars per teensy jar. Though I'm often disappointed with jarred condiments, I still encourage you to try them when you can fit them into your budget. Every now and then you hit it big and find a low-calorie, richly flavored all-purpose kind of product you can use to perk up suppers *and* add to your pantry inventory. A dash, a pinch, and a pour is a great way to liven up a dish that would otherwise be just okay. So don't give up. In the meantime, try this recipe—you're gonna like it, unless you hate onions.

ABOUT 1 CUP

2 cups thinly sliced sweet onions (about 1 medium-large)
¾ cup balsamic vinegar
1 tablespoon brown sugar

PLACE onions, balsamic vinegar, and brown sugar in a 2-quart nonreactive pot with tall sides over medium-high heat. Bring to a boil, stirring constantly. Immediately reduce heat to low, cover, and simmer, stirring occasionally, until thickened and marmalade-like, about 1 hour.

SHORTCUT CHEF
Slice onions the night before but seal them in plastic and then wrap them in foil or you'll stink up the whole refrigerator and everything in it.

MORPH This is great spread on warm toasted bread and served as a savory accompaniment to roasted chicken, steaks, or maybe that leftover turkey. It's great on sandwiches and pizza, too.

Guyometer:
I really like this,
so it must not be
good for me.

Cooking Thin with Chef Kathleen

Caramelized Onions

This is similar to the Balsamic Onion Marmalade on the facing page. Caramelized onions are such a wonderful flavor ingredient and all-around great condiment to have on hand. ■ Caramelized onions are superb served with just about any roasted meat or vegetable, or use as a pizza topping, burger condiment, or sandwich spread.

ABOUT 2 CUPS; ENOUGH TO TOP 2 PIZZAS WITH SOME LEFT OVER

3 tablespoons olive oil

3 pounds Bermuda onions, peeled and thinly sliced (about 6 medium)

3 cloves garlic, peeled and thinly sliced

1 bay leaf, broken in half

6 sprigs fresh thyme

Coarse-grained salt

IN a large heavy-bottomed pot, heat oil over medium-high heat. When hot but not smoking, add onions, garlic, bay leaf, and thyme. Stir until evenly coated. Reduce heat to medium, add salt to taste, and cover. Cook for 1 hour 15 minutes, stirring frequently, until onions are very soft and reduced to one third their original volume. Remove lid, increase heat to medium-high, and cook, stirring often, until excess juices have reduced and thickened, about 30 minutes more. Onions will take on a jamlike consistency and should not be watery. Remove bay leaf and thyme sprigs. Cool to room temperature. Refrigerate in an airtight container until ready to use.

SHORTCUT CHEF
Cut the onions the night before but store them in totally airtight containers or you'll stink up the refrigerator.

MORPH Make a double batch and freeze half for those nights when you just don't feel like cooking.

If the onions are ever in danger of burning, add a little water and turn down the heat.

Bread and Butter Zucchini Pickles

Judy Rodgers of Zuni Café in San Francisco makes the world's best mustard zucchini pickles. I weep for her pickles. They are that good. If you're ever in her neighborhood (1658 Market Street) you must stop in. All the food is wonderful. Don't bother trying to count calories, either. Judy's food is something to save up for. ■ Recognizing how obsessed I am with Judy's pickles and knowing I'd long ago forgotten the recipe, my mom tried to come up with a surrogate version. After years and years of trying, I finally fell in love with these. They're not as great as Zuni's (don't tell my mom I said that) but they're very, very good.

2 PINTS

6 cups washed, trimmed, and thinly sliced (about ¼ inch thick) zucchini

1 cup thinly sliced sweet onions

¼ cup plus 1 teaspoon coarse-grained salt

6 cups ice cubes

2 cups apple cider vinegar

1½ cups sugar

1½ teaspoons mustard seeds

1½ teaspoons celery seeds

½ teaspoon turmeric

IN a large bowl, combine zucchini, onions, and ¼ cup of salt. Toss to combine. Cover with ice cubes and let stand 3 hours at room temperature. Drain well.

IN a large pot over medium-high heat, combine vinegar, sugar, mustard seeds, celery seeds, turmeric, and remaining 1 teaspoon salt. Bring to a boil, stirring occasionally until sugar dissolves. Remove from heat and let cool to room temperature. Divide zucchini and onion mixture between two 1-pint jars. Pour brine into jars, cover, and refrigerate until ready to serve. Keeps up to 1 month refrigerated.

Guyometer:
Never thought
they'd be any good,
but they are.

SHORTCUT CHEF

If you haven't gone out and bought that must-have plastic mandoline, this is another perfect excuse to do it. Plan ahead by purchasing pint jars in advance; otherwise, you'll be running to the store in the middle of the recipe. I hate when that happens.

MORPH Make a double batch; this is a great low-fat snack to have on hand.

Prepare this recipe on a day you plan on being in more than out, since the pickles need to stand on ice for three hours.

Herbed Ricotta Cheese Spread

One should never be without a tub of herbed ricotta. It's got a lot less fat than mayonnaise and a whole lot more character and flavor. To me mayonnaise was invented as an excuse for stale bread—unless we're talking about homemade mayonnaise, which in my opinion is worth the 10K race you'll surely have to run to burn it off. Although the recipe will work just fine with grocery store brands, try to find a good source for freshly made ricotta cheese. The soft fresh curds are cloud-puff fluffy and the taste is so farm fresh you can almost hear the cows mooing.

ABOUT ¾ CUP

8 ounces skim-milk ricotta cheese

1 teaspoon chopped Microwave "Roasted" Garlic
(page 256) or more to taste

2 tablespoons roughly chopped herbs
(such as basil, thyme, parsley, oregano, and chives)

1 tablespoon freshly grated Parmesan cheese

Coarse-grained salt and cracked black pepper

*Guyometer:
Honey, what is
this? Some weird
new cream cheese
or what?*

PLACE ricotta, garlic, herbs, and Parmesan in a small bowl and fold together until blended. Add salt and pepper to taste.

MORPH Herbed ricotta can be used as a spread on sandwiches, crackers, breadsticks, or bagels (with a thick slice of tomato you're in lunch heaven), or as a topping on baked potatoes or pizza. You'll think of a few hundred uses of your own.

If you like the strong flavor of fresh garlic, skip the roasted and mince two cloves fresh to use instead.

If there's a crowd showing up for Sunday brunch: Lay out a bowl of herbed ricotta, a platter of sliced tomatoes, a nice plate of lox, a basket of bagels, a few thinly sliced sweet onions, a carafe of freshly squeezed orange juice, and perhaps a pitcher of mimosas if you're in the mood, and you've got a no-fuss spread to please almost any crowd.

Cooking Thin with Chef Kathleen

Nancy Smith's Buttermilk Biscuits

If you're too tired to make buttermilk biscuits from scratch, see if you can get a table at Mrs. Smith's restaurant, the Washington Street Inn, in historic Lewisburg, West Virginia. Built of massive ancient oaks and locally fired bricks back in 1808, this house-turned-restaurant is filled with Civil War and nineteenth-century memorabilia and is known today for its gracious dining and extraordinary culinary creations. If buttermilk biscuits aren't on the menu, it simply means Margaret's back in the kitchen turning out pans and pans of the world's best dinner rolls, so sweet and tender and savory you'll have to pace yourself or you won't have room for the hot berry cobbler. By the way, biscuits are a once-in-a-while treat worth saving up for.

10 BISCUITS

2 cups flour

2 teaspoons baking powder

1 teaspoon baking soda

½ teaspoon salt

5 tablespoons cold unsalted butter, cut into tiny pieces

¾ cup buttermilk

PREHEAT oven to 400°F. In a mixing bowl, sift together flour, baking powder, baking soda, and salt. Using a fork, cut in butter until mixture resembles coarse meal. Pour buttermilk directly into center and continue mixing with a fork until dough starts to hold together.

TURN dough onto a lightly floured large cutting board or directly onto the counter. Knead only enough to form an 8 × 5-inch rectangle, about ¾ inch thick. Cut into 8 squares. Place on a nonstick cookie sheet or a pan lined with parchment paper. Bake 12 minutes, or until lightly golden.

I didn't call for egg wash because I'm lazy. But if you're serving the biscuits to guests or you're in the mood, beat 1 whole egg and brush the top of the biscuits with the egg just before you put them in the oven.

I don't fuss with biscuit cutters because you end up with scraps that need to be rolled again. The more you work the dough, the tougher the biscuits will be. But it's up to you.

Grandma's Apple Butter

Nancy Smith's grandma had the most beautiful backyard. "As little girls, my cousin Mary and I loved to play there and get lost among the apple trees and flowers. When there were more apples than we could eat, Grandma made apple butter in a huge black pot on legs set right in the middle of the backyard. Daddy lit the fire under the kettle early in the day so Grandma could make her apple butter. Sometimes the sun would set before it was done. Daddy would drive his old Ford right up to the pot and shine his headlights so Grandma could finish." ▪ Since we couldn't find giant back-yard kettles at a decent price, we came up with a microwave version of Grandma's apple butter.

4 TO 6 CUPS

3 pounds apples (6 to 7 large), peeled, cored, and cut into same-size pieces

PLACE apples in a large microwave-proof bowl. Microwave on high about 55 minutes, or until thickened and mostly smooth. Check after 20 minutes and then every 15 minutes until done.

Plum Apple Jam

If you're thinking, I can buy this in a jar, think again. **Not only can you not buy it in a jar, but I guarantee you've never tasted anything this good. I'm telling you this multi-use sauce is over-the-top great and you** *need* **to make it. It's outrageous slathered on toast, plopped smack in the center of steaming hot oatmeal, or served as mock chutney with sliced roasted breast of turkey.**

4 TO 5 CUPS

6 cups plum wedges (about 8 large)

3 cups peeled, cored, and sliced apples

$\frac{1}{2}$ cup sugar (or a teensy bit more if plums are quite sour)

PLACE plums and apples in a large microwave-proof bowl, sprinkle with sugar, and toss to coat. Microwave on high for 20 minutes. That's it. If you're a paranoid cook or just don't trust your microwave, check the plums after 10 minutes.

MY IDEA OF A GREAT DINNER

Sautéed pork tenderloin (page 326) topped with this fantastic plum jam, Buttery Mashed Potatoes (page 185), and plain old steamed or boiled green beans.

Strawberry Rhubarb Jam, Sauce, and Dessert Topping

I had come up with this kind of name because this concoction is not only a fabulous topping for ice cream or angel food cake, but also a decidedly delicious jam for toast and hot biscuits and a wonderful afternoon pick-me-up (think applesauce). Spoon strawberry rhubarb sauce over angel food cake, top with sliced fresh strawberries and a few mint sprigs, and you'll have 'em lined up around the block. ■ One more thing: if you're an "Ew, ick, what's rhubarb?"–type person, change your act. Rhubarb is scandalously delicious, naturally healthful, and simple to deal with. If you can cut celery, you can cut rhubarb. Looks the same, crunches the same, cuts the same—now go get some. Hurry.

6 TO 7 (½-CUP) SERVINGS

1 quart strawberries, rinsed and hulled

4 cups ½-inch-thick rhubarb slices

½ to ¾ cup sugar

PLACE strawberries and rhubarb in a microwave-proof bowl large enough to hold them. Sprinkle fruit with sugar and toss to coat evenly. Microwave on high for 20 minutes. Darlings, it doesn't get any simpler than that.

If the queen's coming for dinner: Serve the sauce over pound cake. I think she stopped watching her weight years ago.

You don't need the world's most perfect berries for the sauce. In fact, if the only fresh ones available are no less than 3,562 miles from home and all you have parked outside is a mule, you can use frozen berries. But the better the berry, the better the sauce, so don't be lazy.

Cooking Thin with Chef Kathleen

Light Meals, Vegetarian Entrées, and Entrée Salads

When the air conditioner craps out and you do, too

UNDERSTANDABLY, WHEN WE'RE FEELING

blah or out of sorts, feeding ourselves becomes somewhat of a challenge. It's

only natural to pick up the phone and order the next pants size up. "Send me

an extra-large all-meat pizza, a Greek salad with extra dressing, and some gar-

lic bread, too." Add up how many meals you don't make at home each week and do a quick calorie-count reality check. The numbers are probably not in your favor. Losing weight and keeping it off for good are achievable but we must become creative culinary thinkers, plan-ahead types, doers, certainly not carryout call girls.

Light meals are a good habit to get into because they're quick to prepare and they get the job done. Luckily, we have a few internal gauges to jump-start what really ought to become routine. For instance, when the air conditioner inevitably craps out or when we feel like all our stuffing is falling out from fatigue or flu, and certainly when the jeans are a teensy bit too tight from too much celebrating, we instinctively revert to light meals.

Nature kicks us into the light meal groove—we've got the dog days of summer, holidays, and flu season covered (it's all a matter of how you look at things). To keep up the habit throughout the year, deem light meal nights as license to have dessert. Once you start eating light meals every now and then, you'll want them more often, especially if you have dessert only on light meal nights.

Tuna and White Bean Salad

"Supping on canned goods again, Kathleen?" Much to the chagrin of my "real" chef friends, I love pantry suppers. I don't care if the ingredients come from a bag, box, or tin can. I've handpicked them, so I know they're good. Shortcuts rule. Besides, you can throw this meal together in a matter of minutes. Certainly quicker than you can schlep across town for fast food.

4 SERVINGS

Guyometer:
Well, he didn't roll
over and die.

Two 14-ounce cans white beans, rinsed and drained

¼ cup thinly sliced scallions (white and green parts), about 3

2 tablespoons fresh oregano or 1 teaspoon dried

¼ cup loosely packed, roughly chopped flat-leaf parsley

¼ cup red wine vinegar

2 tablespoons extra-virgin olive oil

2 tablespoons fresh lemon juice

Coarse-grained salt and cracked black pepper

Two 6-ounce cans white albacore tuna packed in water, drained

1 cup diced celery

PLACE beans in a large serving bowl (why get a mixing bowl dirty, too?). Add scallions, oregano, parsley, vinegar, olive oil, lemon juice, salt and pepper to taste, tuna, and celery. Stir until combined. Taste and adjust seasonings. Serve immediately.

If the queen's coming for dinner: Garnish the salad with grated hard-boiled eggs, parsley sprigs, and a wedge or two of lemon. Or serve half a soft-cooked egg on each plate.

SHORTCUT CHEF

Make it the night before. It's delicious the second day.

MORPH Turn this into a heartier meal by serving the salad on a bed of lettuces with tomatoes. If you're starving or just want more, dig around the fridge and see if you can scare up some leftover blanched green beans, potatoes, carrots, or freshly sliced cucumbers.

FROM MOM'S LIPS TO YOUR EARS

Cook up a batch of dried beans if you have the time, or use fresh beans if you can possibly get your hands on them. They're worth the trouble.

BLT Salad

Waiting for tomato season must be what it's like waiting for the baby to be born, and when drip-down-your-arm good tomatoes finally do arrive in the markets, they aren't around long enough. I can't get them worked into menus fast enough. In peak tomato season, I've been known to eat BLTs several times in the same week. ■ So, embarrassed by my obsession with the sandwich, I came up with this clever variation, the BLT salad. Not able to part with the classic BLT ingredients list, I left in the bacon, lettuce, and tomato and added a few new flavors, too.

4 SERVINGS

1¼ pounds small white or red new potatoes

5 tablespoons extra-virgin olive oil

Coarse-grained salt and cracked black pepper

1 large sweet onion, peeled, cored, and cut into 4 thick slices

2 tablespoons balsamic vinegar or other vinegar you like

2 tablespoons roughly chopped fresh basil leaves

3 medium tomatoes, peeled, cored, and cut into large chunks

¼ pound bacon, cut crosswise into ½-inch strips

12 cups loosely packed washed salad greens (such as arugula or a variety of mixed greens)

2 ounces crumbled blue cheese

PREHEAT oven to 425°F. Cut larger potatoes into quarters, smaller ones into halves. Place potatoes in a plastic bag and pour in 1 tablespoon of olive oil; seal bag. Shake and toss bag until potatoes are evenly coated. Pour onto a cookie sheet. Add salt and pepper to taste.

PLACE onion slices in bag you used for potatoes. Don't add any oil—there will be enough left in bag. Turn until onions are coated; do not break up onion slices. Place on cookie sheet with potatoes and bake, turning once, until potatoes and onions are golden, 40 to 45 minutes.

MEANWHILE, place tomatoes in a large bowl. To make dressing, whisk together remaining 4 tablespoons olive oil, balsamic vinegar, and chopped basil in a small bowl. Season with salt and pepper. Pour about one fourth of dressing over tomatoes. Set aside.

IN a large nonstick pan over medium-high heat, cook bacon until brown and crispy. Drain on paper towels. When potatoes and onions are cooked, divide among 4 serving plates. Place salad greens in bowl with tomatoes and toss with remaining dressing. Taste and adjust seasonings with salt and pepper as necessary. Arrange salad greens on the serving plates. Top with bacon and sprinkle with blue cheese.

A sweet onion is an onion that's bred to be sweet. They're different in nature from cooking onions, which are stronger in flavor and not usually sweet at all. Common sweet varieties include Walla Walla, Granex, Bermuda, Vidalia, Texas Sugar Babies, and Maui onions. And of course they're widely available. I wouldn't send you on a goose chase for an onion.

Light Meals, Vegetarian Entrées, and Entrée Salads

Sesame-Ginger Shrimp and Spicy Black Bean Salad

This recipe can be made the night before and is fantastic left over. A few of the ingredients sound a little exotic but all of them can be found in gourmet or specialty Asian markets. Not in the mood for shrimp? Serve the salad over grilled and thinly sliced steak, grilled chicken, or all by itself.

4 SERVINGS

FOR THE SHRIMP

1 pound large shrimp, peeled and deveined

2 teaspoons sesame oil

1 tablespoon minced fresh ginger

1 teaspoon minced garlic

1 tablespoon white sesame seeds

2 teaspoons olive oil for sautéing

FOR THE DRESSING

¼ cup plus 2 tablespoons fresh lime juice

¼ cup plus 2 tablespoons rice wine vinegar

1 teaspoon sesame oil

1 tablespoon olive oil

1 teaspoon fish sauce

1 tablespoon sugar

½ teaspoon hot chili paste or red pepper flakes

2 teaspoons minced fresh ginger

FOR THE SALAD

3 cups cooked black beans or two 15-ounce cans black beans, rinsed and drained

1 medium cucumber, peeled, seeded, and cut into ¼-inch slices

1 mango, peeled, pitted, and cut into ½-inch chunks

3 scallions, thinly sliced (white and green parts)

½ cup roughly chopped cilantro leaves

PREPARE SHRIMP: In a medium nonreactive bowl, combine shrimp, sesame oil, ginger, garlic, and sesame seeds. Set in refrigerator until ready to cook, up to 2 hours ahead.

PREPARE DRESSING: In a small nonreactive bowl, whisk together lime juice, rice wine vinegar, sesame oil, olive oil, fish sauce, sugar, chili paste or red pepper flakes, and ginger. Taste and adjust seasonings as necessary.

PREPARE SALAD: In a large nonreactive bowl, place black beans, cucumber, mango, scallions, and cilantro. Pour dressing over salad, toss to coat well, and set aside.

SAUTÉ SHRIMP: In a nonstick skillet, heat 2 teaspoons olive oil over medium heat until hot but not smoking. Sauté shrimp until cooked thoroughly, turning once, about 3 minutes. Divide salad among 4 serving bowls and garnish with equal portions of shrimp.

SHORTCUT CHEF
Skip marinating the shrimp if you want, but it's not that complicated and you can do it the night before. In fact, make the dressing a day ahead if you can spare the time. Use canned black beans but choose the best-quality beans you can get your hands on. I know you can only go by the labels, so buy two different brands if you're not sure which is the better product and do side-by-side tests.

MORPH Make a double batch and stuff tomorrow's lunch box with Asian-style wraps. Roll the salad into flour or corn tortillas.

Chicken and Asian Noodle Salad

This is a nice way to use up last night's leftover chicken and some vegetables that didn't get eaten. Or you can deliberately cook some extra chicken and vegetables to have either a luncheon or a light supper partially prepared. My grandmother, who had a two-hour commute between New York City and her home in Roslyn, Long Island, was a master at half preparing the next night's dinner while putting the finishing touches on today's.

SHORTCUT CHEF

Make the dressing the night before. It's a shake, a whisk, and a stir, and voilà, dressing. I keep sesame-miso vinaigrette on hand for all salad emergencies. A great marinade for chicken and meat, it's very, very flavorful. No one has to know your kitchen secrets. Build out the dressing by adding scallions, garlic, or fresh herbs. Experiment or use it as is. So little fat, so much flavor.

We used to serve this salad in a papaya at my Maui restaurant when papayas were plentiful. Obviously this salad can be served without the papaya, so if the papayas in your market are anything less than spectacular, don't use them.

4 SERVINGS

5 tablespoons rice wine vinegar

2 tablespoons white or yellow miso

¼ teaspoon sesame oil

Two 6-ounce boneless, skinless chicken breasts, cooked and thinly sliced

4 ounces dried Chinese plain or somen noodles, cooked according to package instructions

1 cup cherry tomatoes, halved

1 cup green beans, blanched

2 ounces arugula or other baby lettuce (about 2½ cups loosely packed)

¼ cup loosely packed, roughly chopped cilantro

2 papayas, halved, peeled, and seeded (optional)

IN a small nonreactive bowl, whisk together rice wine vinegar, miso, and sesame oil until well combined. Set aside.

IN a medium-size bowl, combine chicken, noodles, tomatoes, green beans, arugula or other salad greens, and cilantro. Drizzle miso vinaigrette over salad and toss until evenly coated. Taste and adjust seasonings with more miso or vinegar, if desired. If using papayas, place one papaya half on each of 4 plates. Divide salad evenly among papaya halves or serve in cool Asian-style bowls if you're entertaining.

If the queen's coming for dinner: Dress up the salad with any variation of the following: red and yellow tomatoes, Yukon Gold or purple potatoes cut into chunks, blanched yellow wax beans, chunks of mango and/or avocado, marinated beets, or any combination of seasonal vegetables you like, but keep in mind, you may need to make extra dressing.

FROM MOM'S LIPS TO YOUR EARS

I told Kathleen she shouldn't make you run all over the planet for hard-to-find ingredients but I made an exception here. Miso practically lasts forever in the refrigerator and the dressing really is delicious. Look for yellow or white miso in the Asian foods section of your supermarket or in Asian specialty markets. It's usually kept refrigerated near the fresh tofu.

Light Meals, Vegetarian Entrées, and Entrée Salads

Italian Sausage Potato Salad Supper

I have a hard time sticking to a single portion of potato salad, any potato salad. I love potatoes. I figured out a way to turn potato salad into an entrée by adding lettuces, a tasty vinaigrette, and some cooked sausage. You'll have a hard time convincing meat eaters that this is dinner, so I wouldn't introduce this type of entrée to the leery until you're well into the healthy-living, cook-at-home routine. They might abandon ship. Be sure to plate the food individually to control portion sizes.

4 TO 6 SERVINGS

3 pounds Yukon Gold or russet potatoes

3 tablespoons white wine vinegar

2 tablespoons Dijon mustard

¼ cup white wine

¼ cup extra-virgin olive oil

Coarse-grained salt and cracked black pepper

1 tablespoon minced chives

½ cup roughly chopped flat-leaf parsley leaves

2 tablespoons water

¾ pound low-fat Italian sausages (2 large or 3 medium)

16 cups salad greens, washed and dried

PLACE potatoes in a large pot and cover them with cold water. Over high heat, bring to a boil, immediately reduce to a simmer, and cook until potatoes are just done, 25 to 30 minutes. Do not overcook.

MEANWHILE, prepare dressing. Whisk together vinegar, Dijon mustard, white wine, olive oil, and salt and pepper to taste. Set aside.

WHEN potatoes are cooked through, drain and cool slightly. While potatoes are still warm, peel and cut into ½-inch-thick slices. Place potatoes in a large mixing bowl. Season with salt and pepper, chives, and parsley, then add dressing. Set aside.

PLACE water and sausages in a small nonstick pan set over medium heat. Cover and cook until sausages are firm to the touch and cooked through, 10 to 12 minutes. Let sausages rest 5 minutes, then cut on the diagonal into ½-inch-thick slices.

COMBINE salad greens and dressed potatoes and toss until all greens are well coated. Divide greens and potatoes evenly among individual serving plates and top with equal portions of sausage.

Guyometer:
I smell sausage.
Yum.

SHORTCUT CHEF
Prepare the dressing, wash and dry the lettuces, cook the sausages, and set out the tools you'll need. The potatoes are lovely warm but I suppose you could start them early.

Cook extra potatoes and throw them into a frittata (pages 134–140) later in the week.

Portobello Mushroom Salad with Blue Cheese

Admittedly this didn't rate very high with my father. However, when my mom and I pointed out to him that this was a savory, creative way to eat healthy and that bland steamed dinners were always an option, too, I do believe we heard a begrudging grunt of approval.

4 SERVINGS

1 pound portobello mushrooms

2 tablespoons water

4 cups hand-torn bread crumbs (fingertip size)

½ pound green beans, trimmed and blanched

3 red bell peppers, roasted, peeled, seeded, and cut into bite-size pieces or strips

20 cups loosely packed salad greens, washed and dried

2 tablespoons extra-virgin olive oil

1 to 2 tablespoons balsamic vinegar

Coarse-grained salt and cracked black pepper

4 ounces Maytag blue cheese or feta cheese, crumbled

Guyometer: Where's the beef?

SHORTCUT CHEF

While you're watching TV, prep the bread crumbs, wash the lettuces, and roast the peppers, or at the very least, read the recipe through, making sure you have all the ingredients and the necessary tools on hand. Anything you can do ahead will pay off. To save more time, cheat and use jarred roasted peppers. You know the drill—rinse them first.

MORPH Make a double batch minus the lettuce. Turn it into a sandwich for tomorrow's lunch. Try it with roasted turkey or chicken breast.

PREHEAT oven to 350°F. Spray mushrooms with olive oil or non-stick cooking spray. Place them in a single layer in a baking dish just large enough to hold them. Add water to dish and cover tightly with foil. Bake, turning once at the halfway point, until mushrooms are completely cooked through and softened, 25 to 35 minutes. When cool, cut into ½-inch slices.

MEANWHILE, scatter bread crumbs on a cookie sheet and bake 20 to 25 minutes, or until golden. Cool.

IN a large bowl, toss together mushrooms, green beans, roasted peppers, and salad greens. Add oil, vinegar, and salt and pepper to taste. Toss until completely coated. Add bread crumbs, toss once more, taste, and adjust seasonings. Divide salad among 4 serving plates. Top with crumbled cheese.

If the queen's coming for dinner: Toss bread crumbs with the lettuces separately and arrange on plates first. Top greens with beans, peppers, mushrooms, and finally the cheese. It makes for a lovely presentation.

Culinary heads-up: Bake mushrooms and bread crumbs at the same time, and blanch the green beans while you wait. Choices, choices—spray the bread crumbs with oil and season with salt and pepper if you like. We tested them seasoned and unseasoned, and for the purpose of this salad, the extra work didn't pay off. Baked, cooled, and tossed into the finished salad, the plain bread crumbs absorbed dressing and seasonings on their own and added a pleasing crunch to the overall dish. So don't bother preseasoning them if you're not in the mood or just want to avoid the extra calories.

Light Meals, Vegetarian Entrées, and Entrée Salads

Salad Niçoise
(Tuna and Potato Salad)

This is a great recipe to plan ahead for. When you're blanching green beans and cooking potatoes this week, make enough for this salad, and most of the work will be done. Don't tell Julia Child you heard this from me, but any good vinaigrette will do. Of course it won't be authentic *salade niçoise* but it will be authentically yours. *Bon appétit!*

6 SERVINGS

FOR THE VINAIGRETTE

1 shallot, peeled and minced

¼ cup red wine vinegar

Juice of 1 lemon

Coarse-grained salt and cracked black pepper

3 anchovies, rinsed and chopped to a paste

¼ cup extra-virgin olive oil

FOR THE SALAD

8 cups loosely packed salad greens, washed

1½ pounds small potatoes (such as Yukon Gold or new potatoes), cooked and cut in half or into 1-inch pieces

½ pound green beans, trimmed and blanched

4 very ripe tomatoes, cored, peeled, and cut into 1-inch chunks

Two 6-ounce cans white albacore tuna packed in water, drained

2 or 3 large eggs, hard-boiled

20 niçoise or 16 kalamata olives

PREPARE VINAIGRETTE: Place shallot in a small mixing bowl with vinegar, lemon juice, and salt to taste. Let stand 1 hour or more (this softens flavor and removes peppery bite of the shallot). Whisk in pepper, anchovies, and olive oil.

PREPARE SALAD: Place greens in a large mixing bowl, pour one third of dressing over all, toss to coat evenly, and divide among plates. Place potatoes, green beans, and tomatoes in same bowl, pour in one third dressing, toss to coat evenly, and divide among plates. Place tuna in same bowl, toss with remaining salad dressing, and divide among plates. Garnish each plate with half of one egg and several olives.

SHORTCUT CHEF
Prepping ahead will really pay off here. Cook potatoes and green beans the night before. Whenever you find yourself with a few extra minutes (just after you put the kids on the bus, right after lunch, while the darlings are doing their homework) squeeze in a quick prep job. Cook the eggs or prepare the vinaigrette. Prepping ahead is an important habit to get into; you'll eat at home more often. Use the prewashed bag lettuces if you don't have time to wash your own.

MORPH Turn the leftover salad niçoise into your own version of an Italian Country Loaf Sandwich (page 122).

My mom and I argue about this constantly: I like the eggs cooked just to the point of jiggly centers (about an 8-minute egg) and Mom likes them cooked to golf-ball-like texture (a 9½-to-10-minute egg).

Grilled Shrimp and Chopped Vegetable Salad

You know how I'm always telling you to throw extra veggies on the grill to get a jump start on tomorrow's dinner? This is one of those recipes. If you've got the BBQ fired up, it's always safe to throw on a few extra red peppers. ■ Choose the sweetest corn you can get your hands on. By all means choose a variety of lovely, flavorful, sweet and peppery salad greens. Iceberg just won't do. If you're not sure what constitutes sweet and peppery, ask the nearest produce person. Bring home different lettuce varieties and try them out.

4 SERVINGS

8 bamboo skewers (see sidebar on facing page)

I pound medium or large shrimp, peeled and deveined

4 teaspoons plus 3 tablespoons extra-virgin olive oil

6 to 7 ears corn, shucked

8 scallions

Coarse-grained salt and cracked black pepper

2 red bell peppers

8 to 12 cups loosely packed salad greens

2 tablespoons fresh lemon juice

¼ cup balsamic vinegar

SHORTCUT CHEF

Whisk the vinaigrette together ahead of time, shuck the corn at the store, skewer the shrimp the night before, and/or clean the lettuces and the scallions, too. Do the following only if it's the difference between your trying this recipe or not: use frozen corn, prewashed packaged lettuces, and/or jarred roasted, peeled peppers. Freshest is always best, but you knew that.

PREHEAT grill. Skewer shrimp by holding 2 skewers side by side and slightly apart and threading each shrimp onto both skewers, which will make them easier to work with on the grill. Rub shrimp with 2 teaspoons of olive oil and set aside in refrigerator.

PLACE corn cobs and scallions in a plastic bag (I use the one I bought them in). Pour 2 teaspoons olive oil into bag and season with salt and pepper. Seal bag. Shake and turn bag to distribute oil and seasonings evenly.

WHEN grill is ready, place red peppers over hottest flames and cook, turning, until charred on all sides. Place in plastic bag. When cool enough to handle, peel, stem, and seed peppers, cut into 1-inch pieces, and place in a very large salad bowl.

WHILE peppers are roasting, grill corn, scallions, and shrimp. When corn is cooked and cool enough to handle, cut kernels from cobs directly into bowl with red peppers. Thinly slice scallions (white and green parts) and add to bowl with vegetables. Remove shrimp from skewers and add to bowl. Add greens to bowl. Pour lemon juice, balsamic vinegar, salt, pepper, and remaining 3 tablespoons olive oil over salad. Toss until all ingredients are evenly distributed. Taste and adjust seasonings. Serve immediately.

If the queen's coming for dinner: Choose delicate salad greens, such as fancy mixed greens or arugula. Toss lettuces separately, divide among serving plates, and serve chopped salad in center of greens.

Roast the peppers first, throw them right into the plastic bag they came in, close the bag, and let them steam so they're ready to peel when you're through grilling. Grilled, peeled, stems removed, cored, and seeded, they keep well in the refrigerator or freezer, covered tightly.

Soak bamboo skewers in water the night before or at least 1 hour ahead so they won't burn (at least that's the theory). I've found that they don't burn as quickly and it does make a difference, but if you forget, proceed anyway. You won't lose any shrimp on the barbie.

If you've got a great sense of adventure and a little extra time on your hands, add other vegetables to your heart's desire. All of the summer squashes, any sweet onion, or any meaty mushroom (white button, brown, portobello, shiitake, or porcini) would be a delicious addition to this salad.

Oven-Roasted Tomato and Sweet Corn Gratin

This is a delicious vegetable side dish but I usually serve it as the entrée for an all-vegetarian dinner. I love a good steak, but I thoroughly enjoy all-veggie dinners once a week or so, too. Diving into heaping portions of good-for-you foods without having to worry about excess calories is what I call guilt-free-eating-with-abandon.

4 SERVINGS AS AN ENTRÉE, OR 8 AS A SIDE DISH

1 tablespoon plus 1 teaspoon olive oil

2 medium onions, peeled and finely chopped

1 tablespoon water

2 cups fresh whole-wheat or sourdough bread crumbs (4 to 6 slices bread)

Coarse-grained salt and cracked black pepper

3 ears corn, shucked

½ cup loosely packed, roughly chopped flat-leaf parsley leaves

4 to 6 medium tomatoes (about 1 pound), peeled, cored, cut into ¼-inch slices

PREHEAT oven to 350°F. In a nonstick skillet, heat 1 tablespoon olive oil over medium-high heat until hot but not smoking. Add onions; stir to coat evenly with oil. Add water to pan and cover. Cook, stirring frequently, until onions are softened, 15 to 18 minutes. While onions are cooking, season bread crumbs with salt and pepper. Set aside. Break corn cobs in half, then slice off kernels.

WHEN onions are thoroughly cooked, turn off heat. Add corn to onions; stir until corn and onions are evenly distributed. Season with salt, pepper, and parsley.

LIGHTLY spray a 9-inch square baking dish with olive oil or cooking spray. Spread one third of bread crumbs in baking dish. Top with a layer of tomatoes, then half of onion and corn mixture. Repeat layers, finishing with tomato slices. Spray (or drizzle 1 teaspoon) olive oil over tomatoes. Bake 35 to 40 minutes, or until heated through. Serve immediately.

SHORTCUT CHEF
Use frozen corn but buy the best you can get.

Cooking Thin with Chef Kathleen

Simple Corn Cakes

If I had to make a top-ten list of favorite recipes in this book, this recipe would be on it. These corn cakes are delicious, especially at the height of corn season. Even when I've made them with frozen corn, they're still great. This is a base recipe that stands on its own but feel free to add mint, basil, or even cheese, such as feta or Parmesan. I like to eat them plain but they're a wonderful backdrop to grilled shrimp topped with **Mango Papaya Salsa** (page 251).

4 SERVINGS

6 large eggs

4 cups fresh corn kernels (about 8 ears)

¼ cup minced sweet onion (such as Vidalia)

½ cup flour

2 tablespoons sugar

1 teaspoon coarse-grained salt

1 tablespoon butter, melted

¼ teaspoon cracked black pepper

1 teaspoon olive oil

PREHEAT oven to 200°F. In a large bowl, beat eggs until blended. Stir in corn, onion, flour, sugar, salt, and butter. Season with pepper. Place olive oil in a large nonstick skillet over medium-high heat. When oil is hot but not smoking, ladle batter into pan, using about 2 tablespoons batter for each corn cake. Cook 2 to 3 minutes per side, or until golden. It shouldn't be necessary, but if pan requires more oil add another teaspoon to cook second batch of cakes. Keep first batch warm in oven until all corn cakes are cooked.

Six eggs divided among four people isn't excessive, but if you want to cut calories, cut back on the yolks (for every yolk you delete, add two egg whites).

Potato, Tomato, and Onion Casserole

I know, I know, where's the cheese? Where's the cream? Where's the butter? Entrées like this leave plenty of room for dessert. Isn't that where you'd rather spend calories anyway? Listen, this is good, clean, soul-satisfying food—a nourishing wintertime supper (if you can get good tomatoes) or a perfect room-temperature summertime meal.

4 SERVINGS

2 pounds potatoes (Yukon Gold or russets), peeled and thinly sliced

3 tablespoons extra-virgin olive oil

I medium sweet onion (such as Vidalia), peeled, cored, and cut into ¼-inch slices

I tablespoon fresh thyme or lemon thyme leaves

2 tablespoons water

Coarse-grained salt and cracked black pepper

5 medium tomatoes, cored, peeled, and cut into ¼-inch slices

PREHEAT oven to 425°F. Bring a large pot of salted water to a boil. Add potatoes and blanch for 4 minutes. Remove potatoes with a slotted spoon and set aside in a large bowl with the tomatoes.

HEAT 1 tablespoon of olive oil in a large nonstick skillet over medium-high heat, add onion and thyme, and toss until well coated. Add water to pan, reduce heat to medium-low, cover, and cook until onion is translucent and cooked through, 10 to 12 minutes. Remove from heat and season with salt and pepper.

SHORTCUT CHEF

Peel and slice the tomatoes the night before and/or cook the onion. Peel potatoes and store overnight covered in water. If you blanch the potatoes, you can assemble the entire dish a day ahead. Cook the casserole if you've got the time. It's great left over.

If you're skipping dessert and have a few calories to spend, sprinkle a little freshly grated cheese between the layers—an imported Parmesan or aged provolone perhaps. Just know the cheese doesn't make the dish. The recipe is delish as is.

If you've never peeled a tomato, here's how: Fill a medium pot with water and bring to a boil. Set the pot of water in the sink. Plunge the tomatoes into the hot water for a minute and remove. Water that spills over will go down the drain instead of all over the stove. When tomatoes are cool enough to handle, core and peel.

Cooking Thin with Chef Kathleen

SEASON potatoes and tomatoes with salt and pepper. Assemble casserole in a 3-quart baking dish. Drizzle 1 tablespoon of olive oil over dish bottom and spread evenly. Place one third of onion in dish, add one third of potatoes, and top with one third of tomatoes. Continue to layer ingredients, finishing with a layer of tomatoes. Drizzle remaining 1 tablespoon olive oil over top of casserole. Cover loosely with foil, bake 20 minutes, remove foil, and bake 20 minutes longer, or until potatoes are cooked through.

FROM MOM'S LIPS TO YOUR EARS

If you can't find sweet onions, don't make the dish. The onion has to be sweet or you'll be up all night with indigestion. If you're thinking of using a moldy old onion with huge green sprouts, don't bother. And shame on you for keeping rubbish like that in the house.

Ratatouille on the Grill

My mom is the world's laziest cook and I'm second. We're forever trying to figure out ways to get the job done quicker, with the least amount of cleanup conceivable. In the summertime, on especially unbearable hot and humid days, we hate to even turn on the stove. Somehow, grilling seems easier to cope with.

4 SERVINGS AS AN ENTRÉE, OR 6 AS A SIDE DISH

FOR THE DRESSING

2 cloves garlic, minced

1 tablespoon sherry vinegar

3 tablespoons olive oil

1 cup loosely packed, roughly chopped fresh herbs (such as basil, mint, parsley)

Coarse-grained salt and cracked black pepper

FOR THE RATATOUILLE

2 teaspoons plus 1 tablespoon olive oil

1 large onion, peeled and cut into $\frac{1}{2}$-inch slices

4 ears fresh corn, shucked

2 small zucchini, cut lengthwise into $\frac{1}{4}$-inch slices

3 small eggplants, cut lengthwise into $\frac{1}{4}$-inch slices

12 mushrooms, cut in half

Coarse-grained salt and cracked black pepper

4 medium tomatoes, cored

1 red bell pepper

PREPARE DRESSING: In a small bowl, whisk together garlic, vinegar, olive oil, herbs, and salt and pepper to taste. Stir until combined. Taste and adjust seasonings.

PREPARE RATATOUILLE: Preheat grill. Using a pastry brush and 2 teaspoons of oil, brush onion slices lightly on both sides, but don't gob oil on. Place corn, zucchini, eggplants, and mushrooms in a plastic bag (I use the one I bought them in). Pour 1 tablespoon olive oil into bag and season with salt and pepper. Seal bag. Shake and turn bag to distribute oil and seasonings evenly.

WHEN fire is hot, arrange all vegetables on grill. Place red pepper over hottest flames and tomatoes over coolest flames. Cook red pepper until charred on all sides. Place in plastic bag. When cool enough to handle, peel, stem, seed, cut into 1-inch pieces, and place in a salad bowl. Cook tomatoes until softened and just beginning to fall apart. When cool enough to handle, peel off skin, which will have blistered and lifted partway off on its own. Cut each tomato into 6 or 8 pieces, right over serving bowl, so juices become part of the dressing.

GRILL all remaining vegetables until cooked through and tender. Cool slightly, cut into smaller pieces, and place in salad bowl with pepper and tomatoes. Cut corn kernels off cobs directly into salad bowl. Pour dressing over ratatouille and toss to combine. Taste and adjust seasonings; serve immediately.

SHORTCUT CHEF
Prepare vegetables to the point of grilling the night before. Store them right in the plastic bags you bought them in.

MORPH If you've got meat-loving hungry diners, serve this with thinly sliced grilled chicken or steak. Leftover ratatouille is divine served sandwich style, with Italian country loaves, baguettes, or even toasted pitas. Toss leftovers with cooked pasta; sprinkle with fresh herbs.

Read through the book to find other recipes that utilize grilled vegetables. Throw those veggies on the barbie while you've got it fired up and this week's dinners will be in the bag.

Asparagus Tart with Roasted Tomatoes

A tart can be composed of just about anything you've got on hand and need not be a complicated affair. Leftover cooked potatoes, grilled portobello mushrooms, sautéed onions, corn cut off the cob, blanched green beans, steamed broccoli, and even cooked greens make wonderful tart fillings. ■ If you can make Toll-House cookie dough, you can make tart dough. This recipe doesn't require prebaking.

The roasted tomatoes are easy to prepare, but do require three hours in the oven.

SHORTCUT CHEF
Bake the tomatoes a day ahead. Make a double batch of tart dough and keep it in the freezer up to 1 month, wrapped tightly in plastic and foil.

Read the recipe through start to finish. This isn't something you should start at four o'clock. Tarts for dinner are really very simple once you get into the tart-making groove. Your first tart experience should be wonderful, so plan to cook this on a day you have time. Shop for the ingredients in advance and you'll need a tart pan with a removable bottom.

This is not a weight-watcher meal, but it's not too over-the-top, either. Serve simple vegetable sides, such as steamed green beans, carrots, or peas. Keep the side dishes clean and have fruit for dessert instead of something heavy. Balance your calories.

10 SERVINGS

1 ½ pounds Roma tomatoes (about 8), peeled, cored, and cut into quarters

½ cup whole basil leaves

3 cloves garlic, peeled, cut in half lengthwise, and sprout removed

1 tablespoon grated lemon zest

1 ¼ cups flour

½ teaspoon coarse-grained salt

7 tablespoons cold unsalted butter, cut into small pieces

4 to 5 tablespoons ice water

8 ounces aged provolone cheese, grated

1 pound asparagus, bottoms trimmed, cut into 1-inch pieces

Guyometer: Silly girl food, but surprisingly good for something I thought I'd hate.

PREHEAT oven to 300°F. Place tomatoes, cut side up, in a shallow baking dish and bake 3 hours, or until shriveled but not blackened.

Cooking Thin with Chef Kathleen

TO make the crust, place basil, garlic, and lemon zest in bowl of a food processor. Pulse until finely chopped. Add flour and salt and pulse until just combined. With motor running, add butter a few pieces at a time and mix until there are no lumps larger than small peas. Add water a tablespoon at a time, pulsing to combine after each addition. When dough appears to be coming together to form a ball, remove from processor and mold into a ball by hand. Flatten dough into a 6-inch disk, wrap tightly in plastic, and refrigerate 1 hour.

PREHEAT oven to 375°F. On lightly floured surface, roll dough into a 14-inch circle, and press into a 10-inch tart pan with a removable bottom. Fold overhanging dough inside to build an even rim and pinch or crimp as you would pie crust. Sprinkle tart bottom with half of cheese and then all the asparagus. Arrange tomato segments over asparagus and top with remaining cheese. Bake 1 hour, or until crust is golden and cheese is bubbly brown. Serve hot, warm, or at room temperature.

If the queen's coming for dinner: She'll positively never leave. Tarts are really very beautiful. In fact, they're perfect for entertaining, especially when you want to enjoy time with your guests. It's perfectly acceptable to serve tarts at room temperature. They're wonderful for lunch, brunch, or dinner. If you cut very thin slices, you could even serve a tart as an appetizer.

FROM MOM'S LIPS TO YOUR EARS

Aged provolone is worth the trouble it takes to find it. You need to have a chunk of Parmesan and a chunk of aged provolone around all the time. They don't have all the calories and fat of creamier cheeses and because they're so strong and dry, a little goes a long way. And if you weren't paying attention at the beginning of the book, you need to have grated mozzarella in the freezer at all times, too. Replace this stuff as you run out. You can't live without toilet paper, right? You don't run out of that very often. So don't run out of staples.

Zucchini-Tomato Torta

This torta is a big hit in my house and definitely worth the time it takes to make. This version is made with zucchini, but the sky's the limit here, so try using several varieties of summer squash, eggplants, and roasted peppers. Looking for a way to use up summer's abundance of fresh herbs? Try layering in some of your favorites, such as basil, oregano, parsley, or thyme.

4 SERVINGS

6 medium yellow squash or zucchini

1 tablespoon plus 2 teaspoons extra-virgin olive oil

Coarse-grained salt and cracked black pepper

2 medium cloves garlic, minced

1¾ cups canned crushed tomatoes with juice (or crush canned whole tomatoes yourself)

¼ cup loosely packed, roughly chopped basil leaves

8 ounces skim-milk mozzarella cheese, shredded

¼ cup freshly grated Parmesan cheese

PREHEAT oven to 400°F. Trim ends from zucchini; cut crosswise into ¼-inch-thick slices. Place zucchini in a plastic bag with 1 tablespoon of olive oil. Seal bag, shake, and turn until all slices of zucchini are coated with oil. Lay zucchini slices on 2 large baking sheets. Sprinkle with salt and pepper. Bake, turning once at the halfway point, just until zucchini slices start to brown, about 25 minutes.

WHILE zucchini are in oven, prepare sauce. Place garlic in a medium nonstick saucepan with remaining 2 teaspoons of olive oil. Turn heat to medium and sauté until golden, 1 to 2 minutes. Add tomatoes and simmer until thickened, about 15 minutes. Stir in basil and season with salt and pepper to taste.

LINE bottom of a 9-inch nonstick springform pan (or 9-inch square pan) with a layer of zucchini slices; do not overlap. Spoon one third of tomato sauce over zucchini and sprinkle with a generous one third of mozzarella and one third of Parmesan. Repeat process, making 3 layers of zucchini, tomato sauce, and cheese.

BAKE until top of torta is golden brown and sauce is bubbling, about 30 minutes. Cool on a rack 15 minutes.

If the queen's coming for dinner: We ask that you build the torta in a 9-inch springform pan. It looks so pretty when you present it to ungrateful diners who'd rather be eating burgers and fries. Nonetheless, if your springform pan leaks the way mine does, use a 9-inch square pan. Cut and serve as you would lasagne.

SHORTCUT CHEF

You can skip the garlic or use the jarred variety. Of course by now you've got pregrated mozzarella in your freezer, so you can cut that little chore out. No? Tsk. Tsk. Work with me, people. Keep grated mozzarella and coarse and fine bread crumbs in your freezer— they come in so handy.

Zucchini, Scallion, Onion, and Cheese Pancakes

Okay, so you don't need a griddle to make them and thank goodness for that—how many of us have one? They're not pancakes in the breakfast sense. They're more on the order of potato pancakes, which can be served anytime. These are dinner or weekend entertaining pancakes. I wouldn't recommend them for breakfast unless it's a special brunch-type meal.

4 SERVINGS

4 cups grated zucchini

Coarse-grained salt

1 cup crumbled feta cheese

½ cup slivered scallions

¼ cup loosely packed, roughly chopped basil

2 tablespoons loosely packed, roughly chopped mint

⅓ cup flour

Cracked black pepper

8 large egg whites

2 tablespoons olive oil

½ cup plain low-fat yogurt, for serving

PLACE grated zucchini in a large colander. Season with salt to taste. To drain zucchini of excess water, press it down with a plate and a heavy weight or a plastic bag filled with water for 1 hour.

PREHEAT oven to 200°F. In a large bowl, combine zucchini, feta cheese, scallions, basil, mint, and flour. Season with salt and pepper to taste. Beat egg whites to stiff peaks, but not dry and grainy. Gently fold egg whites into zucchini mixture.

IN a 10- or 12-inch nonstick skillet over medium-high heat, drizzle only enough oil to coat pan bottom. When oil is hot but not smoking, ladle batter, ¼ cup per pancake, into pan. Cook as you would breakfast pancakes, until golden, about 2 minutes per side. Place cooked pancakes on a cookie sheet and keep warm in the oven until you've cooked the last one. Serve immediately with a dollop of yogurt.

Guyometer:
Good. But can
we have steak
tomorrow?

SHORTCUT CHEF

Grate the zucchini ahead. Crumble the feta, slice the scallions, and separate the eggs.

If you hate feta cheese, use blue cheese or Parmesan or skip the cheese altogether. It's not absolutely necessary.

If you want to cut back even further on fat calories, lightly mist the pan instead of using olive oil straight from the bottle. But be sure to *lightly* mist it or you'll end up using the same amount or more. If you keep your pan at an even steady heat, you won't need to use the entire 2 tablespoons of oil called for.

Light Meals, Vegetarian Entrées, and Entrée Salads

Fish

AS KIDS WE'D TROMP HOME from school and talk about

what dinner might be. On days when we slammed open the front door (with

a force only schoolchildren possess) and got a smelly whiff of frying fish, we'd

scream, "Oh, ish! It's fish! Gross, Mom. We don't want any dinner."

Fish is good for you and you know it. They tell us we're supposed to have

two or more servings per week; the sooner we do, the better our health will be. Fish is one of the quickest meals you can get on the table. There's nothing hard about plopping a piece of salt-and-peppered fish in a nonstick pan and throwing it into the oven for 10 to 12 minutes, is there? Snap out of it! With a couple of great veggie sides, you're home free.

True, fish can be a little pricey, but so is a trip to the cardiologist. Splurge a little. You're worth it! Now that you're totally motivated to do what you know you must, you're probably thinking, Kathleen, how do I wade through all those choices, what's good, what's not? How do I know if it's fresh? Is my husband going to like it?

One thing at a time! First of all, it's easier to look at a whole fish and assess its freshness or lack thereof: clear, bulging eyes, bright red gills, scales adhering so firmly to the flesh that you notice only that the fish looks wet and glassy and, of course, firm-to-the-touch flesh. That said, most of us don't buy whole fish, let alone bounce quarters off one to determine firmness. But where there are fish fillets and fish steaks, there are whole fish! Examining the whole fish on display at your fish counter is a clear indication of the quality of the rest of the inventory. You with me, secret agents?

Choosing fish fillets and steaks is a little trickier, but if you can raise kids, tend to families, and manage careers inside and outside the home, you can select great fish for dinner. Increase your odds by frequenting stores that really move their merchandise, and shop around until you find a consistent source. Fish displays should look clean and the product should look well cared for and appetizing. If it doesn't, move on.

Fit-to-purchase fish fillets and steaks will be perky, brightly colored, firm looking as opposed to waterlogged and soggy, and they'll smell clean—hopefully, of their home waters. If you're trying out a new vendor, buy only enough for the evening meal. When you've hit the fresh-fish jackpot, you might consider buying extra and freezing some for later. Fresh is better than frozen and eating it on board the boat it was caught from is better too, but we're talking about maintaining a lifestyle here.

For those of you who don't fry fish because "it stinks up the house," we don't, either (we took away Mom's frying pan). We realized that baking fish substantially reduces its odors. These preparations are guaranteed to be "little stinkers," as in they won't stink up the curtains. Cooking fish outside is another way of keeping the smell away, but you knew that.

Oven-Baked Salmon with Ginger and Lime

If you're committing to a healthy lifestyle, useful tools are essential. A cast-iron broiling pan is a small investment worth every penny. Cooking chicken, fish, shrimp, and even beef kabobs under the broiler takes just a few minutes. Because the cast-iron holds so much heat, the "meat" sears on the outside and remains moist on the inside.

4 SERVINGS

2 tablespoons fresh lime juice

2 teaspoons grated ginger

One 1¼-pound salmon fillet, skin removed

Coarse-grained salt

2 limes, cut in wedges

PREHEAT oven to 450°F. If you're using a cast-iron broiling pan, place in oven 10 to 15 minutes ahead to preheat.

IN a small bowl, whisk together lime juice and ginger. Place salmon fillet in a shallow dish; season with salt on both sides. Pour marinade over salmon, turning fillet over to distribute evenly. Cover salmon with plastic wrap and let stand, refrigerated, until you are ready to cook it, no more than 30 minutes.

SPRAY broiler pan with oil. Place salmon on pan and cook for 10 to 15 minutes, turning once at the halfway point, or until cooked to your liking. Cooking time will vary with thickness of fillet. Serve immediately with lime wedges.

You can prepare the salmon in a nonstick skillet over medium-high heat for 6 to 8 minutes per side, or until cooked to your liking. The marinade will keep the salmon from sticking to the pan, so you should not need additional oil.

Salmon is fine with lemon and a little salt and pepper, Kathleen. All that fancy stuff (ginger and lime) is just busywork. People are busy enough already.

Fish

Oven-Baked Salmon with Cucumber Salad

This recipe almost didn't make the cut because wasabi sounds intimidating. I decided to keep it in because wasabi is precisely the kind of ingredient you need to gravitate toward. It adds a lot of flavor and great character to the finished dish, leaving you satisfied with good-for-you calories. It's easy to throw butter and oil into food to make it taste better. It's just as easy to throw in high-impact flavor ingredients like wasabi once you learn how. Wasabi, the root of an Asian plant, has a horseradish-like flavor and is available in paste and powder form in most grocery stores in the Asian ingredients section. Adding water to wasabi powder constitutes prepared wasabi.

4 SERVINGS

2 cucumbers, peeled, seeded, and cut into ½-inch chunks

Coarse-grained salt

¼ cup fresh lemon juice

⅓ cup rice wine vinegar

1 teaspoon finely chopped pickled or grated fresh ginger

1½ tablespoons sugar

1 teaspoon prepared wasabi

One 12-ounce salmon fillet, skin removed

Cracked black pepper

2 teaspoons extra-virgin or good-quality olive oil

PLACE cucumbers in a colander and season with salt. Fill a gallon-size plastic bag with water, seal, and place on top of cucumbers to press out excess water. Let stand 1 hour.

IN a medium nonreactive bowl, whisk together lemon juice, rice wine vinegar, ginger, sugar, and wasabi and stir until completely dissolved. Add cucumbers and stir to coat.

TWENTY minutes prior to cooking the salmon, heat oven to 450°F. Season salmon with salt and pepper. Oil a baking pan and add salmon. Bake until salmon is cooked through, 12 to 15 minutes. Cut salmon into 4 pieces and place 1 piece on each serving dish. Spoon cucumber salad over salmon and serve immediately.

Guyometer:
What is this
supposed to be?
It's pretty good.
Unusual, but
good.

Prep the cucumbers early in the day, squeeze the lemon juice, gather all other ingredients, and set out the tools you'll need.

If you can't find wasabi, use the same amount of horse-radish instead. It's not exactly the same but it's a very good substitute. On the other hand, if you don't want the spicy element in your salad, skip it altogether.

Baked Fish with Soy Dill Sauce

Too tired to cook? Don't. You'll hardly have to put in any effort at all to get this dinner on the table. The trip to the market to pick up the fish will take longer. Have your partner pick up the catch of the day. If you don't have dill, use basil, mint, parsley, or any combination of fresh herbs that appeals to you. You might grate in a bit of fresh ginger if the spirit moves you, and if you're feeling ambitious, add a little chopped garlic to the mix.

4 SERVINGS

3 tablespoons low-sodium soy sauce

2 scallions, thinly sliced (white and some green parts)

¼ cup loosely packed, freshly chopped dill

Cracked black pepper

1¼ pounds tilapia or other good-to-bake fish (ask at the fish counter for recommendations or try any white fish or salmon)

PREHEAT oven to 425°F. In a 7 × 11-inch baking dish (any baking pan that will hold the fish in a single layer will do), mix together soy sauce, scallions, dill, and pepper. Stir until combined. To coat fish with marinade, place it in pan and turn over a few times, ending with the fish skin side down if your fish has skin. Bake 10 minutes, or until thickest part of fish is slightly firm and springs back lightly. Remove skin and serve.

Guyometer:
That was fast,
and good.

Fresh ginger keeps almost forever (or at least two weeks) in the refrigerator. Just cut off the dried-up part when you want to use it next.

Swordfish with Olive Oil, Lemon, and Parsley

This is mock pan-fried fish, the kind of fried that won't send you to the cardiac wing. Buttery swordfish steaks are my favorite fish for this quick pan supper. I can't imagine anyone not loving them, but if you don't or they're too expensive, this recipe will work with just about any thin fish. Remember to adjust the cooking time.

4 SERVINGS

1 pound skinless swordfish steak, cut ⅜ inch thick

Coarse-grained salt and cracked black pepper

Grated zest of 1 lemon (use the microplane grater—
  do you have it yet?)

¼ cup loosely packed flat-leaf parsley leaves

2 teaspoons good-quality olive oil

4 lemon wedges

Guyometer:
Great. For fish.

SEASON fish with salt and pepper. Sprinkle both sides of fish with lemon zest. Press parsley leaves onto both sides of fish. The leaves will stick to the fish the way postage stamps stick to envelopes. Okay, that's a stretch, but they'll stay in place long enough for you to get the fish in the pan, which is where they'll really stick.

HEAT olive oil over medium-high heat in a large nonstick skillet. When oil is hot but not smoking, add fish to pan and cook, turning once, until golden and fork-tender, about 2 minutes per side. Serve with lemon wedges.

If the queen's coming for dinner: Use
sage leaves instead of parsley. They're
so pretty pressed into the fish that
she'll surely come to dine again.

Ask your fishmonger to remove the skin for you.

Fish

Pan-Fried Paprika Sole

If you're too tired to cook, cook this anyway. It's very, very easy. This is one of those dinners you really can get on the table almost as fast as you can bring a large pot of water to a boil. In fact, bring a pot of water to a boil and throw in a few ears of corn and some green beans for lickety-split veggie sides. Customize this cook-at-home routine to your everyday reality and you'll be way, way ahead of the game.

4 SERVINGS

½ cup flour

1 tablespoon fresh thyme leaves or 1 teaspoon dried

2 teaspoons paprika

⅛ teaspoon cayenne pepper

1 teaspoon coarse-grained salt

¼ teaspoon cracked black pepper

½ cup milk

1 pound sole or other white fish fillets

½ cup fresh lemon juice

¼ cup loosely packed, roughly chopped flat-leaf parsley leaves

2 tablespoons roughly chopped fresh chives

2 teaspoons capers, rinsed

Guyometer:
Pretty good for a
healthy dinner.

PLACE flour in a plastic bag large enough to hold and shake fish. Add thyme, paprika, cayenne, salt, and pepper. Shake until evenly distributed. Place milk in a shallow dish and dip one piece of fish at a time into milk. Make sure fish is coated with milk, shake off excess, and place in bag with flour. Gently turn fish over in bag until it is coated on all sides with flour mixture. Shake off excess flour coating. Set fish aside in a single layer. Repeat until all fish fillets are coated.

PLACE a large nonstick skillet on stove over medium-high heat. Using olive oil spray, coat pan bottom evenly with a fine mist. When pan is hot but not smoking, place fish in pan in a single layer. Spray fish with a fine mist of olive oil. Cook 1 to 2 minutes per side, until fish is firm to the touch. Remove fish from pan; keep warm in a 200°F oven if making a large batch.

INCREASE heat to high; add lemon juice, parsley, chives, and capers to pan. Reduce until slightly thickened, about 1 minute. Pour over fish and serve immediately.

If the queen's coming for dinner: Place lemon wedges and sprigs of parsley on each plate before serving.

Make up the flour mix the night before.

Don't use bottled lemon juice. It will never do. If you don't have lemons, use limes or serve the fish with Horse-radish Sauce (page 245).

Pan-Fried Potato Fish Cakes

Over Cheerios one morning, my mom said to me, "What do you want with your cod cakes for dinner?" An air sickness bag came to mind. She said, "No, really." "Mom, people aren't going to want cod cakes for dinner. Crab cakes, salmon cakes, maybe, but cod cakes?" ▪ Defiantly pushing on to prove her hunch that you'd be interested in eating cod cakes for supper, she declared, "James Beard's mom used to make them for him." "Mom, no one's going to eat them just because James Beard's mom thought they were a good idea." "They have ginger in them." "And that's supposed to be a selling point?" "Well, they've got butter, cream, and eggs, too." "Mom, I hardly think people want to blow dessert calories on fish cakes." "Well, what would you put in them, Miss Smarty-Pants?" ▪ "Can we lose some of the butter? How about a couple of egg whites instead of the whole eggs and let's skip the cream altogether. A few scallions or chives could be good." And that's how we came up with the best cleaned-up fish cakes you'll ever eat.

4 SERVINGS

1 pound white fish fillets (such as cod)

1 tablespoon white vinegar

1 teaspoon pickling spice

4 cups plain (no seasonings, butter, or milk) mashed potatoes, hot

2 tablespoons unsalted butter, softened

1/2 cup loosely packed, roughly chopped flat-leaf parsley leaves

4 scallions, thinly sliced (white and green parts)

1/8 teaspoon cayenne pepper (or more to taste)

3/4 teaspoon coarse-grained salt (or more to taste)

1/4 teaspoon cracked black pepper

1 lemon, cut into 8 wedges (optional)

1/2 cup plain yogurt (optional)

Guyometer:
If nothing is the alternative, these are pretty good, but I'd rather have steak any day.

Cooking Thin with Chef Kathleen

PLACE fish, vinegar, and pickling spice in a pan just large enough to hold fish and add enough water to cover fish. Remove fish and bring liquid to a boil; immediately reduce heat to low and place fish in pan. Poach 7 to 9 minutes at a very gentle simmer, or until fish flakes and is cooked through. Drain.

PLACE fish in a mixing bowl with hot potatoes, butter, parsley, scallions, cayenne, salt, and pepper. Mix until completely incorporated.

USING your hands, form fish mixture into 3-inch patties, about ¼ inch thick. Coat a large nonstick skillet with olive oil spray. Cook fish cakes until hot all the way through and golden and crispy outside, 3 to 4 minutes per side. Serve with lemon wedges and plain yogurt.

If the queen's coming for dinner: Serve fish cakes with the Quick Roasted Red Pepper Sauce on page 246. The flavors in the sauce complement the fish cakes beautifully, and the presentation is very haute cuisine without a whole lot of fuss.

Plan this supper by preparing mashed potatoes earlier in the week as a side dish. Remember to take out the 4 cups required for this recipe before seasoning them.

This recipe calls for plain mashed potatoes and poached fish, so be sure to read the recipe from start to finish and allow enough time.

Fish

Lemony Poached Cod

You're probably thinking that you'll never be able to sell poached fish to your family, but this recipe is a lovely room-temperature Italian dish, which means you can prepare it ahead. In fact, it's best served cooked at least 2 hours ahead of serving.

4 SERVINGS

FOR POACHING

4 cups water

I bay leaf

I scallion, roughly chopped

2 parsley sprigs

I teaspoon salt

I pound cod fillets

FOR THE DRESSING

2 scallions, thinly sliced (green and white parts)

¼ cup loosely packed, roughly chopped parsley leaves

2 tablespoons chopped fresh thyme or I teaspoon dried

I tablespoon grated lemon zest

¼ cup fresh lemon juice

2 tablespoons extra-virgin olive oil

Coarse-grained salt and cracked black pepper

POACH FISH: Pour 4 cups or enough water to cover fish into a skillet just large enough to hold fish. Add bay leaf, scallion, parsley, and salt. Bring water to a boil. Using a spatula, slide fish into water and reduce heat to low. Cook 7 to 9 minutes, or until fish is firm but not hard. Remove fish to a serving platter.

PREPARE DRESSING: Place ¼ cup poaching liquid in a small mixing bowl, discarding bay leaf and remaining liquid. Add scallions, parsley, thyme, lemon zest, lemon juice, and olive oil; mix well. Add salt and pepper to taste. Spoon over fish. Serve warm or at room temperature.

Cod might be the best choice or maybe not. Ask the person behind the fish counter to sell you the best piece of fish for poaching purposes.

Cooking Thin with Chef Kathleen

Meat

SADLY, SINGLE-SERVING 32-ounce porterhouse steaks are

now a thing of the past. The meat police strictly enforce 3-to-4-ounce

servings, roughly the size of a deck of cards. My father is still trying to find

a loophole in this law. But my mother manages to fool him into thinking he's

getting big servings by slicing and fanning the meat and by keeping his plate full

of vegetables and potatoes. Hey, listen, whatever works.

Use meat as a flavoring and a condiment rather than the main focus of your meal, because it's a high-calorie item no matter how you slice it. You just don't get much bang for your calorie buck with some meats. The sooner you come around to this way of thinking, the easier life will be. At least you still get to eat meat. Besides, you save lots of money at the grocery store. Fennel isn't usually over ten dollars a pound.

To wean meat eaters, I recommend gradually scaling back on the number of times meat is served as the main entrée each week. Certainly never eat meat two nights in a row or you'll blow your weekly meat allotment before Wednesday. Meat's rich characteristics and intense flavors account for its intoxicating draw. Construct equally exciting meals with sturdy gusto and the meat eaters won't catch on. Try polenta or Spaghetti with Baby Back Rib Sauce (page 206), Chili Pork Stew (page 325), quick pan-fried Pork Tenderloin with White Wine Sauce (page 326), or Chicken Burgers (page 328).

Where's-the-beef dinner expectations will end a lot sooner if you stick to having dessert only on light meal nights. Meat for dinner, fruit for dessert. Soup for dinner, chocolate for dessert. They'll catch on pretty quickly, trust me.

BBQ Spare Ribs

Who'd think spare ribs could be part of a naturally healthful diet? They're certainly not a "free" food (something you can eat with abandon), but an occasional dinner of spare ribs is perfectly acceptable. Most of my tricks for keeping this supper slim have to do with planning, shopping, and portion control. ▪ At the butcher, you'll have a choice of restaurant-style spare ribs, plain old spare ribs, and baby back spare ribs. Choose baby back ribs, which are the most succulent and the easiest to prepare; they also contain the least fat. They happen to be the most expensive but they're the best. ▪ Plan on three ribs per person. Fred Flintstone would have you believe an entire rack is a single serving. This is just not the case, and if you're trying to live healthy, serve plenty of delicious side dishes, and no one will miss the extra calories. ▪ Choose a barbecue sauce high on flavor and short on fat, or make Jack's BBQ Sauce if you've got time. Nothing you can buy will come close to this outrageous sauce. Otherwise, read the labels on the store-bought varieties; you'll be surprised at the calorie differences.

4 SERVINGS

1 slab baby back ribs (about 2 pounds)

Salt and pepper

¾ to 1 cup barbecue sauce (see Jack's BBQ Sauce, page 242)

Guyometer: Eat slow. If your wife's anything like mine, you're not going to get seconds.

SHORTCUT CHEF
Make Jack's BBQ Sauce ahead. It's really quick to throw together.

You're going to have to serve plenty of vegetable side dishes, because you just can't serve a slab per person unless you're not watching your calorie intake. Check out these side dishes: Buttery Mashed Potatoes (page 185), Quick and Spicy Carrot Slaw (page 147), and how about plain steamed green beans or a quick tossed salad?

Ribs are sold in slabs, so you may end up buying more than three ribs per person. In that case, cut off the extra ribs before you cook them and save them for Spaghetti with Baby Back Rib Sauce (page 206).

PREHEAT oven to 400°F. Season baby back ribs with salt and pepper. Place in a 7 × 11-inch baking pan or your oven broiler pan. Cover tightly with foil. Bake 1 hour. Remove from oven, discard foil, and pour off liquid that has accumulated in pan bottom. Pour barbecue sauce over ribs, turning once to cover both sides evenly. Return to oven for 10 minutes. Remove from oven. Cut between ribs, portioning 3 ribs per person. Serve immediately.

Flank Steak and Roasted Vegetables with Crispy Potatoes

Instead of pouting on those gloomy winter weekends, re-create summer's luscious char-grilled flavors indoors. But when you can prepare this on the backyard grill, do. Grill extra veggies and save them for veggie sub sandwiches midweek.

6 TO 8 SERVINGS

One 1¼-pound flank steak

⅓ cup fresh lime juice

Coarse-grained salt and cracked black pepper

2 large potatoes, peeled and thinly sliced

2 tablespoons olive oil

1 yellow squash (such as crookneck), cut into ½-inch slices

1 zucchini, cut into ½-inch slices

1 large red bell pepper, cored, seeded, and cut into quarters

1 tablespoon red wine vinegar

⅓ cup loosely packed, chopped fresh herbs (such as basil, parsley, and mint)

PREHEAT oven to 425°F. Season steak with salt and pepper and place in a sealable plastic bag. Add lime juice; refrigerate for 1 hour.

PLACE potatoes in a plastic bag with 1 tablespoon of oil, salt, and pepper. Shake to coat. Arrange potatoes in a single layer on cookie sheets. Bake 24 to 26 minutes, turning once at the halfway point.

PLACE squash, zucchini, and red pepper in a plastic bag with remaining 1 tablespoon oil. Shake to coat and arrange in a single layer on a cookie sheet; season with salt and pepper on each side. Bake 16 minutes, turning each vegetable halfway through.

PREHEAT broiler to high. Place steak on a broiler pan. Broil, turning once, to desired doneness, 7 to 9 minutes for medium rare. Let steak rest 10 minutes and then cut into thin slices.

DIVIDE cooked potatoes among serving plates in a single layer. Cut roasted peppers into strips and place with remaining vegetables in a large salad bowl with steak slices. Add vinegar and herbs and toss until well combined. Taste and adjust seasonings. Serve on top of potatoes.

SHORTCUT CHEF
Entertaining? Cooking for friends you want to impress doesn't get much easier than this. Prep everything up to the point of cooking, the day before the big bash. Slice and season the veggies and marinate the steak. Go wild and grill the veggies hours ahead of party time. This entrée is delicious served hot or at room temperature.

MORPH If you're serving fewer than 6 people, the leftovers make great take-to-work sandwiches.

You don't have to use yellow squash *and* zucchini; use all one or the other or any veggies you want, for that matter. Ask for a small flank steak unless you're feeding a crowd.

Flank Steak, Grilled Onion, and Tomato Sandwiches

Flank steak is a rich and beefy cut of meat that loves a good marinade. Good certainly doesn't mean complicated. After testing dozens of rubs, spice mixes, and marinades, I found this to be my favorite way to dress this quick-cooking steak. ■ The onions must be sweet. Don't accept that an onion is an onion. Choose a variety that's bred to be sweet, such as Granex, Walla Walla, Maui, Vidalia, or Texas Sugar Babies. The tomatoes have to be ripe, too, or leave them out. There's nothing worse than a flavorless tomato—you might as well chew on foam.

6 SERVINGS (WITH SOME MEAT LEFT OVER)

1 ½ pounds flank steak

½ teaspoon coarse-grained salt

¼ teaspoon cracked black pepper

¼ cup fresh lime juice

1 tablespoon extra-virgin olive oil

2 large sweet onions, cut into ½-inch slices

2 large tomatoes, cored and sliced

6 focaccia buns, cut in half horizontally

4 tablespoons Salsa Verde (page 252)

Guyometer:
Meat!

SPRINKLE steak with salt and pepper on both sides. Place in a sealable plastic bag. Add lime juice and olive oil. Seal bag. Shake and turn until lime juice and olive oil are evenly distributed. Place in refrigerator for ½ hour.

IN a large nonstick pan over medium-high heat, heat 1 tablespoon of marinade from bag with steak. Add steak to pan and sauté until medium rare, 5 to 7 minutes per side. You may add extra marinade if necessary.

Cooking Thin with Chef Kathleen

REMOVE steak from pan and let rest on a cutting board 10 minutes. Meanwhile, add onion slices to pan with any remaining marinade. Sauté until softened and translucent, 4 to 5 minutes per side.

USING a sharp knife, cut steak into thin slices across the grain. Place 1 tomato slice on each bun bottom. Lay 5 to 7 thin slices (3 ounces per person) of steak over each tomato slice. Top each sandwich with onions, 2 teaspoons of salsa verde, and a bun top. Cut in half diagonally and serve immediately.

If the queen's coming for dinner: Ask her if she can come another night and invite the boys over instead. They'll appreciate this meal more than she will.

SHORTCUT CHEF
The Salsa Verde drizzled over the sandwiches is outrageous. Make it a day ahead—it's great left over, but if you don't want to fuss with it, add a slice or two of avocado instead.

MORPH Buy a bigger flank steak and pack up sandwiches for the lunch box or add to a salad.

If you're preparing this meal on an outdoor grill, spear onion slices on bamboo skewers that have been soaked in water up to 1 hour before. This will prevent the skewers from burning and the onion slices from falling through grill grates.

FROM MOM'S LIPS TO YOUR EARS
Buy fresh bread—focaccia if it's available, but don't kill yourself looking for it if it's not. Choose another soft, "baked that day" bread to soak up the delicious meat juices. Weather permitting, this is a great meal to prepare on an outdoor grill.

Pretty Quick Beef Stew

I was going to call this beef stew with carrots, potatoes, parsnips, and mustard but I figured I'd lose half of you. You wouldn't try it because it sounded weird and hard. It's neither. It's pretty quick to throw together and very, very satisfying. It positively won't take you all day to prepare and really doesn't require a lot of prep, unless you consider washing and cutting a few vegetables a lot of work.

4 TO 6 SERVINGS

1 tablespoon olive oil

¾ pound beef stew meat, trimmed of all visible fat, cut into 1-inch cubes

1 medium sweet onion, cut in half and thinly sliced

1 pound carrots, peeled and cut into 1½-inch chunks

1 pound parsnips, peeled and cut into 1½-inch chunks

1 pound new potatoes (or larger potatoes, peeled and cut into 1½-inch chunks)

6 cups Chicken Stock (page 95), Vegetable Stock (page 96), or canned broth

Coarse-grained salt and cracked black pepper

2 tablespoons coarse-grained mustard

PREHEAT oven to 375°F. In a large ovenproof soup pot, heat olive oil over medium-high heat. Add meat and cook, stirring occasionally, until browned on all sides, 5 to 7 minutes. Add onion to pot and cook, stirring often, until it begins to soften, 5 to 7 minutes more.

ADD carrots, parsnips, potatoes, and stock to pot. Season with salt and pepper. Bring to a boil, then turn off heat. Taste and adjust seasonings. Cover pot with its lid or aluminum foil. Bake

SHORTCUT CHEF

Peel the carrots and parsnips, cut into chunks, and store in plastic bags, refrigerated. Peel and slice the onions. If you're not using small new potatoes, peel the potatoes, store in a container covered with water, and refrigerate until you're ready to cut them into chunks.

MORPH Make extra, a double batch even. It's the perfect kind of recipe to freeze. Package stew in individual or family-size portions. You'll love defrosting this hearty meal on nights you're too tired to cope with cooking. You can thank me later.

for 1½ to 1¾ hours, or until vegetables and meat are fork-tender. Using a slotted spoon, remove vegetables and meat to a large serving dish (not a platter, or the broth will spill over). Set pot over medium-high heat and bring broth to a boil; stir in mustard. Cook a minute or so, or until mustard is blended. You're not looking to make a thick sauce but I suppose you could cook it down if you wanted to. Pour sauce over vegetables and meat. Serve immediately.

Guyometer:
Mmm. Meat and
potatoes. Oh yeah.

It's very important that you cut all the vegetables except the onions into like-size pieces so they cook evenly. Choose a chunk size and stay with it.

Meat

Super Pot Roast Supper

This was one of my grandma Genevieve's favorite dinners as a child and remained so throughout her life. Her mother used to fix it for her, and when my mom was old enough she took over pot roast preparations and has handed down the recipe to all of us. There are no mystery ingredients in the recipe; the preparation is really quite simple. I think the memories were made by the fact that no one missed dinner on pot roast night. It's turned into our family's way of having Thanksgiving dinner once a month or so.

6 TO 8 SERVINGS

One 2-pound boneless beef chuck roast, trimmed of all visible fat

1 teaspoon coarse-grained salt

½ teaspoon cracked black pepper

1 tablespoon olive oil

6 thyme sprigs

1 bay leaf

¼ cup water

One 28-ounce can diced or whole tomatoes with juice

2½ cups thinly sliced onions (about 2 small)

4 cups 1-to-2-inch carrot chunks (6 to 10 carrots)

2 cups ¾-inch celery slices (about 4 stalks)

1½ pounds Yukon Gold or russet potatoes, peeled and cut into 2-inch chunks

PREHEAT oven to 350°F. Season meat with salt and pepper. In a large, heavy-bottomed pan, heat olive oil over medium-high heat. When oil is hot but not smoking, add meat to pan and brown on all sides, about 5 minutes per side. Turn off heat. Remove meat from pan and pour off any fat. Add thyme sprigs, bay leaf, water, and canned tomatoes with juice. Return meat to pan and place onions over meat. Cover and bake 1 hour.

REMOVE cover; continue baking uncovered for 1 more hour. Add carrots, celery, and potatoes to pan. Cover and bake until meat is tender and vegetables are fork-tender, about 1 hour more. Meat is done when tender to touch and falls apart easily. Remove and discard thyme sprigs and bay leaf.

TO STORE OVERNIGHT: Lift out carrots, celery, and potatoes and place in a bowl. Taste sauce and adjust seasonings. Refrigerate meat with sauce in pot. Refrigerate vegetables in a separate container. Remove hardened fat. Return vegetables to meat and reheat in the oven, on the stovetop, or in the microwave.

TO SERVE ON SAME DAY YOU MAKE IT: Remove meat from pot and place on a serving platter. Using a slotted spoon or tongs, gently lift vegetables from cooking liquids and place on serving platter with meat. Pour remaining liquid into a glass measuring cup large enough to hold it. Using a turkey baster, draw out sauce by placing baster at bottom of cup (the fat will have risen to the top). Pour defatted sauce over meat. Discard fat.

Guyometer:
A real meat-and-
potatoes dinner.

SHORTCUT CHEF

Make this a day ahead for even better flavor and easier fat removal. Refrigerate overnight (right in the pot if you're as lazy as I am). Any remaining fat will rise to the top and harden for simple removal. To reheat, just place the pot on the stove over medium-low heat and heat until the meat and vegetables are hot all the way through, about 20 minutes. This is a good trick to use with any stew, braised dinner, or soup that may have hidden fat.

MORPH Sick and tired of cooking? Make a double batch and freeze it. This dinner is better the second day, which makes it a perfect make-ahead-and-freeze-it candidate. As always, think about how you're going to reheat the pot roast from the freezer and store it accordingly. Do you need to put it in a microwave-proof container or a plastic bag set inside a refrigerator dish? Think it through so defrosting and reheating can be done by the troops.

Brisket for Dave

Whenever I could, I'd cook for my friend Dave. He was up there in years and didn't get out to his favorite restaurants as often as he wished. So we traded services: food for wisdom. I think I may have come out ahead in the deal, but I know he enjoyed the meals, too. ■ I'll never forget the first time my mom and I cooked brisket for Dave. She arrived home with a gigantic butcher-wrapped package that was at least 2 feet long. "Kathleen, what on earth are we going to cook this in? We don't have a pan big enough." We hated to do it, but we cut the brisket in half crosswise. I can hear Jewish moms all across America gasping, but it was either that or build a makeshift stove in the bathtub. Besides, it turned out beautifully. Dave talked about that brisket to his last day.

10 SERVINGS WITH LEFTOVERS

5 pounds or so lean brisket of beef, cut in half. (Ask for "first cut" brisket—it's leaner. Your butcher will know what you're asking for. Don't worry if it weighs more, the recipe will work just fine.)

Coarse-grained salt and cracked black pepper

1 tablespoon flour

2 tablespoons olive oil

8 medium onions, thickly sliced

2 cloves garlic, thinly sliced

2 tablespoons tomato paste

Scrubbed small potatoes (3 to 4 per person)

Peeled carrots, cut into 1½-inch chunks (1 to 2 medium per person)

PREHEAT oven to 375°F. Using a sharp knife, remove and discard some of visible fat from brisket. Remainder can come off before serving. Season generously with salt and pepper. Sift flour over meat on all sides.

PLACE 1 tablespoon of olive oil in an ovenproof soup pot (largest one you have), or if you're lucky enough to own a giant brisket-size ovenproof casserole, use that. Heat oil over medium-high heat. Add first piece of brisket to pan and brown on all sides until golden. Remove from pot; set aside. Add remaining 1 tablespoon oil and brown second brisket piece on all sides; then remove from pot. Add onions and cook, stirring often, until golden, 10 to 15 minutes. Turn off heat and add garlic to onions; stir to combine.

PLACE brisket pieces back in pot over onions. Using a rubber spatula, spread tomato paste over brisket tops. Cover tightly and place in oven. Bake 2 hours. Remove from oven. One at a time, cut brisket pieces into ¼-inch-thick slices and carefully return to pot, keeping them as close to "whole" as possible. Once all brisket is back in pot, slightly angle brisket slices in neatest row(s) possible. Don't make yourself nuts.

ADD potatoes and carrots to pot, pushing them down into liquid. Taste broth and adjust seasonings. Cover tightly. Return to oven for 1¼ to 1½ hours.

REMOVE vegetables from pot. Lift brisket out of juices, arrange on a platter, and surround with vegetables. Taste sauce, adjust seasonings, and spoon over brisket platter. Serve immediately.

Guyometer:
You're a fool if you miss brisket night.

SHORTCUT CHEF

Get ahead on your veggie prep. Peel and slice the garlic, scrub the spuds, peel and slice the onions and carrots when you get a free minute, and store them in separate plastic bags.

Figure on cooking the brisket 30 to 35 minutes per pound of meat. If the onions start to stick during cooking, add a teaspoon or so of water, but not too much—remember, you're browning the onions.

Putting a lot of food on the table makes people overeat. So don't do it. Prepare everyone's plate individually. Freeze leftover brisket in family-size portions and cook up fresh vegetables each time you serve it.

FROM MOM'S LIPS TO YOUR EARS

You have to serve meat once in a while. Load up on the vegetables and don't exceed proper portion sizes. Behave and you don't have to go without.

Meat

Meat Loaf

SHORTCUT CHEF
Make the meat loaf up to
the point of baking ahead.

MORPH Make a double
batch and freeze the second
meat loaf. It's very nice to
come home to savory meals
you loved the first time
around. You don't have to
stand at the foot of the
stove seven nights a week.
It's just not a requirement.
Again, the key to high-
quality defrosted fare is
storing it properly. Use
good-quality containers,
plastic wrap, and aluminum
foil. Take a few extra minutes and label the food.
Otherwise, you're going to
be staring at unidentifiable
miscellaneous freezer
bombs. You could end up
defrosting panty hose if
you're not careful.

Our recipe calls for three
types of ground meats. You
can use whatever you want.
We wanted to show some-
thing a little different and this
combination is particularly
moist and flavorful. You can
use a mini chopper if you
have one to prepare the
mushrooms and garlic.

Gone are the high-fat ingredients and proportions that hiked calorie counts over the top. Living a healthy lifestyle doesn't mean a life of chicken and fish. There's always room for a savory meat loaf and Buttery Mashed Potatoes (page 185). Anything in moderation.

6 TO 8 SERVINGS

2 slices bread, crusts removed

¼ cup white wine

2 teaspoons olive oil

1 cup finely chopped mushrooms

2 cloves garlic, minced

½ pound lean ground veal

½ pound lean ground pork

½ pound lean ground beef

3 large egg whites, beaten

½ cup low-fat or nonfat sour cream

1 teaspoon salt (or more to taste)

½ teaspoon freshly cracked black pepper

PREHEAT oven to 400°F. In a large mixing bowl, toss bread slices with wine until evenly coated; set aside to soak. In a medium nonstick pan, heat olive oil over medium heat until hot but not smoking. Add mushrooms and garlic. Sauté until mushrooms have released their water and are cooked through, 6 to 8 minutes. Tear up soaked bread to make crumbs. Place meats in a mixing bowl with bread crumbs. Add mushroom-garlic mixture, egg whites, sour cream, salt, and pepper. Mix until all ingredients are well combined. Form meat mixture into a log and place in a loaf pan or on a cookie sheet with sides. Bake 45 to 50 minutes, or until cooked through, or until loaf reaches 165°F on an instant-read meat thermometer.

Cooking Thin with Chef Kathleen

Cheddar Cheeseburger Deluxe

You don't have to give up your favorite foods, and there's nothing wrong with a juicy cheeseburger every now and then. The trick to keeping this supper slim is to monitor portion sizes, choose the leanest ground beef you can buy, and choose bakery fresh buns with no added sugar or fat. Don't go for giant-size buns, which may end up being too much bun for the burger and too many calories. ▪ You can cook the burgers indoors in a nonstick pan, but it's best to grill them outdoors for the added smoky flavor whenever you can.

4 SERVINGS

12 ounces lean ground beef

Coarse-grained salt and cracked black pepper

1 very large sweet onion, cut into 4 thick slices

1 teaspoon olive oil

2 ounces cheddar cheese, coarsely grated

4 hamburger buns

2 medium tomatoes, cut into thick slices

4 large lettuce leaves, washed

FIRE up the backyard grill. Divide ground beef into 4 equal portions. Form into patties and season with salt and pepper. Skewer onion slices. Using a pastry brush, coat onion slices with oil. When coals are ready, place onions over direct heat. When onions are cooked on one side, 5 to 7 minutes, turn over. Place burgers over direct heat and cook about 3 minutes. Turn patties over, top with cheese, and cook 3 to 4 minutes more, until cheese has completely melted and burgers are cooked to desired doneness. Serve cheeseburgers on buns piled high with cooked onions, tomato slices, and lettuce.

Soak four bamboo skewers in water overnight or at least 1 hour ahead so they don't burn.

Porcupines

My grandmother used to feed these to my mother as a child. They're called porcupines because they look like porcupines to a child. All the rice sticks out of the meatballs. If you've got finicky kids, you might talk them into these.

4 SERVINGS

¾ cup diced onion

1 teaspoon oil

1 tablespoon water

1 pound lean ground beef

2 cups cooked brown rice or long-grain white rice

Coarse-grained salt and cracked black pepper

One 28-ounce can crushed tomatoes with juice (or crush canned whole tomatoes yourself)

1 bay leaf

Guyometer:
Outrageous!

SHORTCUT CHEF

Make the rice the night before (see Perfect Microwave Rice on page 236). You can really make the entire dish the night before up to the point of baking.

MORPH These are great wrapped in blanched cabbage leaves, too.

If you don't mind crunchy onions, don't bother adding the water or cooking them covered. I prefer my onions soft and sweet, so I take the extra time, but it's entirely a matter of taste.

PREHEAT oven to 350°F. Place onion and oil in a nonstick skillet over medium heat and stir until onion is coated with oil. Add water to pan, cover, and cook until onion is completely softened, 15 to 20 minutes. Place meat and rice in a mixing bowl; add onion, season with salt and pepper, and mix to combine. Form into 8 sleeping porcupines (round balls) and place in a baking dish just large enough to hold but not squish them. Pour tomatoes with juice over porcupines; season with salt, pepper, and bay leaf. Bake 1 hour. Remove bay leaf before serving.

If the queen's coming for dinner: Serve something else— this is too homey.

Cooking Thin with Chef Kathleen

Chili Pork Stew

We really weren't sure what to call this dish, which has a bit of an identity crisis. It's a cross between a really great chili and a hearty soup yet has elements of a good stew. Serve it with a simple salad of garden lettuces and Quick Corn Bread (page 231) if you've got the time. It's hearty, though, so don't feel that you need a bunch of side dishes.

4 SERVINGS

2 teaspoons olive oil

1 pound pork or beef stew meat, cubed

1 cup diced onion (about 1 medium)

1 tablespoon chili powder (or more to taste)

One 28-ounce can diced tomatoes with juice

Coarse-grained salt and cracked black pepper

3 cups green beans, trimmed and cut into 2-inch pieces

2 cups corn kernels (fresh is best—3 to 4 ears)

IN a 3-quart pot, heat oil over medium-high heat. Add meat and brown on all sides, stirring often, about 5 minutes. Reduce heat to medium, add onion and chili powder, and cook until onion softens, 7 to 10 minutes more. Add tomatoes, salt, and pepper and cook on low heat for about 30 minutes. Add beans and corn and cook 20 minutes more, or until you're starving and can't wait another minute. Taste and adjust seasonings.

Guyometer: Now this is more like it.

SHORTCUT CHEF

This is another great dish to make and freeze, and as you know by now, it takes very little effort to cook a double batch. You could use a break next week.

Who needs part of a can of tomatoes hanging around in the refrigerator and why do recipes call for partial cans? What is that about? When a recipe calls for part of a can, look at the recipe, give it a thought, and decide whether you'd like to throw the rest out, watch it mold, or make more sauce. I usually like extra sauce, so I throw in the whole can. Remember this is just dinner. It's only food. Recipes don't have to be followed to the letter. Go with your instincts.

FROM MOM'S LIPS TO YOUR EARS

Cooking times in recipes are highly flexible. If you've got a hair appointment, lower the heat, get your hair done, and come home to a pot of stew. On the other hand, if you're in a hurry, turn up the heat, pay attention to what you're doing, and cook it less.

Pork Tenderloin with White Wine Sauce

Want faster than drive-through food? Quicker than you can tear those little ketchup packets open with your teeth, you can be sitting down to dinner fit for a king. This recipe works equally well with pounded chicken or very thin fish fillets.

4 SERVINGS

One 12-ounce pork tenderloin, cut crosswise into 8 or 12 slices

3 tablespoons flour

Olive oil

1 cup white wine

⅓ cup loosely packed, roughly chopped flat-leaf parsley

Coarse-grained salt and cracked black pepper

PREHEAT oven to 200°F. One at a time, place pork slices, cut side up, between 2 sheets of plastic wrap. Using a meat pounder or bottom of a heavy pot, pound pork to ⅛ inch thick. Work from center out. Place flour in a shallow dish. Dredge pork slices in flour, shaking off all excess. Place pork slices on a rack or cookie sheet but don't let them touch one another or the flour will gum up.

COOK pork slices in a 12-inch nonstick skillet (or largest one you have). Heat just enough oil to coat pan bottom (or use spray oil if you have it) over medium-high heat. When pan is hot, add as many pork slices as you can fit into pan without overlapping. Cook, turning once, until done, 1 to 2 minutes per side. Keep cooked slices warm on a plate set in oven.

SHORTCUT CHEF

Keep prepounded pork tenderloin in your freezer and you won't be sorry. Don't roll your eyes. If you follow some of this easy advice, cooking healthful fast meals can become an everyday reality.

MORPH Leftover cooked pork makes a great sandwich. Or cut the pork into little strips and add them to a stir-fry, fried rice, or soup.

IMMEDIATELY after removing last pork slices, turn heat to high, pour wine into pan, and reduce to ⅓ cup. Add parsley and salt and pepper to taste. There won't be tons of sauce, just enough to drizzle a little over each portion.

There's nothing complicated about pork tenderloin. It's very lean, highly flavorful, and easy to deal with. Weigh the whole tenderloin (or have your butcher weigh it for you) so when you're eyeballing slices, you'll have some sort of an idea how big the slices should be. Bottom line, you're aiming for 3-to-4-ounce portions per person.

No, you don't have to use white wine. You could use chicken stock or apple juice or a combination of the two. There's also a wonderful alcohol-free winelike product called Ver Jus. It's made from wine grapes and is tart with a hint of sweetness. It's available in gourmet markets near the wines or sometimes tucked in with the vinegars or fancy bottled gourmet mustards and capers. Experiment with it; try it in quick pan sauces, salad dressings, or in place of wine in any recipe, because if you think it might work, it probably will. Remember that the key to loving naturally healthful food is keeping it quick, simple, and interesting. So latch on to any flavor ingredient that appeals to you. Don't go on wild-goose chases for ingredients. Get in the habit, though, of exploring grocery store aisles. Keep a list in your wallet of ingredients and products you've read about or seen, and anytime you're someplace new, see if you can locate one of them.

Chicken Burgers

You never could have talked me into chicken burgers in my past life. I was a Whopper-with-cheese kind of girl. These chicken burgers are so profoundly flavorful I've given up fast food burgers for good. Okay, for the most part. You may be tempted to serve these hamburger style on a bun but they're devilishly good on their own.

4 TO 5 SERVINGS

1 pound ground white meat chicken

2 cups coarse to fine fresh bread crumbs

½ cup low-fat milk

3 tablespoons grated sweet onion (or finely, finely minced)

¼ teaspoon cayenne pepper

¾ teaspoon coarse-grained salt

Cracked black pepper

1 tablespoon olive oil

*Guyometer:
Now you're
talking!*

Be sure to use ground white meat chicken. If you're buying your ground chicken from the grocery store, ring the bell and ask if they've got what you're looking for or if they'll grind some chicken breast for you. You can also grind it yourself in a food processor. Remove all excess fat and cartilage from boneless, skinless chicken breast and tenders, cut into 1-inch cubes, and pulse until coarsely chopped.

Make a double or triple batch and freeze individual patties. Be sure to portion them out properly. As we know, size matters.

FROM MOM'S LIPS TO YOUR EARS

You can make fresh bread crumbs ahead. It takes only a few extra minutes. Remove the crusts from good bread (or don't remove the crusts), tear into chunks, and pulse in a mini chopper or food processor. Make a giant batch and freeze it so next time you can skip this step.

PLACE chicken in a mixing bowl. Using a rubber spatula, fold in ½ cup bread crumbs, milk, onion, cayenne, salt, and pepper to taste. Mixture will be very wet, so it will be a bit icky forming it into patties, but forge ahead. Place remaining 1½ cups bread crumbs on a dinner plate or cookie sheet. Divide chicken mixture into 4 or 5 piles (you decide which portion size is best for you) and, using your hands, shape into patties. Coat each patty with bread crumbs. Heat oil in a large nonstick skillet over medium heat and when hot, fry patties until golden and cooked through, about 5 minutes per side. Serve immediately.

If the queen's coming for dinner: Serve the burgers sans bun with Tomato Relish (page 241) or Tomato Mushroom Sauce (page 248).

Cooking Thin with Chef Kathleen

Fast Fried Chicken Tenders

When I am craving Colonel you-know-who's famous fried chicken, I make this instead. It is just as satisfying and has only a fraction of the calories. With a little advanced planning and a well-stocked pantry, you can throw this together on a moment's notice.

4 SERVINGS

12 ounces boneless, skinless chicken breasts, cut into 1-inch-wide strips, or chicken tenders

1 teaspoon coarse-grained salt

½ teaspoon cracked black pepper

2 tablespoons Dijon mustard

2 teaspoons minced garlic

1 teaspoon grated lemon zest

2 tablespoons fresh lemon juice

1 cup fresh bread crumbs

1 to 2 tablespoons olive oil or olive oil spray

1 lemon, cut into wedges

Guyometer:
Real meat.
Mmmmm.

If the queen's coming for dinner: Season the bread crumbs with salt and pepper and 1 tablespoon of chopped fresh herbs, such as thyme, oregano, and basil. She'll be duly impressed.

SEASON chicken pieces with salt and pepper. In a shallow baking dish, whisk together Dijon mustard, garlic, lemon zest, and lemon juice. Add chicken, turning several times to coat evenly. Cover with plastic wrap and refrigerate 30 minutes or overnight.

REMOVE chicken pieces from marinade and dredge in bread crumbs, coating evenly.

PLACE a large nonstick skillet over medium heat. When it is hot, add 1 tablespoon of oil or spray pan with a fine mist of oil, adding more only if necessary. Add chicken and cook until crispy and golden brown, about 3 minutes per side. Serve with lemon wedges.

SHORTCUT CHEF
Make the bread crumbs ahead, trim and slice the chicken, mince the garlic, and make the Dijon marinade, too, if you've got the time. If you do make the marinade ahead, dump the marinade ingredients in a sealable plastic bag. Squish them around until well combined, add chicken pieces, and refrigerate.

When a recipe calls for bread crumbs, I always make extra. I store them in my freezer in freezer-safe bags. Of course I always buy and freeze extra chicken breasts, wrapping each one separately so I don't pull out too many or too few.

Spicy Chicken Kabobs over Rice

Don't go turning the page because the ingredients list looks a bit lengthy. This is a shake, stir, and dazzle recipe. It's not at all hard to get on the table and it's a nice change. The great thing about this recipe is that the marinade flavors the kabobs and serves as sauce for the rice. I bet you have a few marinade recipes of your own to which you can apply this same principle. You'll need 8 to 12 skewers, 2 per serving.

4 TO 6 SERVINGS

Juice of 3 limes

1 tablespoon extra-virgin olive oil

¼ cup plain low-fat yogurt

4 cloves garlic, grated

¼ teaspoon coarse-grained salt

¼ teaspoon ground cardamom

1 teaspoon ground turmeric

½ teaspoon ground allspice

¼ teaspoon cracked black pepper

½ teaspoon ground cumin

1 pound boneless, skinless chicken breast, cut into 1-inch cubes

FOR THE RICE

2 cups long-grain rice

3½ cups Chicken Stock (page 95), canned broth, or water

½ cup dried currants or raisins

Coarse-grained salt

PLACE lime juice, olive oil, and yogurt in a bowl. Add garlic, salt, cardamom, turmeric, allspice, black pepper, and cumin. Mix until completely combined. Taste and adjust seasonings. Divide marinade in half, placing second half in refrigerator to be used later for the rice.

PLACE chicken in sealable plastic bag; pour unrefrigerated half of marinade over chicken. Seal bag and turn until all chicken is completely coated with marinade. Place in refrigerator at least 1 hour or overnight if possible. Place skewers in water and soak 1 to 2 hours.

PREPARE RICE: Place rice, stock or water, currants or raisins, and refrigerated marinade in an 8-cup glass measuring cup or any microwave-safe bowl. Rice expands during cooking, so choose a container large enough to accommodate the final product. Microwave on high, uncovered, for 10 minutes. Microwave on medium-low, uncovered, for 15 minutes. Do not stir rice at any time during cooking process. Fluff with a fork just before serving. Season with salt to taste.

MEANWHILE, preheat outdoor grill to hot or turn broiler to high. On an oiled rack, grill or broil chicken on skewers 4 to 6 minutes per side, or until fork-tender and cooked through. Serve kabobs over rice.

Guyometer: They weren't too spicy.

If the queen's coming for dinner: Go wild and get fancy. Add chunks of onion (or whatever veggie appeals to you) and pineapple to the skewers before you cook them. Cut the veggies the same size as the chicken and allow a few extra minutes of cooking time.

SHORTCUT CHEF
Marinate the chicken the night before.

Most newer microwaves have a rice setting. Follow their directions and if you're not satisfied, follow my instructions next time; they work every time.

Use two skewers per kabob so food won't twist all around on the skewer.

Seared Breast of Chicken with Orzo and Mushrooms

To eat well now and forever, the food must be deeply satisfying, affordable, and quick to prepare. This recipe meets those criteria. It's simple to prepare, yet the flavors are pleasingly complex. Not your average, run-of-the-mill, nondescript chicken dinner. Buy the best mushrooms your budget will allow. Cremini, portobello, shiitake, chanterelle, and porcini are wonderful in the recipe but not essential.

4 SERVINGS

2 cups uncooked orzo pasta

6 teaspoons olive oil

3 cups coarsely chopped wild and/or white button mushrooms

4 cloves garlic, peeled and minced

1 sweet onion, chopped (about 2 cups)

2 tablespoons balsamic vinegar

12 to 16 ounces boneless, skinless chicken breasts

Coarse-grained salt and cracked black pepper

½ cup loosely packed, freshly chopped herbs (such as parsley and thyme)

1 lemon, cut into quarters

COOK orzo according to package directions. Save ½ cup pasta water. In a large non-stick skillet, heat 2 teaspoons of olive oil over medium-high heat. When hot but not smoking, add mushrooms to pan. Increase heat to high and cook, stirring often, until softened. Add garlic and cook until pan juices dry up and mushrooms start to brown. Remove mushrooms and garlic from pan and set aside.

WITHOUT bothering to wash skillet, place it back on stovetop over medium-high heat. Add 2 teaspoons olive oil and onion. Stir onion to coat evenly with oil. Cook, stirring often, until onion caramelizes but retains its crunch and crispness. Turn off heat and add vinegar to pan. Stir to combine. Pour onions over mushrooms.

RETURN skillet to stovetop over medium-high heat. Add remaining 2 teaspoons olive oil to pan; when oil is hot but not smoking, add chicken breasts to pan. Season with salt and pepper. Cook, turning once at the halfway point, until golden and cooked through, 4 to 6 minutes per side. Place chicken breasts on cutting board to rest.

RETURN onion and mushrooms to skillet along with pasta and reserved pasta water. Stir to combine just until heated through. Remove from heat, add fresh herbs, and toss to combine. Taste and adjust seasonings. Slice chicken breasts on the diagonal and serve over pasta. Serve with lemon wedges.

SHORTCUT CHEF
Cook pasta the night before or if you're really feeling ambitious, make the entire recipe ahead minus the chicken.

Spicy Buffalo Chicken Wings

Sadly, I can't eat these with the same abandon I used to, but they're still on the menu and that's all that counts. This is a quick modified version of classic Buffalo chicken wings, using Frank's Red Hot sauce. The difference: almost no fat. By eliminating the butter and frying and by removing all traces of excess chicken fat and most of the skin, you reduce the calories significantly.

Guyometer: Great! Real food! Not too greasy.

4 SERVINGS

SHORTCUT CHEF

I buy my wings in batches of 6 pounds and remove the skin. I set my cutting board up in front of the television set and I'm usually done in 20 minutes or so. I freeze half of the wings for the next time. If you have never removed the skin from chicken, ask your butcher—who is sure to give you a few pointers. Use a very sharp knife.

The recipe calls for 1 cup of hot sauce to dip the wings in, but start out with ½ cup so you don't contaminate the whole cup. You can use any leftovers to pour over baked wings.

FROM MOM'S LIPS TO YOUR EARS

Taking the skin off is something you can deal with. Try it. You can do it.

½ cup flour
¼ teaspoon coarse-grained salt
Cracked black pepper
16 whole chicken wings, fat, tips, and skin removed
½ to 1 cup bottled hot sauce (such as Frank's Red Hot sauce)

PREHEAT oven to 400°F. In a large sealable plastic bag, combine flour, salt, and pepper. Shake until salt and pepper are evenly distributed. Add chicken wings and shake until wings are evenly coated with flour. Pour wings into a mesh strainer and gently shake off excess flour. Place ½ cup hot sauce in a small bowl. Dip chicken wings, one at a time, into hot sauce until evenly coated. Add more sauce to bowl if necessary. Place in a single layer on a baking sheet that has been coated with olive oil spray. Roast for 30 minutes, turning once at the halfway point. Serve immediately.

If the queen's coming for dinner: Serve something else. Queens never pick up food with their fingers or watch football games.

Cooking Thin with Chef Kathleen

One-Pot Chicken with Tomatoes and Vinegar

I highly recommend that you take two seconds and throw in a batch of Creamy Baked Polenta (page 227) or Perfect Microwave Rice (page 236) before you get started. They practically cook themselves, and this dish just screams to be served over something, unless you serve it in a big soup bowl with a slice of crusty Italian bread.

4 TO 6 SERVINGS

One 3-to-4-pound chicken, washed, patted dry, skinned, and cut into 10 pieces (cut breast into quarters)

Coarse-grained salt and cracked black pepper

1 teaspoon olive oil

1¼ cups red wine vinegar

2 cups canned diced tomatoes with juice

1 cup Chicken Stock (page 95) or canned broth

¼ cup loosely packed, roughly chopped flat-leaf parsley leaves

1 tablespoon butter

SEASON chicken thoroughly on both sides with salt and pepper. In a large nonstick skillet, heat olive oil over medium-high heat. Sauté chicken pieces until golden brown, 5 to 7 minutes. Turn chicken over and cook 3 minutes more. Slowly add vinegar to pan and cook until vinegar is reduced by half, turning chicken several times so it soaks up the flavor. Add tomatoes with juice and chicken stock; reduce heat to medium-low, cover, and simmer until chicken is cooked through, about 15 minutes more. Stir in parsley and butter. Serve in shallow bowls or over polenta, rice, or pasta. This makes lots of sauce.

MORPH This is one of those perfect recipes to make and freeze for later. By that, I mean make a double batch and you've got a perfect reheat meal for a night you're too tired to cook.

A word about vinegars: They're an essential flavor ingredient in low-fat dishes, so choose them carefully. Each time you can fit a different vinegar into your budget, try one. Buy high-acid (6 or 7 percent) red wine vinegar; lower-acid vinegars are often watered down, resulting in flat vinaigrettes and sauces. I like champagne, sherry, red wine, and balsamic vinegars.

It doesn't take any brains to get the skin off chicken. Pull it. It's a little tough getting it off the legs but with a tiny bit of effort it will come off. Use a sharp knife for the wings and legs—the rest you can literally pull off by hand. Skin the chicken after it's cut up.

Chicken with Tomatoes and Zucchini Rice

Don't freak out at the length of this recipe. I could have kept it shorter but for convenience' sake (yours, darlings), I incorporated a quick rice recipe to serve with the chicken. The prep steps have been merged so you can see how it is possible to cook dinner from start to finish in less time than it takes to complete seasonal road repairs. Make like a restaurant chef and cook everything at once. Combine prep steps, sauté garlic for two dishes at the same time, use the same pan over and over, blanch green beans in the pasta water. Culinary cheaters prosper.

4 TO 6 SERVINGS

FOR THE RICE

1 tablespoon extra-virgin olive oil

2½ cups ¼-inch cubes zucchini

Coarse-grained salt and cracked black pepper

½ cup finely chopped onion

2 teaspoons minced garlic (about 2 cloves)

1½ cups long-grain rice

2¾ cups water or stock

Pinch red pepper flakes

FOR THE CHICKEN

One 3½-pound chicken, washed, patted dry, and cut into 10 pieces

Coarse-grained salt and cracked black pepper

1¼ cups red wine vinegar

5 sprigs fresh thyme or 1 teaspoon dried

1 bay leaf

1½ pounds ripe tomatoes (about 6 small), cored and peeled (or not peeled)

½ cup loosely packed, roughly chopped fresh basil or flat-leaf parsley leaves

PREPARE RICE: In a 10-inch nonstick skillet, heat ½ tablespoon of olive oil over medium-high heat. Add zucchini to pan. Season with salt and pepper. Cook, stirring often, just until it begins to soften, 3 to 4 minutes. Remove from pan; set aside. Using same pan, add onion, garlic, and remaining ½ tablespoon olive oil; reduce heat to medium-low, cover, and cook until onion has softened, 12 to 14 minutes. If onion begins to stick, add 1 tablespoon of water to pan, cover, and continue cooking. Remove onion and garlic from pan and set aside.

PLACE half of cooked onion-garlic mixture in an 8-cup glass measuring cup or similar-size microwave-safe container. Rice expands during cooking, so choose a container large enough to accommodate the final product. Add rice, water or stock, and red pepper flakes. Stir until combined. Microwave on high, uncovered, for 10 minutes. Microwave on medium-low, uncovered, for 15 minutes. Do not stir rice at any time during cooking process. When rice is done, add zucchini, season with salt and pepper, and combine by fluffing with a fork. Don't mix or stir rice too hard or you'll end up with a giant zucchini rice ball.

PREPARE CHICKEN: Season chicken with salt and pepper. Heat same skillet you used for onions over medium heat. Brown chicken, skin side down, until golden, 10 to 12 minutes. Turn chicken over; cook second side until golden, 8 to 10 minutes more.

PLACE remaining onion-garlic mixture back in pan with chicken. Add vinegar to pan, turn heat to medium-high, and cook until most of vinegar has evaporated, 4 to 6 minutes. Add thyme and bay leaf. Cut tomatoes into ¾-inch pieces and add to pan. Cover tightly and simmer 10 minutes. Uncover, remove, and discard thyme and bay leaf. Reduce liquid by half (or to desired consistency), about 10 minutes more. Swirl in chopped fresh herbs and serve over rice.

Meat

SHORTCUT CHEF

Move the TV into the kitchen. Relax, unwind, and make Wednesday's dinner Tuesday night after the dishes have been cleared. While you're watching TV, chop the garlic, peel the tomatoes, cut the zucchini, cut up the chicken and season it. Heck, make the whole dinner the night before if you've got the time.

Most newer microwaves have a rice setting, so skip my directions and hit the rice button. Next time, if you're not satisfied, try it this way—it works every time.

Use canned peeled whole tomatoes or don't bother peeling fresh tomatoes if you don't mind their skins. To peel tomatoes, bring a medium pot of water to a boil. Take the pot off the stove and place it in the sink. Drop the tomatoes into the water and let stand 1 minute. Remove the tomatoes and core and peel them.

The recipe doesn't call for any oil to be added to the pan prior to browning the chicken. Don't worry. There's plenty of fat in the skin to get the job done. Speaking of chicken fat, don't eat the skin. It's a complete waste of fat calories. Ben & Jerry's or chicken fat, you decide.

Dee Dee's Quick Broiled Chicken

I have to be careful, because I don't want to offend my friend Dee Dee by revealing her lazy culinary ways in print, but this incredibly talented woman has a knack for getting supper on the table faster than you can set out the napkins, plates, knives, forks, and spoons. She's a mom and a full-time CPA and tax attorney. Let's just say she's got a few tricks up her sleeve, and as I extract them from her, I'll pass them on to you. I couldn't resist dolling up her famous chicken. I added slivered scallions, grated ginger, and lime zest and you can, too, unless you opt for Dee Dee's original salt and pepper version, which is quick and equally delicious.

4 TO 6 SERVINGS

One 3½-to-4-pound whole fryer chicken (giblets and cavity fat removed)
Coarse-grained salt and cracked black pepper
½ cup thinly sliced scallions (white and some green parts)
2 tablespoons grated fresh ginger
I teaspoon grated lime zest

USING a sharp knife or poultry scissors, cut through bones on either side of backbone. Remove and discard backbone or save for soup stock. Place chicken, breast side up, on a cutting board. Flatten chicken by placing heel of your hand over breastbone and pressing down firmly. Season chicken generously on all sides with salt and pepper.

MIX scallions, ginger, and lime zest together in a small bowl. Rub mixture over breast meat, directly under breast skin; this is done by slipping fingers between skin and breast meat, loosening membrane as you go (it's not as gross as it sounds). Spread rub under skin to cover breast completely and evenly. Do the same with legs and thighs to the extent that you can. Refrigerate overnight or let stand at least 1 hour in refrigerator.

BROIL chicken on lowest rack of oven for 45 minutes, turning once at the halfway point, until an instant-read thermometer reads 160°F in thickest part of thigh, or until juices run clear. Serve immediately.

MORPH Chicken wraps, chicken tacos, chicken salad, chicken sandwiches . . .

Listen, your doctor would roll her eyes if she knew you were cooking chicken with the skin on, but chicken has skin. That's the way they sell it. That said, just because it's there doesn't mean you should eat it. Don't, but it keeps the meat moist during cooking.

The recipe works perfectly fine with a whole chicken cut in half, quarters, eighths, or any which way.

Roasted Chicken and Apple Salad

Everything you expect from Mom's homemade chicken salad: rich flavors, smooth creamy textures, and velvety divine dressing. It's very easy to prepare, too. Okay, so maybe your definition of easy doesn't include roasting a chicken just so you can eat a sandwich. But how hard is it to throw a chicken in the oven and let it roast while you relax or get twenty-five things done? Anyway, this makes great sandwiches, but don't count this out as dinner. It's quite refreshing in the fall, when apples are just starting to flood the markets.

6 SERVINGS

One 3-pound chicken, roasted, or Dee Dee's Quick Broiled Chicken (page 338)

I medium apple, peeled and diced (or unpeeled—skin adds color)

I stalk celery, cut into ¼-inch slices

I tablespoon capers, rinsed

FOR THE DRESSING

2 tablespoons Dijon mustard

¼ cup regular or low-fat mayonnaise

¼ cup plain low-fat yogurt

2 tablespoons fresh lemon juice

Coarse-grained salt and cracked black pepper

SHORTCUT CHEF
Cook chicken the night before while you're watching TV and your partner's getting the kids off to bed and folding the laundry. Pull chicken meat off the bone ahead of time. Got 5 extra minutes? The dressing can be made ahead, too.

MORPH Serve chicken salad over garden lettuces with any combination of fruits or vegetables that appeals to you: chunks of tomato, blanched green beans, roasted beets, blanched carrots, chunks of mango, papaya, or avocado.

REMOVE skin from roasted chicken and discard. Remove meat from bones; discard all fat and bones. Pull and shred or dice meat into pieces. Place in a bowl. Add apple, celery, and capers to chicken and toss.

PREPARE DRESSING: In a small mixing bowl, whisk together Dijon mustard, mayonnaise, yogurt, and lemon juice. Stir until combined. Add salt and pepper to taste.

POUR dressing over salad and toss to combine. Serve immediately.

Ask your butcher to remove the backbone from your chicken or carefully do it yourself. It will cut the cooking time in half. If you're really pressed for time or just plain lazy, buy an already roasted chicken.

Season the chicken generously with salt and pepper the night before roasting if you can, or at least 1 hour ahead. Stuff a few slivers of garlic and/or fresh herbs under the skin of the chicken breast before you roast it. The meat will pick up these marvelous flavors.

Choose a crisp, firm-textured, sweet and tart apple such as a Granny Smith. Avoid baking apples, which can be a bit mealy and soft.

Split-Roasted Chicken and Vegetables

In case you haven't noticed, I'm a big fan of roasting chickens without their back-bones. They cook faster, the skin comes off easily after cooking, and there's not much to it. I'm game for any quick-cook solution. Is this the leanest way to eat chicken? Probably not, but it's certainly better for you than take-out pizza and super-size burger meals.

6 TO 8 SERVINGS

3 scallions (white part only)

1 clove garlic, peeled

¼ cup loosely packed fresh cilantro leaves

2 teaspoons ground cumin

1½ teaspoons sweet paprika

⅛ teaspoon cayenne pepper

Coarse-grained salt and cracked black pepper

One 3½-pound chicken, backbone removed

1 pound tiny peeled carrots (the kind you should be snacking on at work)

2 cups peeled pearl onions (you can buy them peeled and frozen)

PLACE scallions, garlic, and cilantro leaves in a mini chopper or food processor. Pulse until minced. Or place ingredients on a cutting board and, using a sharp knife, chop by hand. Place in a small bowl, and add cumin, paprika, cayenne, and salt and pepper to taste. Stir until well combined and pastelike.

NOW comes the messy part. Rub paste all over chicken, into cavities, especially over breast meat, directly under breast skin; this is done by slipping fingers between skin and breast meat, loosening membrane as you go (it's not as gross as it sounds). Spread rub under skin to cover breast, thighs, and legs completely and evenly. Refrigerate overnight or let stand at least 1 hour in refrigerator.

Cooking Thin with Chef Kathleen

PREHEAT oven to 500°F. Spray oven broiler pan bottom with nonstick cooking spray. Spread carrots and pearl onions evenly over pan bottom. Place broiler pan rack over vegetables.

PLACE chicken, skin side up, on broiler pan rack. Move legs up onto breast as far as possible to ensure more even cooking. Roast chicken 40 to 45 minutes, rotating pan once, until an instant-read thermometer reads 160°F in the thickest part of the thigh, or until juices run clear. Let chicken rest for 10 to 15 minutes before serving on a warm platter surrounded by vegetables.

SHORTCUT CHEF

Ask the butcher to remove the backbone from the chicken. If you don't frequent a specialty butcher shop (seriously consider it—the products can be far superior in freshness and flavor) ring the bell at the grocery store meat counter—the butcher will be happy to oblige you.

MORPH Make two chickens and turn the second one into Roasted Chicken and Apple Salad (page 340). Freeze everything else for chicken stock.

Remove all the skin and excess fat from the chicken before serving or let diners do it themselves (we're a self-serve house).

Small round potatoes cut in half or parsnips are wonderful vegetable additions or substitutions.

Lemony Garlic Roasted Chicken

Roasted chicken is an easy plan-ahead dinner you can get on the table without a whole lot of fuss. In the summertime I sometimes use hyssop and lemon thyme if any of my spring-planted seeds have turned into usable potted herbs. Use whatever combination of fresh herbs you happen to have on hand. Dried herbs are no substitute for fresh, so if they're all you've got, skip them and use a simple spice rub instead, keeping in mind that coarse-grained salt and cracked black pepper season a bird just fine. Don't be too heavy-handed with fresh herbs—too many sprigs and you could end up with Pine Sol–flavored chicken.

4 TO 6 SERVINGS

One 3½-pound chicken, rinsed and patted dry

Coarse-grained salt and cracked black pepper

2 cloves garlic, thinly sliced

4 marjoram or oregano sprigs

6 lemon thyme or regular thyme sprigs

1 lemon, cut in half

SHORTCUT CHEF
Season the chicken the night before.

MORPH Turn the leftover chicken into Roasted Chicken and Apple Salad (page 340). It's no extra work to throw in a second chicken. Leftover chicken meat off the bone is great in soups and frittatas and on BBQ Chicken Pizza, too (page 126).

ONE DAY or at least 4 hours ahead, season chicken generously with salt and pepper. To stuff garlic and herbs over breast meat and under skin, you must first loosen skin. Begin at the neck end by sliding one hand between skin and breast meat until loosened. Do this with each breast. Tuck half of sliced garlic and half of herbs over breasts and between breasts and thighs.

Cooking Thin with Chef Kathleen

SQUEEZE lemon over and around chicken, throwing rinds inside cavity of bird. Store in refrigerator until you're ready to roast.

JUST BEFORE COOKING, preheat oven to 500°F. In a roasting pan fitted with a rack or on a cookie sheet with sides, place chicken breast side down. Cook for 20 minutes. Carefully turn chicken breast side up and continue cooking another 8 minutes. Reduce oven temperature to 325° and cook 15 minutes more, or until an instant-read thermometer inserted in thickest part of thigh reads 160°F, or until juices run clear. Let chicken rest for 10 to 15 minutes. Carve, remove skin, and serve.

This super-quick cooking method for roasting chicken yields a moist bird with crunchy golden skin, but there will be a lot of smoke. Not to worry—turn on fans and open the windows.

Roasted chicken is not lean cuisine. If you want to enjoy it, don't eat the skin, don't sop up bird juices and fat with bread, and stick to the white meat. Serve yourself a proper portion and load up on delicious veggie side dishes. Moderation is key.

Split-Roasted Chicken and Potatoes

If you're looking for a very lean dinner, this is not the right recipe. However, it's a very easy dinner to get on the table and it's a much better choice than eating bad food out. You know all about proper portion sizes and that you have no business eating the skin no matter how crispy it is. So behave yourself and you can enjoy good old-fashioned roasted chicken every now and then.

4 TO 6 SERVINGS

One 3½-to-4-pound fryer chicken (backbone, giblet, and cavity fat removed)
Coarse-grained salt and cracked black pepper
1 tablespoon olive oil
2½ pounds russet or Yukon Gold potatoes (4 to 5 medium), peeled and cut into ⅛-inch slices

SHORTCUT CHEF

Keep an extra whole fryer on hand in your freezer so when you're tempted to call for less nutritious carryout, you've got a back-up plan and a simple recipe you can whip up faster than the delivery boy can get to your door (if you've remembered to defrost it).

MORPH The recipe serves four to six, with plenty of chicken and bones left over. Make Roasted Chicken and Apple Salad (page 340) with the leftover meat if you've got enough. Freeze everything else for chicken stock.

FLATTEN chicken by placing heel of your hand over breastbone and pressing down firmly. Season with salt and pepper all over and let stand, uncovered, in refrigerator as long as possible or overnight.

JUST before cooking, place oven rack in lower-middle position and preheat oven to 500°F. Pour olive oil into bottom broiler pan and spread evenly. Place a layer of potatoes in broiler pan and season with salt and pepper. You don't have to line them up or anything—the only reason you're layering them is so you can season each layer with salt and pepper. For some reason it works better this way than placing potatoes, salt, and pepper in a bag with oil and shaking until well coated. Broiler pan bottom needs extra oil to keep potatoes from sticking. Make 2 or 3 layers of potatoes.

PLACE broiler pan rack over potatoes. Place chicken breast side up on rack. Roast chicken 40 to 45 minutes, rotating pan once, until an instant-read thermometer reads 160°F in the thickest part of thigh, or until juices run clear. Let rest 10 to 15 minutes before serving on a warm platter surrounded by potatoes.

You really need to prepare this recipe in an oven broiler pan with a rack.

If you have to remove the backbone yourself, place the chicken on a cutting board set atop a wet towel (which will keep the cutting board from slipping). Using a sharp knife or poultry scissors, cut through the bones on either side of the backbone. Remove and discard the backbone or save for soup stock. Don't try to rush this task—it will take several minutes until you've done it a few times.

If time allows, season the chicken generously with salt and pepper and let sit in the refrigerator, uncovered, overnight. You will notice a significant improvement in the overall flavor and texture of the cooked skin (if you're indulging in it).

If the boss is coming for dinner: This is a great recipe to prepare when you're entertaining. The chicken comes out of the oven golden and crispy and the potatoes are to die for. Yes, it's because they're basted in chicken drippings, which is precisely why you cannot eat more than a modest portion. If you do, you'll just have to work it off later.

FROM MOM'S LIPS TO YOUR EARS

This is one meal you really have to plate up so no one overeats. It's a little richer than most of the recipes in the book. I serve it with steamed green beans and a tossed salad so diners fill up on vegetables instead of begging for more potatoes.

Chicken Pan Supper with Peppers, Onions, and Fettuccine

This kid-tested recipe passed with flying colors. My dad—who loves eating lunch out because it's the only time my mom's not reminding him about the dangers of butter, sugar, fat, and cream—brown-bagged the leftovers. Now *that's* a good supper. Read the recipe through from start to finish the night before. It's not too time intensive. This is a great recipe to make with an assistant.

6 SERVINGS

One 3½-pound chicken, cut into 12 pieces, visible fat and excess skin removed
Coarse-grained salt and cracked black pepper
1 large sweet onion, thinly sliced
3 cloves garlic, thinly sliced
5 yellow and/or red bell peppers, cut into ½-inch strips
8 ounces uncooked fettuccine or other pasta
¼ cup loosely packed, chopped fresh basil leaves

SEASON chicken with salt and pepper. Place chicken skin side down in a large nonstick skillet. Over medium-high heat, brown on all sides, 10 to 15 minutes. Remove chicken from pan, place in 3-quart saucepan, and set aside. Add onion and garlic to skillet, reduce heat to medium, and cook until softened, stirring often, 5 to 7 minutes. If onion isn't releasing its water quickly enough and is in jeopardy of sticking, add ¼ cup water. When onions have softened, turn off heat and pour over chicken. Arrange peppers over onion and garlic. Turn heat to low and cook, covered, until chicken is cooked through, about 25 minutes. Taste and adjust seasoning. Remove from heat.

MEANWHILE, in rapidly boiling salted water, cook pasta according to package directions until al dente. Drain and season with salt. Add basil to chicken; stir until evenly mixed in. Spoon chicken and sauce over noodles. Serve immediately.

Desserts

"KATHLEEN, YOU DON'T NEED DESSERT every

night. When you're not around, your father and I never have dessert." Of

course, she's right, but I don't have to like the fact that it's best not to con-

sume sugary desserts every night. Despite my elephantine efforts, I've never

really been able to come to terms with that stodgy old no-dessert mind-set,

so I've changed my definition of dessert.

Creamy pies, three-tiered cakes, and old-fashioned ice cream sundaes aren't entirely out of the question, but they're not everyday desserts for me anymore. I'm certainly not suggesting you give up desserts entirely.

What's a birthday without cake? Who ever heard of Thanksgiving without pumpkin pie, and what would Valentine's Day be without chocolate? It's only natural to associate particular desserts with specific occasions. I enjoy real desserts in between holidays, too, but I've learned to make room for them in my diet by cutting back before and after dessert days and increasing my workout a little, especially around the holidays. I also live by dessert rule number one: higher-calorie desserts on light-meal nights only, fresh fruit more often.

If I'm staring at peak-season, perfectly ripened pears with a lovely blush to them throughout dinner, it's all I can do to hurry up and finish my entrée so I can bite into one. Ben and Jerry who? I didn't change my tastes overnight. It's still an all-the-time effort, but the results are worth it. The key is planning ahead. I've made it a priority to shop for small quantities of the best and to keep the fruit bowl clean and fresh. No yucky blemished specimens allowed.

The grocery store markets fruit to you—do the same for your family. At my house, if there's only one left, everybody wants it, so buy a few pieces at a time. One more tip: Rearrange the fruit around 4:00 P.M. Add a different variety of fruit for dinner. Bananas are great for breakfast or an afternoon snack, but a plain old peeled banana isn't my idea of dessert.

Some of the desserts in this chapter are naturally low calorie and, well, others aren't. Eat small portions of a quality dessert, which is a whole lot better than too much of a bad thing. Try a slice of Lemon Loaf (page 356) with plum sauce, Rhubarb Applesauce (page 377), or the Ultra-Lite Pecan Chocolate Chip Cookies (page 370).

Karen's Angel Food Cake

Our friend Karen had a passion for baking angel food cakes. Her husband, Ray, once told me, "Our kids were never cake kids and knowing it was cake we couldn't even get them to try it. That was fine for me because I had the whole thing to myself. But I must have appeared to be enjoying it too much because my daughter, Heather, tried some and loved it. She told her brothers and all of a sudden I had only one-quarter of a cake to myself at best." Karen's cake has become a family favorite in our house, too.

10 SERVINGS

1 ¼ cups egg whites (about 9 large eggs),
   at room temperature

¼ teaspoon salt

1 teaspoon cream of tartar

¼ teaspoon pure almond extract

1 ½ cups sugar, sifted

1 cup cake flour, sifted 3 times

Guyometer:
If my wife says it's a healthier option, then it must be, but it tastes just as good as regular cake.

PREHEAT oven to 325°F. In a large mixing bowl, using an electric mixer, beat egg whites until frothy; add salt, cream of tartar, and almond extract. Continue beating until they form stiff but not dry peaks. Using a rubber spatula, gradually fold in sugar a few tablespoons at a time. Using same rubber spatula, gradually fold in flour, one quarter at a time. Be sure that you use a true folding motion, gently turning spatula from bottom of bowl to the top, folding in air with each stroke, as opposed to beating or stirring. You just went to all that work to whip up the egg whites, so don't beat them to death now.

POUR batter into an ungreased 9-inch angel food cake pan (you know, the one with the tube in the center—but not a bundt pan). Bake 1 hour, then remove from oven. Cool in pan 10 minutes and then invert pan and let cake stand upside down for an hour, or until cooled. You might let cake stand over a plate in case your oven was

Chocolate you're craving? Karen's secret to instant chocolate-glazed cakes was to melt a single-size chocolate bar (milk or dark) and pour it right over the cake. Optional show-stopping toppings: Scatter a pint of fresh raspberries or sliced strawberries over the chocolate-glazed cake. Dip fresh strawberries into melted chocolate and arrange them on top of the cake. Sprinkle entire cake with confectioners' sugar for a fancy finish.

The recipe calls for you to sift the flour three times. Doing so really makes a difference. You have to sift the sugar once, too. Don't cut corners here; the cake is perfect.

FROM MOM'S LIPS TO YOUR EARS

Don't overdo the almond extract. It's perfect the way it is.

funky and cake plops out of the pan prematurely. Hey, it happens. If it behaves and stays in, run a table knife around tube and edges when cake is completely cool. Invert on plate. Serve on its own, with a dusting of confectioners' sugar, or with World's Easiest Fruit Sauce (page 353).

DIVINE VARIATIONS

Chocolate angel food cake: Replace ¼ cup of flour with ¼ cup sifted cocoa powder and 1 teaspoon instant coffee. Substitute vanilla extract for almond extract.

Christmas angel food cake: To sifted flour, add 1 teaspoon cinnamon, ½ teaspoon ground cloves, ½ teaspoon ground allspice, and ½ teaspoon freshly grated nutmeg. Use vanilla or almond extract, depending upon your tastes. Just before baking, fold in 1 tablespoon grated orange rind. My dad loves this topped with cranberry sauce or applesauce (and real whipped cream if my mom isn't around).

If the queen's coming for dinner: You must serve this cake. Presented on a cake stand, it makes a dramatic entrance even a queen can appreciate. I'd probably serve it to her with heaps of sugared berries poured over the cake (page 376) and dollops of real whipped cream.

World's Easiest Fruit Sauce–Filled Angel Food Cake

The key to getting this super dessert on the table faster than the coffee brews is a little advance planning. I highly recommend you set aside a little time to bake a fresh angel food cake, but you can use a store-bought one (just this once) if you're fresh out of time.

8 TO 10 SERVINGS

8 cups mixed fruit, washed, drained, peeled, seeded, and hulled as necessary

⅓ cup sugar (or more or less to taste)

2 tablespoons fresh lemon juice

1 recipe Karen's Angel Food Cake (page 351) or store-bought cake

Guyometer: Can I have seconds?

PLACE fruit, any natural juices, sugar, and lemon juice in a large, nonreactive bowl. Toss to coat evenly and let stand 30 minutes or up to 1 hour, stirring occasionally.

WHILE fruit is macerating, slice angel food cake in half horizontally. Place bottom half of cake on a serving plate. Hollow out a ½-inch-deep by 1-inch-wide tunnel all the way around the cake.

TO serve cake, pour half the fruit mixture into and over tunnel. Don't worry if it's messy. Place top half of cake over fruit. Spoon remaining fruit over and around entire surface of cake, letting juices and a few pieces fall down sides. Slice and serve.

If the queen's coming for dinner: You must make Karen's Angel Food Cake. You'll probably want to garnish the cake with freshly whipped, lightly sweetened cream or nondairy whipped topping. Whip the cream already—it takes only 2 minutes.

SHORTCUT CHEF

Cheat and use frozen fruit that has been completely thawed but not strained.

FROM MOM'S LIPS TO YOUR EARS

Use any combination of fruits you like; just be sure to take advantage of seasonal varieties available to you. We've had this with peaches alone or peach, plum, and nectarine combos. Kathleen's favorite is strawberry-mango but she won't touch her father's favorite: raspberry-blackberry.

Desserts

Apple Crumb Cake

I love to eat dessert. A little extra cardio in exchange for an occasional slice of cake is totally worth it to me. This cake is heavenly divine and it's not too over the top calorie-wise compared to the usual temptations out there.

8 TO 10 SERVINGS

FOR THE CRUMB TOPPING

$1/3$ cup brown sugar

2 tablespoons butter, melted

$1/4$ cup chopped pecans

2 tablespoons flour

$1/2$ cup old-fashioned rolled oats

FOR THE BATTER

1 $1/4$ cups flour

$1/2$ teaspoon salt

$1/2$ teaspoon baking soda

$1/2$ cup brown sugar

$1/2$ cup granulated sugar

$1/4$ cup ($1/2$ stick) butter

1 large egg

$1/2$ cup buttermilk

1 $1/2$ cups peeled, diced tart cooking apples

Guyometer:
Great dessert.

PREHEAT oven to 350°F. Butter and flour a 9-inch nonstick springform pan; set aside.

PREPARE CRUMB TOPPING: In a small bowl, mix together brown sugar, butter, pecans, flour, and oats.

PREPARE BATTER: In a separate bowl, sift together flour, salt, and baking soda. Set aside. In a large mixing bowl or bowl of an electric mixer, cream together brown sugar, granulated sugar, and butter until combined. Add egg and buttermilk and mix until completely incorporated. Slowly add dry ingredients to wet, blending thoroughly. With a spoon, fold in apples. Pour batter into prepared pan. Sprinkle topping over cake and bake 25 minutes, or until toothpick inserted in center comes out clean. Cool on a wire rack.

If your mother-in-law is coming for dinner: Serve this to her and she'll forget all about her usual mother-in-law to daughter-in-law speeches.

SHORTCUT CHEF
Make the crumb topping ahead and mix the dry ingredients. Laying out the ingredients and tools for any recipe beforehand really saves time.

If you want to cut calories, skip the crumb topping. Serve the cake warm with a heaping spoonful of Talitha Anne's Microwave Applesauce (page 84). It's a wonderful accompaniment and a great calorie compromise.

Lemon Loaf

I highly recommend eating this warm from the oven; however, my mom prefers it the next day. I must agree that it's delicious the next day, but there's nothing like just-from-the-oven baked goods, especially when the house is filled with heavenly scents. ▪ The original recipe called for cream instead of milk and twice the amount of nuts. We don't think you'll miss the fat. My father thought cranberries would make a great addition to the bread, but then he puts cranberry sauce on anything he can get away with. I happen to agree that cranberries—or blueberries, for that matter—added to the batter would be nice and cranberry sauce spooned over the bread would be delicious, too.

8 TO 10 SERVINGS

1½ cups unbleached flour (okay, you can use regular, but all-purpose unbleached behaves wonderfully in baked goods)

1 teaspoon baking powder

½ teaspoon salt

½ cup (1 stick) unsalted butter

½ cup plus ½ cup sugar

2 large eggs

2 tablespoons finely minced lemon zest (about 2 lemons)

½ cup low-fat or whole milk

½ cup pecans

½ cup fresh lemon juice

Guyometer:
Three yums-up.

PREHEAT oven to 350°F. Butter and flour a 9 × 5-inch loaf pan; set aside. In a medium bowl, sift together flour, baking powder, and salt. Set aside.

MEANWHILE, in bowl of an electric mixer, cream together butter and ½ cup of sugar until light and fluffy. Add eggs and lemon zest and mix until combined. Add dry ingredients, alternating with milk. While there are still bits of flour to be seen, add pecans and mix until ingredients are just combined. Don't overmix or you'll be serving lemon-butter-pecan hardtack. Pour batter into pan and bake in center of oven until bread is golden brown and a toothpick inserted in center comes out clean, 50 to 60 minutes.

PREPARE the lemon glaze while your bread is baking by whisking together lemon juice and remaining ½ cup of sugar in a small bowl. Just after bread comes out of oven, poke holes all over the top with a fork or skewer and pour lemon-sugar mixture over cake. Cool bread in pan on a rack 30 minutes, or as long as you can stand it. Serve warm or at room temperature.

If the queen's coming for dinner: She'll probably prefer clotted cream, real whipped cream, or high-grade vanilla ice cream to cranberry sauce but the bread is fancy enough served alone.

SHORTCUT CHEF
Squeeze the lemon juice ahead, measure and sift dry ingredients the night before, zest your lemons, and/or make the lemon-sugar syrup.

This is not a low-fat dessert by any means. It's a satisfying alternative to those triple-tiered gazillion-calorie desserts I used to eat. Moderate, don't eliminate. Factor these calories into your overall eating plan and add a few minutes to your cardio routine to turn and burn these calories.

Zucchini Apple Cake

Michelle Shaffer gave this recipe to us. Says supermom Michelle, "This cake is so delicious that no one in the family has the slightest inclination it's a reduced-calorie version of the original or that it's got healthful ingredients." ▪ The cake became an instant hit with our family, too, and is now a house favorite. The only real difference is that Michelle serves it with a heavenly cream cheese frosting that I've included because I knew you'd ask. I choose not to frost mine because, darlings, I can't afford the calories. You decide what you've got room for and where you want to spend your calories. ▪ This isn't a no-calorie cake by any stretch of the imagination. But it is a dessert built around some very healthful ingredients and is a better choice than a three-scoop banana split with three toppings, nuts, and a cherry. And that's what this lifestyle is all about: good, better, and best choices.

12 SERVINGS

2½ cups flour

2 cups sugar

1½ teaspoons ground cinnamon

1 teaspoon salt

½ teaspoon baking soda

½ teaspoon baking powder

¾ cup unsweetened applesauce

¼ cup vegetable oil

2 large eggs

2 cups shredded zucchini

½ cup chopped walnuts

¾ cup raisins

4 large egg whites

Confectioners' sugar

FOR MICHELLE'S FROSTING (OPTIONAL)

One 8-ounce package low-fat cream cheese

¼ cup (½ stick) butter, softened

1 tablespoon milk

1 teaspoon pure vanilla extract

2 to 2½ cups confectioners' sugar

PREHEAT oven to 350°F. Butter and flour a 13 × 9-inch pan; set aside. In a large mixing bowl, combine flour, granulated sugar, cinnamon, salt, baking soda, and baking powder.

FOLD applesauce, oil, and whole eggs into dry ingredients until barely mixed. Add zucchini, walnuts, and raisins. Fold until just combined. Whip egg whites to stiff peaks and gently fold in. Do not overmix.

POUR batter into pan and bake 35 to 40 minutes, or until a toothpick inserted in center comes out clean. Cool slightly, sprinkle with a dusting of confectioners' sugar, and serve warm. Or ice the cake with Michelle's Frosting.

TO MAKE FROSTING: In a small mixing bowl, beat cream cheese with butter, milk, and vanilla. Gradually beat in confectioners' sugar and mix until smooth. Spread on cake, and if you want to talk small children into eating it, add a few colored sprinkles. That always gets them. Don't tell them it's cream cheese.

If the queen's coming for dinner: Serve it with the frosting. She's not watching her weight anyway.

SHORTCUT CHEF
Lay out the ingredients and tools in advance. Measure out the dry ingredients and grate the zucchini.

Use Talitha Anne's Microwave Applesauce (page 84) instead of the frosting.

Chocolate Mock-Buttercream Frosting

My sister Carol came over one day and swiped a delicious cookie topped with this frosting before I could tell her we weren't going to use the cookies in the book. "Kath, the frosting is really, really good. Can't you put it in the book?" "No. Who wants a plain old frosting recipe with nothing to frost?" "An easy frosting recipe is a great thing to have. I'm a mom. I have to frost cupcakes, brownies, and cookies all the time. A 1-2-3 frosting recipe that kids will eat is worth its weight in gold." Besides, this one has way less butter as far as frostings go.

ENOUGH TO FROST TWO 9-INCH LAYERS OR 4 DOZEN BROWNIES OR COOKIES

2 tablespoons butter

1 ½ cups confectioners' sugar

½ cup unsweetened cocoa powder

3 to 4 tablespoons milk

CREAM butter, gradually adding confectioners' sugar and cocoa powder. Mix until combined. Slowly add milk, 1 tablespoon at a time, mixing thoroughly after each addition. You may not need all of it but you won't know until you're in the middle of things. When frosting is the perfect consistency to spread, don't add any more milk.

Guyometer:
There can't be
anything healthy
about this.

This keeps well and can be made ahead. Make a half batch if you can't or shouldn't use a whole batch. No sense in keeping temptations within reach. You could freeze it.

Cooking Thin with Chef Kathleen

Chocolate Meringue Drops

I'm the queen of desiring too-huge-for-you portions, so you can imagine my surprise when I found that these tiny (by my standards) cookies packed enough chewy choco-latey rich flavor that a little really was enough. These cookies are so quick to prepare and clean up that you could make baking dessert part of the party.

48 DROP COOKIES

4 large egg whites

2½ cups confectioners' sugar

½ cup unsweetened cocoa powder

2 tablespoons flour

2 teaspoons very finely ground fresh coffee grounds (or powdered instant coffee)

1 tablespoon water

¾ cup finely chopped pecans

PREHEAT oven to 350°F. Line 2 baking sheets with parchment. Using an electric mixer, beat whites until frothy. Add confectioners' sugar, cocoa powder, flour, coffee, and water. Beat on low until combined, turn mixer to high, and beat until marshmallow-topping thick, 3 to 4 minutes. Using a rubber spatula, fold in pecans. Drop by heaping teaspoonfuls onto cookie sheets; bake 15 to 18 minutes, or until tops crack.

If the queen's coming for dinner: If you're a garnishing fool, sprinkle the cookies with confectioners' sugar by pouring sugar through a fine-mesh strainer directly over the cookies just before serving.

Portion out 48 cookies. If you make 24 or 36 or any number less than 48, the portion patrol police will throw you in stationary bike solitary con-finement. You'll have to work off all those excess calories sooner or later. Play by the rules and you can have your cake and be fit, too.

Dark Chocolate Cherry Cheesecake

While testing a dozen recipes for cheesecake using low-fat dairy products, I was disappointed over and over again with the less-than-satisfactory flavors and textures. Nothing tastes as good as the real thing, so I got out fresh eggs, real cream cheese, and semisweet chocolate and made this delicious chocolate cherry cheesecake I know you'll enjoy. Most cheesecakes are made in 9- or 10-inch springform pans and call for double the amount of fat and sugar I use here. I reduced the ingredients and the pan size. This way you can enjoy a smaller portion and fewer calories. Send leftovers to your neighbors or to the office so you won't be tempted to eat slices of cheesecake until it's gone.

12 SERVINGS

FOR THE CRUST

1 ¼ cups fine cookie crumbs (graham cracker or chocolate wafer cookies)

2 tablespoons sugar

3 tablespoons unsalted butter, melted

1 tablespoon water

FOR THE FILLING

8 ounces semisweet chocolate chips (1 ½ cups)

¼ cup brewed espresso or strong coffee

12 ounces cream cheese, softened

¾ cup sugar

½ teaspoon salt

2 large eggs

1 teaspoon pure vanilla extract

¾ cup cherry pie filling

PREHEAT oven to 350°F.

PREPARE CRUST: In a medium mixing bowl, combine crumbs and sugar. Stir until combined. Add melted butter and water; mix until completely incorporated. Pour crumb mixture into an 8-inch springform pan. Using fingertips, press evenly onto pan bottom and ½ inch up sides. Bake 12 to 15 minutes, until crust hardens slightly. Set aside to cool. Reduce oven temperature to 300°F. Place a 9-inch cake pan filled with water on bottom oven rack (this will add moisture to oven so cake will be creamy and dense, not dried out).

PREPARE THE FILLING: In a heavy-bottomed pan, heat chocolate chips and coffee over lowest heat, stirring often, until chocolate is completely melted, 7 to 9 minutes. Cool.

IN a mixing bowl, with an electric mixer on medium speed, beat cream cheese until smooth and creamy. Add sugar and salt. Beat on medium speed 1 minute. Scrape down sides and add eggs, one at a time, beating on medium for 30 seconds and scraping down sides of bowl between each addition. Add melted chocolate mixture and vanilla to bowl, scrape down sides once more, and beat on medium 1 minute. Pour batter into crust. Bake on middle rack for 60 to 65 minutes, or until internal temperature reads 170°F. Take cake's temperature by inserting an instant-read thermometer into center of cake. Turn oven off and let cake stand in oven for 20 minutes more. Remove from oven and cool for 20 minutes on a wire rack. Refrigerate 1 hour. Then freeze 1 hour.

CUT into 12 slices, topping each slice with 1 tablespoon cherry pie filling just before serving. Alternatively, after cheesecake refrigerates for 1 hour, pour entire can of cherry pie filling over cake and refrigerate 2 hours more, or until cake and topping are set.

Pumpkin Pie

This recipe is inspired by one developed by the late Richard Sax, whose book *Classic Home Desserts* is a brilliantly researched compilation of America's best desserts. Probably the most dog-eared book in my collection, it is the kind of book moms need to give their daughters on their wedding day. ■ When you're in the mood for all the calories, go for Richard's version of this pie: it's simply the best pumpkin pie I've ever come across. When you're cutting back on calories and fat, try this slimmed-down version.

8 TO 10 SERVINGS

FOR THE CRUST

11 graham crackers (1 packet)

2 tablespoons water

3 tablespoons butter, melted

FOR THE FILLING

2 cups canned unsweetened pumpkin puree

2/3 cup firmly packed dark brown sugar

2 tablespoons flour

1/2 teaspoon salt

1 1/2 teaspoons ground cinnamon

1/2 teaspoon freshly grated nutmeg

1/2 teaspoon ground ginger

1/2 teaspoon ground allspice

Pinch cracked black pepper

1 cup nonfat evaporated milk

1/3 cup low-fat milk

1 large egg

2 large egg whites

2 teaspoons pure vanilla extract

Guyometer: Richard's pie is better, but my wife won't let me get away with that very often. This hits the spot and is better than no pie at all.

PREHEAT oven to 400°F.

PREPARE CRUST: Place graham crackers in a large mixing bowl or food processor and pulse or mix until finely ground. Add water and melted butter. Pulse until well combined. Press into bottom of pie plate and partway up the sides. Bake 4 to 6 minutes, until set and lightly golden. Cool on wire rack.

PREPARE FILLING: In a large mixing bowl, whisk together pumpkin puree, brown sugar, flour, salt, spices, pepper, evaporated milk, low-fat milk, egg, egg whites, and vanilla. Pour into pie plate.

BAKE until filling is set but still slightly wobbly in center, 35 to 45 minutes.

If the queen's coming for dinner: Naturally, she'll want Richard's pie.

Don't use pumpkin pie filling—it's got spices already in it and probably not in the proportions you'd care to eat.

If you are going to cook your own pumpkin, don't get the Halloween kind. Use "sugar" or "pie" pumpkins. If you want to get ahead, prepare the pumpkin the night before. To roast, preheat oven to 400°F. Cut pumpkin in half horizontally, scrape out the seeds, and place cut side down on a cookie sheet that has been rubbed with just enough oil to keep the pumpkin from burning. Roast until pumpkin is mashed-potato soft and tender, 45 minutes to 1 hour, depending upon the size of the pumpkin.

Chocolate Pudding Pie

Is chocolate calling you? Think a triple-tiered chocolate concoction only a three-star chef could prepare will satisfy your craving? Think again. Rich, dark chocolate pudding pie is as satisfying as any creamy chocolate dessert but has only half the calories of its sumptuous cousin, chocolate mousse pie. The only thing that will be sky high is the deep, dark, and dense flavor of this quick-cooking dessert.

8 TO 10 SERVINGS

FOR THE CRUST

5 ounces chocolate cookie wafers (½ package)

¼ cup finely ground almonds

3 tablespoons unsalted butter, melted

2 tablespoons water

¼ cup sweetened, shredded coconut

Guyometer:
Very rich!

FOR THE FILLING

¾ cup sugar

¼ cup plus 2 tablespoons unsweetened cocoa powder, sifted

¼ cup cornstarch

2 cups skim or low-fat milk

2 ounces bittersweet or semisweet chocolate, chopped

2 teaspoons pure vanilla extract

PREHEAT oven to 350°F.

PREPARE CRUST: In bowl of a food processor, combine cookies and almonds. Pulse until mixture is finely ground. Add melted butter and water. Pulse once or twice. Stir in coconut by hand. Pour crumb mixture into 9-inch pie pan. Using fingertips, press evenly into bottom and up sides of pan. Bake for 12 to 15 minutes, until crust hardens slightly.

PREPARE FILLING: Meanwhile, in a medium heavy-bottomed saucepan, stir together sugar, cocoa powder, and cornstarch. Turn heat to medium-high. Gradually add milk, stirring constantly, until pudding begins to boil and thicken, about 5 minutes. Reduce heat to medium-low, add chocolate, and continue heating 5 minutes more, until chocolate is melted and incorporated and pudding has thickened. Remove from heat; let cool 5 minutes. Stir in vanilla and pour into prepared pie shell. Refrigerate until completely set, about 4 hours or overnight.

If the queen's coming for dinner: You'll probably want to top off the chocolate pudding layer with a layer of real whipped cream that you've sweetened with sugar and vanilla extract. A few chocolate shavings over the top would be lovely, too.

SHORTCUT CHEF

Use a premade chocolate cookie or graham cracker pie crust if you're crunched for time, but the crust recipe is delicious.

If you want to lower the calorie count a little, skip the almonds and cut the coconut and 1 tablespoon of butter from the crust. Or just eat a smaller slice.

FROM MOM'S LIPS TO YOUR EARS

If you want dessert, have the dessert you're craving. Don't settle for something that's not going to do it for you. Speak sensibly to your cravings (i.e., portion control) and be done with it.

Date Bar Cookies

If I lived on a deserted island and had to choose one food to survive on, hands down it would be dried dates. There's nothing more pleasurable than biting into a freshly dried date. Medjools happen to be my favorite variety this week. But I've never tried a date I didn't like. ▪ My three-year-old niece, who's in a phase of eating that excludes absolutely every fruit and vegetable known to man, saw me devouring a date the other day. She curiously inquired, "What chu eating, Auntie Kassie?" Recognizing an opportunity to get some nutrition into the child, I told her I was eating brown sugar candy. Eyeing me suspiciously, giving me a fierce once-over, she tried one. I nearly fainted. She liked it so well she ate the entire date, practically a week's worth of calories for a three-year-old. Now if I can just get her to eat broccoli . . .

THIRTY 2-INCH BARS

FOR THE FILLING

3 cups coarsely chopped dates

¼ cup granulated sugar

1½ cups water

FOR THE CRUST AND TOPPING

1 cup firmly packed brown sugar

1¾ cups flour

½ teaspoon baking soda

1 teaspoon salt

1½ cups old-fashioned rolled oats

¾ cup (1½ sticks) very cold butter, cut into small cubes

PREHEAT oven to 400°F.

PREPARE FILLING: In a nonreactive medium saucepan over low heat, combine dates, granulated sugar, and water. Cook, stirring constantly, until thickened, about 15 minutes. Cool completely.

PREPARE CRUST AND TOPPING: In a large bowl or bowl of an electric mixer, place brown sugar, flour, baking soda, salt, and oats. Mix on low speed until combined. While mixer is running, add butter, a piece or two at a time. Mix until crumblike, with some lumps of butter no larger than pea size.

USING your hands, press and flatten half of crumb mixture into a greased 9 × 13-inch pan. Spread cooled filling into pan over crust. Cover with remaining crumb mixture, patting lightly. Bake until lightly browned, 25 to 35 minutes. Cool slightly and cut into bars while still in the pan. Gently remove cut bars from pan. Serve warm or at room temperature. Date bars, stored in an airtight container, refrigerate and freeze well.

Ultra-Lite Pecan Chocolate Chip Cookies

These cookies are so good you'll have to keep them under lock and key. At least I do—I can't help myself. When they're in the house, I eat more than my fair share. So I send the extras home with anyone who's lucky enough to walk through the door the day I make them. And I've learned not to make them when I'm home alone. I can't be trusted.

50 TO 60 COOKIES

4 large egg whites, at room temperature

¼ teaspoon salt

1 teaspoon pure vanilla extract

¾ cup sugar

12 ounces mini chocolate chips

1 cup chopped pecans

Guyometer:
Mmm.

PREHEAT oven to 250°F. In a large mixing bowl, using an electric mixer, beat egg whites on medium-low until frothy, about 2 minutes. Increase mixer speed to high, add salt, and whip to stiff but not dry peaks. Reduce speed to medium. Add vanilla and then sugar, a few tablespoons at a time. Whip to glossy peaks, about 2 minutes. Gently fold in chocolate chips and pecans. Drop by tablespoonfuls onto cookie sheets lined with parchment. Bake 45 minutes.

TURN off oven and leave cookies in oven overnight without opening oven door. You're really supposed to do that and supposedly they're better, more meringuelike, but it's highly debatable around here. I'm a chocoholic with little self-control, so I usually opt to eat them straight from the oven.

If you want to cut calories back a little further, try reducing the sugar to ½ cup, or cut the chocolate chips back to 8 or even 6 ounces, and/or use only ¾ or even ½ cup of nuts.

Cooking Thin with Chef Kathleen

Baked Apples

My personal dessert motto used to be: If it isn't chocolate, why bother? I'm mostly over that mind-set, although I do revert to it when sumptuous seasonal fruits are scarce and hard to come by. These baked apples are something different *and* they fall in the good-for-you category. The nutrition police would be positively thrilled, which frankly is never my motivation for trying something new. It's the taste-chase first and nutrition second. Okay, that's not entirely true, either—I do try to make sure recipes fit both criteria before trying them, but taste rules.

4 SERVINGS

4 cored Rome Beauty apples

4 to 8 tablespoons raisins (as many as you can fit into each apple core hole)

4 teaspoons brown sugar

½ cup apple juice

PREHEAT oven to 350°F. Cut a strip of peel off each apple around its equator to prevent spontaneous apple explosions in the oven. Depending upon size of apples you're using, a nonreactive 8- or 9-inch baking pan should work nicely, but choose the snuggest fit. Stuff each apple with raisins. Top each apple with brown sugar. Pour apple juice over brown sugar and into pan bottom. Place in oven and bake 1 hour, or until golden and baked through.

If the queen's coming for dinner: She'll be positively pleased with this jewel of a dessert. Tuck a cinnamon stick into each apple for drama and serve them à la mode. Warning: *Beware of à la mode calories. The apples are quite delicious without high-calorie accompaniments.*

Rome Beauties are called for in the recipe only because they're widely available and I didn't want to send you on a wild-goose chase. We tested the recipe with an assortment of different apples and were amazed at all the pleasing taste and consistency variations. If there's an apple authority in your life, ask for recommendations. Otherwise, don't be afraid to try a variety you like. Worst-case scenario: you'll end up with applesauce.

Café Kula Banana Split

This dish was so popular among Maui spa guests dining in my restaurant that they demanded it for breakfast, lunch, dinner, and dessert. It goes over great with kids, too; a "make your own banana split" birthday party was a big hit with my four-year-old sister (she's twenty-one now) and her friends. We set out bowls filled with the season's best fruits, cut into bite-size chunks, and lined up squirt bottles filled with pureed fruits. We gave each child a bowl filled with two different flavors (and colors) of sorbet. They had great fun decorating their banana splits, and each other for that matter. When preparing this recipe, it doesn't matter what kind of fruit you choose; just make sure it's very sweet and ripe—use your favorites.

SHORTCUT CHEF

Read the recipe through start to finish. It calls for sorbets, fruit sauce, and crunchy granola. You do not have to make all those recipes from scratch to enjoy this delicious recipe. But in a perfect world, these three recipes would be part of your culinary repertoire and on hand at all times.

If you're having your banana split for lunch or a dog-day-of-summer light supper, delete the granola and serve it instead with a dollop of yogurt or cottage cheese.

Optional crunch topping variations: toasted nuts or coconut—easy on the coconut, folks. The fat police will be slapping you with violations so fast you'll never get out of cardio class.

I SERVING

I small firm ripe banana

½ cup assorted sliced fruit (mangoes, papayas, kiwis, star fruit, passion fruit, cherries, blueberries, peaches, plums, nectarines, and so on)

Two ¼-cup scoops Fresh Fruit Sorbet (page 374)

2 tablespoons Quick Fruit Sauce (page 375)

2 tablespoons Crunchy Granola (page 81)

SLICE banana lengthwise and place each half along sides of a serving dish. Place fresh fruit between banana halves. Scoop sorbet over fresh fruit. Drizzle with fruit sauce. Sprinkle with granola. Note: This banana split changes with the seasons, which is very exciting. Don't be afraid to use fresh figs or dried fruits, or to try champagne grapes, blood oranges, or pears. The more interesting the variety of fruit, the better the split.

Guyometer:
Now we're talking
desserts.

Cooking Thin with Chef Kathleen

Kathleen's Instant Chocolate Banana Ice Cream

Since I can't give in to all my junk food cravings all the time, I'm forever searching for satisfying alternatives. Reaching for Ben & Jerry's one pity-party-Polly night, I glanced over at a bag of frozen peeled bananas, got chunky-monkey inspired, and came up with this really great alternative to super-fattening ice cream. ■ The recipe calls for frozen bananas, so throw them in the freezer the night before you plan to eat this delicious treat. This ice cream is best eaten as soon as you make it. Refrozen, it loses a lot of its charm, so I prep only as much as I plan to serve. To defrost, microwave 15 to 20 seconds and stir.

SIX ½-CUP SERVINGS

1 pound slightly overripe bananas (about 3 to 4 small)

⅓ cup low-fat milk

1 ½ tablespoons unsweetened cocoa powder (or more or less to taste)

PEEL bananas, break into 1-inch chunks, and freeze overnight in a freezer bag.

TO PREPARE ICE CREAM: Remove bananas from freezer and let stand 20 to 25 minutes or until just beginning to thaw. Place in bowl of a food processor or blender. Add milk and pulse or blend until smooth, scraping down bowl or blender when necessary. Add cocoa powder and blend until completely incorporated. Serve immediately.

Guyometer:
I love Ben & Jerry's.

If plain old chocolate banana won't do it for you, try swirling in a few raspberries, toasted nuts, chocolate shavings, or a splash of crème de menthe. Keep in mind that additions can hike up the calorie counts.

Fresh Fruit Sorbets

Sorbets are a great way to use up an overabundance of fruit or those less-than-perfect pieces no one in the house will touch. Cut out blemishes and bruises, peel and pit fruit, cut into 1-inch cubes, and freeze in freezer bags until you've accumulated enough fruit to make sorbet. Or simply use store-bought frozen fruit. This makes a great treat for children; they'll be eating all-natural fruits.

4 SERVINGS

2½ cups frozen fruit pieces (about 1 pound)

2 tablespoons sugar (or more to taste)

¼ cup cold unsweetened apple juice or fresh apple cider

PLACE frozen fruit and sugar in bowl of a food processor. Puree fruit by pulsing processor on and off while gradually adding apple juice just until sorbet becomes well blended, smooth, and creamy. This will take about 2 minutes. Serve immediately or freeze. To serve frozen sorbet, remove container from freezer and microwave on medium until it softens a bit, checking every 30 seconds.

Try papayas, bananas, pineapple, kiwi, mangoes, star fruit, strawberries, blueberries, blackberries, pitted cherries, even grapes. Anything goes.

You may have to make the sorbet in two batches, depending entirely on the motor of your food processor.

FROM MOM'S LIPS TO YOUR EARS

Getting the little darlings to eat fruit isn't always so easy. A serving of fruit is a serving of fruit. Fresh or disguised as ice cream, it's all the same. Take your victories where you can.

If the Brownie troop is coming for dessert: Make frozen treats on a stick by freezing individual portions in small paper cups with a Popsicle stick in the center.

Guyometer:
Is this that gourmet
stuff? It's good.

Cooking Thin with Chef Kathleen

Quick Fruit Sauce

Originally intended to be drizzled over **Café Kula Banana Split (page 372)**, this sauce
has dressed up many desserts in our house. We've been known to spoon it over angel
food cake topped with plenty of berries, over fruit-filled crepes, pancakes, and waffles, and we've even used it as a layer in ice cream and fruit parfaits. Did I say ice
cream? I meant it. You'd be surprised how far ¼ cup of the best-quality vanilla ice
cream will go when it's layered in a tall parfait glass (or champagne flute) alternately
with lots of fresh fruit and sweet and scrumptious fruit sauce.

2 CUPS

> One 10-ounce package unsweetened frozen berries, thawed, or 2½ cups fresh
>   fruit
> 1 teaspoon sugar, or more to taste (use superfine if available)
> 1 teaspoon fresh lemon juice, or more to taste

USING a colander, drain fruit and discard juices. Place berries in a blender or food
processor and blend until smooth. Pass pureed berries through a mesh strainer to
eliminate any seeds. Add sugar and lemon juice to taste. Keep refrigerated until
needed.

*If Julia Child is stopping by for dessert: Make
two sauces of contrasting color, such as my
favorite combo: mango and blackberry. Pour
sauces into squirt bottles. You can get squirt
bottles at kitchen stores but
you'll pay less at the
drugstore for unused hair-dye
bottles, which work equally
well. Drizzle sauces over
dessert plates and voilà,
you're a pastry chef.*

SHORTCUT CHEF
Use frozen fruit. Set it out
to thaw a couple of hours
ahead or defrost in your
microwave.

You can certainly mix and
match the fruits, but keep
color in mind. Too many fruits
in one sauce and you'll end up
with brown.

Desserts

Berries with Brown Sugar

Some critics might say that this is hardly a recipe. And in a way, they're right. So slap me with a recipe violation citation, what do I care? It's much too important a dessert solution to be just another tip box idea. I didn't want you to miss this. ▪ I certainly don't think I invented this, either—I'm sure moms and grandmas have been feeding their families sugared fruit for hundreds of years, but for some reason you don't see it on dessert menus. I guess it's too plain, which is precisely the point. Most of the time all you really need to satisfy your craving for something sweet is exactly what nature intended, fruit at its best.

4 SERVINGS

4 cups berries or sliced fruit

4 teaspoons dark brown sugar

Guyometer:
This is great. Was it
hard to make?

DIVIDE the berries among the serving dishes and top each serving with brown sugar just before serving. Let all your family mix their own berries with the sugar so they can enjoy the brown sugar before it melts and gets lost. If you forgot what it's like to be a kid, this will surely take you back to sweeter days.

SHORTCUT CHEF
Clean the fruit in advance.

Don't tell anyone, but if you've got overripe or slightly bruised fruit you can trim, this is a great way to use it up.

FROM MOM'S LIPS TO YOUR EARS
Fruit desserts should be served six out of seven nights, if you ask me. How we ever got to the point of expecting baked goods and ice cream seven nights a week I'll never know.

If the queen's coming for dinner: This is a perfectly lovely dessert, especially when you're entertaining. The queen will probably request a dollop of clotted cream. A mint sprig would be nice, too. Serve the berries in tall glasses for a dramatic presentation. Besides, you can't fit more than a tablespoon of cream at the top of a tall glass.

Cooking Thin with Chef Kathleen

Rhubarb Applesauce

Oh hush, you're gonna love it. I'm positively addicted to this stuff. I get the same rush digging into a bowl of this as I do dipping my spoon into a bowl of chocolate ice cream. Okay, that's a lie, but this stuff is good. ▪ Top five reasons you should make rhubarb applesauce:

1. It's a delicious topping for pork chops.
2. It's a great roasted turkey sandwich condiment.
3. It's a great way to perk up plain old oatmeal.
4. It's a safer late-night snack than frozen Snickers bars.
5. Rhubarb applesauce (or Strawberry-Rhubarb Sauce on page 266) is write-home-about good spooned over Karen's Angel Food Cake (page 351).

6 TO 8 CUPS

6 cups apple wedges (4 to 5 apples, peeled, cored, and sliced into eighths)

3 cups sliced rhubarb ($\frac{1}{2}$-inch-thick slices)

$\frac{1}{2}$ cup sugar

PLACE apples and rhubarb in a microwave-safe bowl large enough to hold them. Sprinkle with sugar, tossing to coat evenly. Microwave on high for 20 minutes. Stir to blend. Try not to eat it all straight from the oven.

In a gift-giving jam? Using the strict guidelines set forth by the canning police, give away jars of rhubarb applesauce to those you *truly* love.

Any proportions of fruit that add up to 9 cups will do.

Berry Pudding

This grand finale dessert is quick to prepare and will make a statement on any table. Serve the pudding on a large platter surrounded with sugared berries and sprigs of mint. Serve whipped, lightly sweetened cream on the side. Surprisingly, this pudding is best made with potato bread or challah. If you're counting calories, choose potato bread, which is available from most bakeries and specialty markets. The pudding takes no time to assemble but does require several hours in the refrigerator, so plan to make it a day ahead.

6 TO 8 SERVINGS

4 cups mixed berries, rinsed (hull and slice strawberries)

¼ cup sugar, or to taste

1 tablespoon fresh lemon juice

6 to 8 slices stale bread (such as potato bread or challah), crusts removed

IN a medium nonreactive saucepan, place berries and sugar over medium heat. Bring to a boil, stirring occasionally, and cook until sugar has dissolved and berries begin to release their juices, about 10 minutes. Remove from heat, add lemon juice, and let cool to room temperature.

LINE a 9 × 5-inch loaf pan with plastic wrap, letting 3 inches hang over on all sides. Press plastic wrap into pan, leaving no air pockets.

TRIM bread slices to fit pan and place a single layer in pan bottom. Using a slotted spoon, place a generous single layer of fruit over first layer of bread.

DIP second layer of bread slices into pan with berries for half a minute per side to soak up excess fruit juices. Place over berry layer. Repeat with 2 more layers of fruit and bread, finishing with a layer of bread. Top with remaining juices. Finished pudding should be above top of pan so that when it's weighted down it will compact and absorb all the juices.

FOLD over excess plastic wrap and cover loosely with additional plastic wrap as needed. Place loaf pan on a rimmed cookie sheet to catch any overflowing juices. Cover with a second cookie sheet and place several heavy cans on top to press and weight down pudding. This allows berries to release all their juices into the bread and forces pudding to hold its shape nicely. Refrigerate 8 hours or overnight.

TO UNMOLD, remove top layer of plastic wrap and invert onto serving platter. Lift off loaf pan and peel off plastic wrap lining. To serve, use a serrated bread knife to cut clean slices.

If the queen's coming for dinner: This pudding can be prepared in any mold or nonreactive bowl that is the same volume as a 9 × 5-inch pan. Use a measuring cup and water to compare volumes.

SHORTCUT CHEF
Just because fresh berries aren't in season doesn't mean you can't enjoy this naturally healthful dessert—cheat and use frozen berries.

Washington Street Inn's Peach Batter Cobbler

Nancy Smith is the owner and proprietor of one of the most beautiful restaurants in the United States, the Washington Street Inn, located in the heart of Lewisburg, West Virginia. ▪ As children Nancy and her cousin Mary used to while away the hours by staging grand tea parties at Grandma's house. The little girls especially looked forward to peach season because that was when Grandma served heaping bowls of peaches and cream to her granddaughters on Sunday afternoons. She also made a mouthwatering peach cobbler. ▪ While Grandma sliced peaches, Nancy and Mary were allowed to go upstairs and choose from her hats and pearls. Once dressed in Grandma's Sunday best, the girls would descend the grand staircase and retreat to the parlor, where they were served warm peach batter cobbler. ▪ If you can't get to the Washington Street Inn, you can still enjoy Nancy's grandmother's peach batter cobbler. Nancy was kind enough to share the recipe.

8 SERVINGS

2 tablespoons unsalted butter

¾ cup flour

¾ cup plus 1 tablespoon sugar

1 teaspoon baking powder

¼ teaspoon salt

¾ cup milk (Grandma used cream, but milk works fine)

3 cups peeled and sliced peaches (about ¼-inch slices)

¼ teaspoon ground cinnamon (optional)

PREHEAT oven to 350°F. Place butter in a 9-inch round baking dish. Set pan in oven long enough to barely melt butter. Remove from oven, tilt pan to coat bottom evenly with butter, and set in a warm place.

IN a mixing bowl, stir together flour, ¾ cup of sugar, baking powder, and salt. Add milk and stir until just combined. Pour batter into pan—it will seem a bit thin, but don't worry. Spoon peaches over batter, distributing evenly. In a small bowl, stir together remaining 1 tablespoon sugar and cinnamon, then sprinkle evenly over cobbler. Bake for 40 to 50 minutes, until top is browned. Serve warm.

If the queen's coming for dinner: She'll be positively pleased with your dessert selection.

We like this recipe best with peaches but we've tried it with tart cherries, plums, nectarines, and blueberries and have been quite pleased with the results. In a pinch, we even used frozen peaches, sweetened with 1 tablespoon sugar.

Rhubarb Crisp

I've said it before: If you've chopped celery, you can cut rhubarb. So grab some the next time you see it in the market. This naturally healthful dessert can be thrown together in a matter of minutes, especially if you make the crisp topping ahead. Strawberries are a wonderful addition to this crisp, but just about any combination of sweet fruit plays well against the tangy nature of rhubarb. After a light and nutritious supper, treat yourself to the crisp à la mode (but just a little). Vanilla ice cream is good, but strawberry ice cream is even better. And you don't need to serve it with ice cream—it's fine alone.

8 TO 10 SERVINGS

FOR THE TOPPING

¼ cup roughly chopped walnuts

¼ cup old-fashioned rolled oats

¼ teaspoon ground cinnamon

¾ cup flour

⅓ cup firmly packed light brown sugar

1 tablespoon granulated sugar

4 tablespoons (½ stick) unsalted butter

FOR THE FILLING

2½ pounds rhubarb, cut into ½-inch pieces

½ cup plus 2 tablespoons sugar

3 tablespoons flour

PREHEAT oven to 400°F. Set rack in center of oven.

PREPARE TOPPING: Place all topping ingredients in a food processor. Pulse or mix until the mixture is crumbled to the size of small peas; do not overprocess. Set aside.

SHORTCUT CHEF

Make the topping ahead. In fact, make a double or triple batch and freeze it in single recipe-size packets so you can whip up a crisp on the spot anytime.

MORPH
If you're going to bring rhubarb in the house, you're going to fall in love with it, so you might as well whip up a batch of Strawberry Rhubarb Sauce (page 266) or Rhubarb Applesauce (page 377). They're both super-easy to make.

PREPARE FILLING: Place rhubarb in a large, shallow baking dish, sprinkle with sugar and flour, and stir to coat evenly. Spread crisp topping over entire surface.

BAKE until fruit is bubbly and top is golden brown, 30 to 40 minutes. Serve warm or at room temperature, plain or à la mode.

Guyometer:
Terrific.

Most produce doesn't improve with age, and this is certainly true of rhubarb. Choose rhubarb the same way you choose a good head of celery. Stalks should be virtually blemish-free and firm, not limp. The leaves are most certainly not edible and contain toxic levels of oxalic acid, so discard them immediately. Keep stalks refrigerated.

If the rhubarb you get is particularly thick, you'll need to remove the strings. (Most of the rhubarb you buy will not require this step, however.) Just hold on to the rhubarb and, using a small paring knife, pull strings down the length of the stalk until you've worked your way completely around the stalk, the same as you'd clean a broccoli stem or pull the string off of snap peas.

FROM MOM'S LIPS TO YOUR EARS

Don't give in to the urge to add strawberries or any other fruit until you've tried a rhubarb crisp. It's really, really good and most people won't know what it is because they're sure they hate rhubarb.

Strawberries in Orange Juice

This is a strawberries and wine knockoff dessert. Strawberries and wine are a customary way to finish off a meal in wine-making regions. This is a customary way to finish off a Kathleen-cuisine meal in summer when berries are at their peak. Be sure to use freshly squeezed or premium orange juice.

4 TO 6 SERVINGS

1 quart strawberries, washed, dried, hulled, and cut into quarters

4 teaspoons sugar (less or more to taste)

2 cups fresh orange juice

Guyometer:
Pretty good.

DIVIDE berries among number of guests you're serving. Place in wineglasses. Sprinkle sugar over berries. Pass a pitcher of orange juice around and let guests pour juice over their berries.

IF you're not out to impress guests, place berries in a nonreactive bowl and sprinkle with sugar. Let stand 30 minutes or so and, shortly before serving, pour enough juice just to cover them. Mash a few with a fork, leaving most berries whole. Serve immediately.

MORPH Go with the casual preparation and pour over angel food cake or a teensy portion of vanilla ice cream.

FROM MOM'S LIPS TO YOUR EARS

This is really only as good as the strawberries and orange juice you use, so make the effort.

If the queen's coming for dinner: She'll prefer her berries served in the finest crystal goblets you have or served over pound cake. She's not one to watch her waist, so have freshly whipped, lightly sweetened real cream on hand as well. And don't forget to garnish with mint sprigs.

Quick-Chocolate-Fix Candies

I suppose you could call these chocolate-cherry-almond clusters. If chocolate were forbidden I'd probably be the size of a teenage woolly mammoth. I'd eat it from the minute it was declared "forbidden" straight through to the day the moratorium was lifted. Someone asked me once if chocolate could be part of a low-fat diet. I can't think of a single reason why not. In fact, the scientific community agrees wholeheartedly. No one's recommending the woolly mammoth chocolate diet, but research shows that chocolate is known for being an antidepressant, an aphrodisiac, and an antioxidant.

16 CANDIES

½ cup semisweet chocolate chips

½ cup whole almonds, toasted

½ cup dried cherries or raisins

MELT chocolate in a heavy-bottomed pan set right on a burner of your stove on the lowest setting or microwave on high, stirring every 10 seconds. Hey, it works.

LINE a cookie sheet with wax paper (or use a nonstick cookie sheet). Pour almonds and cherries into bowl with chocolate and mix until thoroughly coated with chocolate. Drop by spoonfuls onto cookie sheet. Let stand at room temperature until set, 4 to 6 hours. Store in airtight container.

Chocolate Pudding

True, at first glance this recipe appears to be similar to the Chocolate Pudding Pie on page 366 but chocolate pudding you can make and eat on the spot is an important enough breakthrough for chocoholics to warrant its own page. It's an entirely different concept. ■ When my sister Talitha was old enough to use the stove, she and her friend Erin would sneak into the kitchen in the middle of the night during their all-night monster movie marathon sleepovers to make this pudding. Instead of waiting for it to cool, they'd eat it warm. ■ Mostly to keep the cupboard slamming, pot clanging, and cleanup to a minimum, my mom, just before she went off to bed, set out the recipe, the measured ingredients, and all the necessary tools so the girls couldn't miss them.

4 SERVINGS

¼ cup sugar

¼ cup unsweetened cocoa powder

2 tablespoons cornstarch

2 cups low-fat or skim milk

2 ounces bittersweet or semisweet chocolate

1 teaspoon pure vanilla extract

Guyometer:
Is there any
left?

IN a medium heavy-bottomed saucepan, stir together sugar, cocoa powder, and cornstarch. Turn heat to medium-high. Gradually add milk and stir constantly until pudding begins to boil and thicken, about 5 minutes. Reduce heat to medium-low, add bittersweet chocolate, and continue heating 5 minutes more, until chocolate is melted and pudding is completely thickened. Remove from heat and let cool 5 minutes. Add vanilla and pour into pudding cups. Eat immediately or refrigerate.

If the queen's coming for dinner: Serve the pudding in champagne flutes topped with whipped cream, a mint sprig, and chocolate shavings.

SHORTCUT CHEF
Copy Mom: Premeasure the ingredients and lay out the tools.

Cooking Thin with Chef Kathleen

Melted Dark Chocolate Sandwiches

This is a heavenly dessert served in other countries for breakfast or an afternoon snack and a treat I like to enjoy on occasion, too. A nifty and satisfying dessert you can serve on those nights when unexpected company arrives, this can be made with any good bread you have on hand. I happen to like the tangy, yeasty flavor of Italian sourdough against the semisweet nature of the slightly bitter chocolate, unless I'm pretending to be on holiday in Paris, in which case I love to make this using a fresh baguette.

4 SERVINGS

4 large slices (center cut) country loaf bread (such as sourdough)

Two 1.2-ounce Hershey's Special Dark bars or other bittersweet or semisweet chocolate

PREHEAT oven to 500°F. Place 2 bread slices on a small cookie sheet. Place 1 candy bar on each slice of bread. You may have to break up the bar to custom-fit the bread. Place remaining 2 bread slices over chocolate. Place sandwiches in oven for 8 minutes, turning once at the halfway point. Cut sandwiches in half (you'll have 4 halves, or 4 servings, which, if you're a chocoholic like me, doesn't seem like enough). Serve immediately.

> *Guyometer:
> What is this? Hey,
> it's good.*

MORPH Wouldn't it be lovely to make extra and take them to lunch every day next week, keep some in your nightstand, a few in your glove box, and a couple in your briefcase? You never know when you're going to need to console yourself with chocolate. I'm just kidding. Don't you dare!

FROM MOM'S LIPS TO YOUR EARS

Don't use Wonder-style bread. If you're going to eat something this simple, it ought to be good. Don't ruin it with the wrong kind of bread. It's a waste of calories. Don't skimp on the chocolate, either.

Quick Chocolate Chip Popcorn Balls

My grandma and I used to eat popcorn together and watch *Dr. Quinn, Medicine Woman* every night. One holiday we decided we wanted popcorn balls, but I knew they were way too fattening. So I set out to come up with a reduced-calorie version we could enjoy without getting into too much trouble. ▓ Some recipes were too hard to follow. Others had me struggling with dangerously hot sugar syrups and caramel so sticky I'm still cleaning the countertops. I tested for days to come up with this simplified, quick-cook method. If this doesn't put a smile on your face, I don't know what will. Grandma loved them.

This is not diet food, okay? You're not going to lose weight eating popcorn balls. Eating desserts is a choice you make. The key is moderation. It's up to you to work an occasional dessert into your weekly food calorie budget. You'll have to cut back somewhere else to even things out, which is not to say that you should factor in desserts every day. Too many restrictions and you're likely to go off the deep end. Learn to enjoy the things you love, sensibly. After all, what fun would life be without treats?

I figured you'd be making these for the Brownie troop or some other group function, so the recipe is for two dozen popcorn balls. If you don't need that many, cut the recipe back.

TWO DOZEN 2-INCH POPCORN BALLS

10 cups air-popped popcorn
2½ tablespoons unsalted butter
One 10½-ounce bag miniature marshmallows
½ cup mini semisweet chocolate chips or mini M&M's

LIGHTLY butter a large mixing bowl and large spoon. Add popcorn to bowl; set aside. Line a cookie sheet with buttered wax paper and set aside.

IN a large saucepan over medium heat, melt butter together with marshmallows, stirring frequently, about 5 minutes. Put popcorn into mixing bowl. Pour melted marshmallow mixture over popcorn, stirring quickly. After 10 strokes, add chocolate chips and continue stirring. It will be a sticky mess and it will seem impossible to combine the ingredients. Fold a few minutes more until popcorn starts to clump together.

BUTTER your hands and form popcorn into 2-inch balls and place on cookie sheet. Serve immediately, or store between layers of wax paper in an airtight container. Eat within a day or two.

Guyometer:
Not very guylike
but good.

Crazy Crunch

There's nothing very healthful about this recipe. It's not something you should make more than once or twice a year, but if you're going to eat caramel corn, you might as well eat really great caramel corn. ■ My mom's friend used to bring packages of her handmade caramel corn to our family Christmas celebrations each year. It was most definitely the preferred treat among the children and is a favorite to this day in our house.

12 SERVINGS

1 cup sugar

½ cup light corn syrup

½ cup (1 stick) butter

12 cups air-popped popcorn

Guyometer:
Got some more?

BUTTER the inside of a bowl large enough to hold the popcorn. Butter a large mixing spoon. Set aside.

PLACE sugar, corn syrup, and butter in a heavy-bottomed nonreactive saucepan over medium-high heat. Bring to a boil, reduce heat to medium-low, and continue boiling until mixture reaches 300°F, is golden in color, and crackles when a spoonful is dropped into cold water.

I'm telling you now, it's hard to stop eating, so don't make it when you're starving and cut the batch in half if you're not making it for a party or to give away.

This is not something you should keep around, but you know that. I make this at Halloween and pack it up in little bags for family and friends who've been known to travel miles and miles out of their way so they don't miss out on the Crazy Crunch.

PLACE popcorn in mixing bowl and drizzle hot caramel over it. Working quickly, stir until all the popcorn is coated with caramel. Cool and store in airtight containers.

Index